MARIANNE MOORE

Poet of Affection

MARIANNE MOORE
Poet of Affection

Pamela White Hadas

SYRACUSE UNIVERSITY PRESS   1977

Library of Congress Cataloging in Publication Data

Hadas, Pamela White.
  Marianne Moore, poet of affection.

  Bibliography: p.
  Includes index.
  1. Moore, Marianne, 1887-1972—Criticism and
interpretation. I. Title.
PS3525.05616Z676   811'.5'2   77-6415
ISBN 0-8156-2162-0

I wish to express
an affectionate gratitude to all my teachers,
but especially to
Kenneth Burke, Howard Nemerov, Allen Mandelbaum,
and my husband.

Pamela White Hadas holds B.A., M.A., and Ph.D. degrees from Washington University, St. Louis, Missouri. A native of Michigan, where she graduated from the Interlochen Arts Academy, she teaches part time at Washington University and is working on a book about Gertrude Stein. Hadas' poetry has appeared in *Poetry*, *Poetry Northwest*, *The Malahat Review*, *New American Review*, and *Ambit*.

CONTENTS

viii

PREFACE

If you are charmed by an author, I think it's a very strange and invalid imagination that doesn't long to share it. Somebody else should read it, don't you think?" Marianne Moore charms us with her "efforts of affection," with her apologies, her questions, and an originality which is the "by-product of sincerity." A persuader and preserver of forms, she spreads her convictions; among them, that "the mind is an enchanting thing," that "voracities and verities sometimes are interacting," that freedom is "the power of relinquishing/ what one would keep." I admit to being charmed and to wanting to share what she has shared.

As early as 1935, when Marianne Moore's *Selected Poems* appeared, T. S. Eliot expressed his conviction "that Miss Moore's poems form part of the small body of durable poetry written in our time." Starting with her involvement with a group of young poets (including William Carlos Williams and Wallace Stevens) in Greenwich Village in 1916, until her death in 1972, she presented a striking figure, a model of conscientious writing and reading, one with the courage of her idiosyncrasies. Yet she maintained her diffidence and privacy. Easily recognizable in the black cape and tricorne hat in which she ventured out to make public appearances in the latter part of her career, her figure presents itself—attending a lecture in Brooklyn on the subject of snakes perhaps, visiting the zoo or posing for *Life* magazine, throwing out the first baseball of the season, chatting with Johnny Carson, modestly informing the guard at St. Elizabeth's Hospital who remarked to her how "good" it was of her to visit Mr. Pound there: "Good? You have no idea how much he has done for me and others."

She wore her authority with naturalness and seldom, to all appearances, lost her poise. When Alfred Kreymborg, baffled and indignant at never having found her at a loss on any topic whatsoever, took her to her first live baseball game to try to show up her ignorance in at least one field, she foiled him. Challenged on the delivery of the first pitch, she remarked, "I've never seen him before, but I take it it must be Mr. Mathewson—I've read his instructive book on the art of pitching—and it's a pleasure to note how unerringly his execution supports his theories." When a herpetologist thought to catch her unawares at a lecture and suddenly placed a large species of snake in her hands, she calmly observed that its skin reminded her of rose petals. When the Ford Motor Company invited her to name a new car, she unabashedly suggested "Andante con moto," "Pastelogram," "The Intelligent Whale," and "Utopian Turtletop." When this figure of Marianne Moore entered a room, everyone naturally rose.

In the present book I have tried to characterize the style of Marianne Moore's literary productions as motivated by a number of intents, primarily survival, conversation, discovery, and selfhood. On the subject of self, Marianne Moore quotes Reinhold Niebuhr: "The self does not realize itself most fully when self-realization is its conscious aim." And she herself says, "In connection with personality, it is a curiosity of literature how often what one says of another seems descriptive of one's self." Consider her observations on Robert Andrew Parker, then: that "one of the most accurate and at the same time most unliteral of painters," combining "the mystical and the actual, working in both an abstract and in a realistic way," "his subjects include animals, persons—individually and en masse; trees, isolated and thickset; architecture, ships, troop movements, the sea." He is "a fantasist of great precision," giving us "masterpieces of construction plus texture, together with a passion for accuracies of behavior. . . . He is in a sense like Sir Thomas Browne, for whom small things could be great things—someone exceptional— *vir amplissimus.*" All of this, of course, may be said of Marianne Moore, who continually discovers herself in what she looks at.

This is not to say she neglects other objectives and methods of discovery, however. Far from it. "Do the poet and scientist not work analogously?" she remarks to Donald Hall. "Both are willing to waste effort. To be hard on himself is one of the main strengths of each. Each is attentive to clues, each must narrow the choice, must strive for precision. . . . The objective is fertile procedure. Is it not?" She discovers herself again.

Many have remarked that the conversation and the art of Marianne Moore were strikingly similar in their procedures. They are, above all, persuasive, and the "three foremost aids to persuasion" are expounded by Moore as humility, concentration, and gusto. She never went anywhere without them. The first, according to her, consists in realizing that it is impossible to be original except as the result of deep and honest feeling; the second consists in an "impassioned explicitness" (her example of this being a letter of the Federal Reserve Board of New York regarding a counterfeit twenty-dollar bill); and the third "thrives on freedom . . . the result of a discipline imposed by ourselves."

Marianne Moore liked to ask and answer the question of why one should write at all. The reason is always survival—not to make a living, but to live. "I was startled, indeed horrified, when a writing class in which I have an interest was asked, 'Is it for money or fame?' as though it must be one or the other—and writing were not for some a felicity, if not a species of intellectual preservation."

It is for her opinions as well as her observations that she survives, as a private person and as a writer. Her pitch is well delivered, and it is a pleasure to note how unerringly her execution supports her theories. *Femina amplissima.*

In addition to and inseparable from Moore's injunctions as to the persuasions of writing are considerations of a more metaphysical sort—of the morality and mystery inherent in things as they are, and of the "confusion that submits its unconfusion to proof." In parts of the present book, I have considered Moore's regard for animals, for "the fight to be affectionate," and for the "hero" armed in her humility who goes in search of some central illumination. In the first, one finds, as Moore herself finds in La Fontaine's work (of which she is a translator), that "indifference to being educated has been conquered, and certain lessons in these fables contrive to be indelible." In the second, one finds, as Moore has found in her poem "Marriage," "a striking grasp of opposites." And in the third one finds, as Moore has found in her description of a frigate pelican (as well as elsewhere), a vision "uniting strength with levity" and the poet herself "whose faith is different/ from possessiveness—of a kind not framed by 'things which do appear'—/ who will not visualize defeat, too intent to cower;/ whose illumined eye has seen the shaft that gilds the sultan's tower" ("Blessed Is the Man").

Throughout my study of Marianne Moore's poetry I have found myself coming back again and again to two particularly intriguing questions that are intimately bound up with all the questions of style and mystery, confusions and morality, which the figure of Marianne Moore poses and persuades us to care about. One is her answer to her own question, "What is more precise than precision?" to which she answers, "Illusion." The other is her question, asked in the late poem "Saint Valentine," "Might verse not best confuse itself with fate?" The answer to this one is strongly implied: yes. The precise illusions that substantiate the humanity of all of us and certain uncertain affirmations of what is too much with us at the same time as it is quite beyond us, are the real subjects of this book. Without "efforts of affection"—those of the poet foremost, and those of the critic not far behind—it is doubtful that we would get very far with them. William Carlos Williams affirms the confidence we have that Marianne Moore generously provides conclusions as well as questions that are worth our efforts, that "the quality of satisfaction gathered from reading her is that one may seek long in those exciting mazes sure of coming out the right door in the end."

I wish to express my gratitude to those who encouraged my interest in Marianne Moore: to Professor Jarvis Thurston for first introducing me to her poems and for reading an early version of this essay; to Professor John N. Morris, who also read my first attempts and pointed out some errors which I have since done my best to eliminate; and to Professor Howard Nemerov especially, who guided me from this book's inception and who was truly heroic in his "mirror-of-steel uninsistence," never allowing his wise and more considered perspectives to interfere with my own necessary bungling toward discovery of my subject, my subject's subjects, and myself. I owe a great deal also to Professor Allen Mandelbaum, whose help was indispensable, who suggested new ways for thinking about style, desirable additions, and necessary modifications of my text, that the book might make a useful contribution to the criticism of Moore already available. Most intense thanks, of course, are due to my husband, who was required to keep the whole of my work in his mind so that when I lost my place in it (as frequently I did) he could remind me of the points I had been wanting to make. He was invaluable in helping me to work out those points in the first place; and he maintained his sense of humor and good nature, as few might have, while I read such poems as "Marriage" aloud at the dinner table, or counted syllables in bed.

I am grateful to the Macmillan Company for permission to quote copyrighted material in the following books by Marianne Moore: *The Complete Poems* (1967), *Collected Poems* (1955), *What Are Years* (1941), and *Selected Poems* (1935). I am grateful also to the Viking Press, Inc., for permission to quote from the poems in *Complete Poems* to which it holds the copyrights; to Farrar, Straus & Giroux, Inc., for permission to quote from *The Dream Songs* by John Berryman; and to Alfred A. Knopf, Inc., for permission to quote from *The Collected Poems of Wallace Stevens* and *The Necessary Angel*.

St. Louis, Missouri   Pamela Hadas
Fall 1976

INTRODUCTIONS

W HERE THERE IS PERSONAL LIKING WE GO." Marianne Moore opens
her poem "The Hero" with this line and in its simplicity, modesty, and generality we can find important insights into this poet's approach, not only to the
"hero" of this particular poem, but to a particular brand of personal heroism
that informs all of her work. The disarming admission of "personal liking" as
a premise from which one proceeds to enter the largely indifferent world and
the peculiarities of one's own life in it is an admission of personal responsibility for the direction of and participation in that life; it is an heroic responsibility, not the less so for its being given to all thoughtful men and women.
Marianne Moore, throughout her work, celebrates this gift to the common
person, that of being able—by the virtues and character of taste, vision, touching, sounding, and the curiosity that leads them on—to choose a certain
ground and to stand on it. "Personal liking" is a modest motive for celebration of life, and a modest motif—to all appearances—in poetry; yet it is heroic
enough in that it can bring the most disparate elements of heaven and earth
together in a single mind. It takes uncommon consciousness to develop common places into imaginary gardens; and it takes uncommon conscientiousness
to let real toads continue to inhabit them. Marianne Moore has these qualities
and does these things consistently; they become her mode of gratitude and
demonstration with respect to the gift of life in all its conjoined uniqueness
and generality. Her poems present the gift of this heroism. Choosing to accept
it is, of course, no more nor less than a matter of personal liking.

   Choice creates the conscious person, even when choice itself is less than
wholly conscious. One chooses to read the poems of a certain poet with
attention because of personal liking. One chooses to talk about them as the
poet has chosen to talk about her own subjects, and one is rewarded with
personal discoveries—the reasons below reason. There is unreason, too, in
everyone's choices, and much to be discovered between the poet and the
critic when the reasonable unreasonableness of both come together. I do not
mean simply to play with words, or to play with affections where Marianne
Moore's poetry is concerned, but when I do I mean it to be, ultimately and

intimately, a serious game. The spirit of affectionate play, games of picking and choosing, and the unpredicted ordinations contained in words seem to me to point to the richest treasures and best strategies for both poet and reader of poems.

Personal liking, determined by so much or so little, is random to a large extent; it precedes deep affections, conversations, and discoveries; it is usefully more democratic than inspiration; and it tempers its opposites, fear and dislike. Liking is a good place to begin to know a world. It is a good place to begin.

Marianne Moore was born on November 15, 1887, in Kirkwood, Missouri, a suburb of St. Louis. Her mother was Mary Warner, and her father, John Milton Moore. After her father's plans for producing a smokeless furnace failed, he suffered a nervous breakdown and left the family. Marianne never met him. Her mother took her and her brother John (seventeen months older than she) to live at the home of their maternal grandparents in Kirkwood, where the Reverend Warner was a Presbyterian minister. (T. S. Eliot's grandfather was a Unitarian minister, also in Kirkwood at this time; it is a pleasing coincidence to remember, though the fact is that the families of the two important poets never met.) When Marianne was seven years old her grandfather died, and the three Moores moved again, to Carlisle, Pennsylvania.

Choosing none of these circumstances, Marianne must have, like any child, been making many choices relating to them during those first years of her life—choices about how to accept the universe and how to survive in it once the acceptance was made. The propitiousness of many of these only surmisable early attitudes is reflected in the childlike wonder and inventiveness of many of Marianne Moore's adult poems. It is inevitable that the despair of others of her feelings should echo too, but it speaks well for the handling of her childhood that the poet never chose to emphasize her melancholy at the expense of wonder. So much for her childhood—so much and no more. Others may report more, but there need not be more for our, or her, style of understanding her work.

Marianne entered Bryn Mawr in 1905 and graduated four years later. (Her brother, meanwhile, was graduated from Yale and ordained as a Presbyterian minister.) Marianne had a personal liking for the subject of English, but the instructors in charge felt that she lacked skills of composition in this area, and she was prevented from taking electives in literature until her last semesters. She did, however, starting in 1907 and continuing for some years after her graduation from Bryn Mawr, have small poems published in *Tipyn O'Bob* (the undergraduate magazine) and in the *Lantern* (the alumnae magazine). Her serious interest in writing is indicated by the fact that she served on the board of *Tipyn O'Bob* from her sophomore year on. She must have brushed shoulders, physically or metaphorically, with Hilda Doolittle (later to become the well-known poet H.D.), as they walked about the same campus during the same years, or with Ezra Pound (later to become one of her mentors and staunch supporters), who was Hilda's suitor during those years. But she had no very close association with either and became most involved with her second choice of majors, biology. This decision seems, in retrospect (and perhaps seemed at the time), to be at least as suitable, if not more suitable a choice than English for one whose eyes possessed infatuated care for form and whose mind was most sensitive to the proper naming and illumination of things. Marianne Moore reports having loved to draw her specimens, and one can feel sure, judging from her poems, that not the smallest detail of leaf or cilia escaped her eye or hand. As she put it in an interview with Donald Hall, "Precision, economy of statement, logic employed to ends that are disinterested, drawing and indentifying, liberate—at least have some bearing on—the imagination, it seems to me."[1]

There is no way of being sure just how much, at this stage of her life, Marianne may have thought of herself as a budding poet or potential artist of any sort, though she does mention (in the interview quoted above) that it had occurred to her to be a painter after her graduation from college. She had also considered medicine. Her modest choice in the end, to attend The Carlisle Commercial College, indicates that she valued sense as much as, if not more than, sensibility. She was perhaps equally endowed with both and accepting of both—a rare enough circumstance among poets, and one which does not make for hoopla biography, though it may have much to do with the particular distinction of her poetry.

In the summer of 1911, Marianne and her mother traveled in Europe, and though one gathers from her few references to it that it was a pleasant experience, the trip seems not to have been earthshaking for her. After this she traveled very little and does not seem to have felt the need to. This was certainly not due to any lack of curiosity, for her reading included items with a large geographical spread. Her poems—for example, "The Web One Weaves of Italy," "Spenser's Ireland," "Camilla Sabina," "England" (about America really), all the poems about strange animals in far habitations, all her poems in fact—testify to the fact that her mind, carrying its own vast geography of reference, could not stay for long in one place.

From 1911 until 1915, Marianne Moore taught English in the U.S. Industrial Indian School in Carlisle. She was working at poetry at the same time, but we can only guess her attitude toward writing. Was it protest or escape for her, "real" vocation or intense hobby? It does not matter, really, whether her poetry took first or second place according to time and circumstance at this point in her life. What does matter is that she came finally to acknowledge it as her most personal liking and most natural occupation.

In 1915, Marianne Moore was first "noticed" as a poet, publishing in *The Egoist* (an English publication edited by Richard Adlington, then married to H.D.) and *Poetry* (edited in Chicago by Harriet Monroe). Choosing to submit her work to these most influential (and subsequently legendary) magazines was certainly no accident; and it was no accident, either, that Marianne Moore gained immediate respect from the central group of young poets writing and reinventing poetry at that time.

In 1916, Marianne's brother John was called to the Ogden Memorial Church in Chatham, New Jersey, and she and her mother moved to Chatham to keep house for him. Here (it was a short trip to New York City) she became involved with the group of poets who contributed to *Others,* a magazine of experimental verse edited by Alfred Kreymborg. She says of his interest in her, "Alfred Kreymborg was not inhibited. I was a little different from the others. He thought I might pass for a novelty, I guess."[2] She passed, of course, for more than that. William Carlos Williams, another one of the Others, has written with affection of the part that Marianne Moore played in this group: "Marianne was our saint—if we had one—in whom we all instinctively felt our purpose come together to form a stream. Everyone loved her."[3] Williams also refers to her figuratively as a "caryatid," a graceful support for new poets and poems, the necessity of her upright stance indisputably more relevant to the structure of the group than the mere novelty of her figure. Kreymborg, in his book of memoirs, *Troubadour,* recalls Marianne Moore as an "astonishing person with Titian hair, a brilliant complexion and a mellifluous flow of polysyllables which held every man in awe. . . . There was no greater pleasure than listening to Bogie and Marianne Moore spinning long subtle thoughts in colloquy. The extreme heights were attained on both sides in an atmosphere of sheer detachment emphasized by the dignified references, 'Mr. Bodenheim,' 'Miss Moore.'"[4]

Marianne Moore reached her poetic maturity at the same time that Pound and Stevens and Williams were also finding their own personal likings in vision and style. Having chosen to live in the geographical center of these experiments more for domestic than for vocational reasons, Marianne Moore's choice of associating with the best of the people and poems that were available at the time was one of intellectual taste and independence. It shows confidence well placed and a certain self-assertion. She was not dragged in by her red hair; she had found something she liked a great deal and she clung to it. Despite all the diffidence for which Marianne Moore is famous, and her persistent claim that what she wrote was not "poetry" (there being, as she points out, "no other category in which to put it"), she worked hard in her own way for what all of the Others were working for—a striking newness. She chose to make—herself—something new.

When, in 1918, John Moore joined the Navy as chaplain, Marianne and her mother moved to Manhattan, the Lower East Side, where they stayed until 1929. Then they moved to the subsequently well-known address on Clinton Hill in Brooklyn, again to be near John. Marianne worked as a secretary in a private girls' school and as a tutor until 1921, when she took a part-time job at the Hudson Park branch of the New York Public Library. In 1921, when she was thirty-four years old, her first book was published by the Egoist Press in London. The whole matter of this publication, including choice and arrangement of poems, was handled by Bryher (Winifred Ellerman) and H.D., without Marianne's knowledge. Certainly, though, she was flattered and encouraged by what she calls "the chivalry of the undertaking." There seems to have been no doubt in anyone's mind, except possibly her own, that she was first rate, that she saw things to say and said things to see that could and should not be overlooked by her contemporaries.

One such oversight was rectified at a party given by Lola Ridge at which both Marianne Moore and Schofield Thayer, one of the publishers of *The Dial,* were present. Marianne was persuaded to read one of her poems and Mr. Thayer immediately requested her to send it to *The Dial.* She told him, "I did send it." And he asked her to send it again. (She did; another's personal liking does wonders on occasion.)

In 1922, Harriet Monroe presented a symposium on Marianne Moore's work in *Poetry,* and in 1923, Moore's long poem *Marriage* was published in England, in the Manikin series. In 1924, The Dial Press brought out her first book to be published in America, *Observations.* The year 1920 had marked her first publication in *The Dial*—certainly the best and most ambitious literary magazine in New York at the time—and, in 1925, she was given The Dial Award, a much-coveted literary prize. In July of that year, she took over as editor of *The Dial* and gave all her creative energy to that occupation (she stopped writing her own poems during these years) until the publication folded in 1929. Of her editorial policy, she told Donald Hall, "It was a matter of taking a liking to things." She may not have wanted *The Dial* to end, but she was pleased this choice had been made for her, seeing it as involving a certain "chivalry" (does this imply a damsel in distress?) toward herself. In any case, this circumstance freed her to go back to even more personal likings, her own poems.

It was certainly not all a matter of personal choices that led to Marianne Moore's commitments to verse. "With me it's always some fortuity," she admits to the interviewer, "that traps me. I certainly never intended to write poetry. That never came into my head. . . . Everything I have written is the result of reading or of interest in people. I'm sure of that. I had no ambition to be a writer." It is simple and spontaneous preference rather than intimations of immortality that leads modest heroes to their tasks. "Someone," remarks Marianne Moore with reference to the morality of choice, "asked Robert Frost (is this right?) if he was selective. He said, 'Call it passionate preference.'" In both her poetry and in her life, Marianne Moore seems always to have made personal choices appropriate to the fortuities; if she regretted any of them we may never know. This is the passion of her style.

As for what was going on in Marianne Moore's life generally between the dates of her publications, between her beginnings and the many announcements of honorary degrees and prizes that came at the end of her career, we do not have much information. Is there another vita besides this one? Of course. We discover no tormenting love affairs or consuming commitments, with the exception of those with and to the world at large. And there seem to be no unbearable disaffections or unnatural separations in Moore's private life save those with and from the world at large. But we assume: conversations, baseball games on the radio, dusting the numerous knickknacks, frequent attendance at the lectures of Brooklyn's Institute of Arts and Sciences, more conversations and correspondences, careful perusal of *Sports Illustrated, National Geographic, The New York Times,* along with miscellaneous monographs, eccentric and less eccentric books and articles, an occasional visit to the zoo, looking out of the window at Clinton Hill, buying odds and ends at the local markets, church on Sunday, and certainly more conversations.

Privacies and quiet fortuities are what seem to have made up the life of this poet aside from poetry. But, then, they are not aside from it. They are its source. Much as one might like a gush of gossip or a tang of scandal to complete a favorite romantic image of Artist, we shall not find them in Marianne Moore's life, nor can their absence be regretted. Thus we can proceed directly to the poems themselves, and to the poet who is "not out/ seeing a sight but the rock/ crystal thing to see—" ("The Hero").

Marianne Moore is a sightseer of virtuosity; she sees what is hidden from the casual scan, including importantly those things that are hidden by their obviousness, and she shares her inspections with wit and grace. Virtuoso definitiveness is often the subject of her verse, as well as its object:

> Neatness of finish! Neatness of finish!
> Relentless accuracy is the nature of this octopus
> with its capacity for fact.
>
> ("An Octopus")

Marianne "Octopus" Moore has a grasp for the detailing and numbering of things: the eight whales on the beach in "The Steeple-Jack," the nine nectarines painted on a plate, the nine eggs a dragon must lay (in order to have the mythologically prescribed nine sons), the six shades of blue in an artichoke, and so on, and it is not frivolous. It leads to the counting of invisible things— the lines and spaces and syllables that give form as it were breath; it leads to reliance on faith in what we do see. She offers us quotations from travel pamphlets, sermons, and *The New York Times;* she gives us footnotes and revisions of visions, all toward the greater precision of life and probity. "We are precisionists,/ not citizens of Pompeii arrested in action," she says in "Bowls." Precision requires a constant activity of the eyes in perception, a constant flow of syllables in expression, and, in affairs of thought and affection, the constant readjustments of a living thing in response to its environment. The octopus-response is to grasp. But one who is determined to be a precisionist of the spirit as well as of the letter and of the thing must inevitably come up against mysteries that are beyond her evidence or her grasp. These mysteries, as well as letters and forms, must somehow be borne by the style of the writer. Style as survival, as conversation, as discovery, as selfhood (a few among many ways of regarding style as it will be handled in the following pages), is a dynamic affair. It gives us, in its various interweavings, a particular sense of the orders of time, morality, and complexities of personality which go beyond precision proper. Style may even verge at times on the improper, unconsciously fastidious as it may seem.

"What is more precise than precision?" Moore asks in "Armor's Undermining Modesty," and her immediate answer is "illusion." The power of the poem on the page intrigues us as a manifest vehicle of hidden properties. We may say that illusion is the final fabric of style, that, as Moore says in the poem "He 'Digesteth Harde Yron,'" "The power of the visible/ is the invisible." We may say that. We may say anything, count anything, say anything counts; that is the first monstrous challenge of style.

Wallace Stevens suggests that Marianne Moore's relentlessly precise observations of nature "make us so aware of the reality with which it is concerned . . . that it forces something upon our consciousness."[5] For the artist to do this most effectively, she must efface herself to some extent in deference to her vision. She must have humility, but not without self-regard. She must have privacy, but not at the price of communicativeness. Marianne Moore is, above all, humble. She never misses a chance to credit a source, admit an ignorance, or praise a thing; yet paradoxically, and beneath it all, humility for her remains a means to knowledge and power that is above it all. Precision of design and the rich possibilities of human illusion are things to be deferred to. True humility within one's self, humility which is carried over into the public presentation of one's self, may be regarded as "the polished wedge that might have split the firmament" ("In This Age of Hard Trying, Nonchalance Is Good"). She is humble, above all.

Humility does not mean resignation to Moore; on the contrary, she seems to feel that by keeping her self as unobtrusive as a desert rat, and her eyes wide open, she may penetrate, or be penetrated by, the world's greatest mysteries. Though one never loses the sense, in reading Marianne Moore's poems, of her "particular possession/ the sense of privacy" ("Injudicious Gardening"), this privacy is never for her a license to commit willed obscurity (the word *willed* to be emphasized). There is no need for superficial mysteries when deep mysteries may be indicated just as well with a superficial objectivity.

The subjects of Marianne Moore's poems are often objects, and these objects are held in an attitude that is close to that of the scientist, where the subject is often an object, and the ultimate objective is truth. As Rémy de Gourmont wrote in his book on style, "The point is not that there is science on the one hand and literature on the other; it is that there are brains which function well and brains which function badly." There is no need to discredit a scientific paper for occasional subjective celebrations, or to mistrust a work of art that procedes with what seems to be "scientific" rigor, so long as the mind behind it is operating successfully toward truth, as Marianne Moore's mind almost unfailingly does. If the object she observes happens to be a porcupine of particular splendor, then her subject, first of all, is the particulars of its appearance and its observable existence; the metasubject is simply splendor. When an animal or an El Greco exists in itself and is "brimming with inner light" that is able to be shared, the accurate description of that object shares its truth. We feel in Moore's poems the truth "of human residence," as Stevens puts it in "Someone Puts a Pineapple Together":

> He must say nothing of the fruit that is
> Not true, nor think it, less. He must defy
> The metaphor that murders metaphor.
>
> He seeks as image a second of the self,
> Made subtle by truth's most jealous subtlety.

Of the idiosyncrasy of Marianne Moore's choice of subjects, T. S. Eliot remarks:

> It would be difficult to say what is the "subject-matter" of "The Jerboa." For a mind of such agility, and for a sensibility so reticent, the minor subject, such as a pleasant little sand-coloured skipping animal, may be the best release for the major emotions. . . . We all have to choose whatever subject-matter allows us the most powerful and most secret release; and that is a personal affair.[6]

Eliot may seem to suggest that "The Jerboa" succeeds *despite* the peculiarity of its subject-matter, as well as *because* of it. Just as we shall note again and again in Moore's most successful poems the correspondence between rhetorical and psychological structures, we shall note the correspondence between the apparent object in its unlikeliness and the hidden objective in its profundity. It is a "personal affair" that includes the reader; as unpretentiously announced idiosyncrasy can invite a precise illusion of intimacy, one treasures the special knowledge of another's predilections, shared or not. This is the basis of many a conversation, many discoveries.

As for survival, in poem after poem, the gleanings of a practiced and practical observation are put into our mouths for us, as by a solicitous mother bird:

> and when
> from the beak
> of one, the still living

> beetle has dropped
> out, she picks it up and puts
> it in again.
>
> ("Bird-Witted")

"Bird-Witted" celebrates the animal perseverance (which becomes moral obligation in human terms) of the mother bird who will half-kill the "intellectual cautious-/ly creeping cat." But only *half*-kill; Marianne Moore is like the mother bird with her intuitions and instincts for survival, but she is also like the cat, ready to devour by calculation the visions so affectionately nourished. It is a matter of style, among other things. As she says of the Russian dance in which one dancer pretends to be two dancers at odds with each other:

> just one person—may, by seeming twins,
>   point a moral, should I confess;
> we must cement the parts of any
>   objective symbolic of *sagesse*.
>
> ("Combat Cultural")

The emotional bird and the intellectual cat: Marianne Moore was aware of the tension between the attitudes of these two while she was still a biology major at Bryn Mawr and saw them then as a subject for poetry. In 1909, the following poem was printed in the Bryn Mawr undergraduate magazine:

A RED FLOWER

> Emotion
> Cast upon the pot,
> Will make it
> Overflow, or not,
> According
> As you can refrain
> From fingering
> The leaves again.[7]

Emotion strong enough to smother, and intellectually cautious creeping toward the source of that emotion: these produce the self-limiting tension, the simultaneous effusiveness and cautions of restraint that make Moore's poems particularly her own. She is by no means alone among poets in having to deal with this problem. In a paper on poetic process I. A. Richards quotes some lines by Trumbull Stickney that are to the point:[8]

> Sir, say no more. Within me 'tis as if
> The green and climbing eyesight of a cat
> Crawled near my mind's poor birds.

It is well known that Marianne Moore did not like to think of what she wrote as "poetry."[9] "Words are constructive/ when they are true; the opaque allusion—the simulated/ flight upward—accomplishes nothing," she says in "Picking and Choosing." At least this is what she says in the 1951 version (*Collected Poems*); in the subsequent printing of the poem in *Complete Poems* (1967), we find she has delicately removed the observation that "words are constructive/ when they are true." Perhaps she decided that the statement was not true enough to be constructive, or that words in themselves are never true enough to comment on themselves with such assurance; in any case, it is an instance of her method of construction and reconstruction, her tenacity in searching for meanings beneath formal ingenuity and easy soundings. She never changes her mind about the uselessness of "opaque allusion"; her object in writing is honest objectivity, as in science, but this does not preclude the illusion and the enchantment that must be a part of any object toward which one's mind is drawn. She says, of the ability of the mind suitable to science and poetry equally, that

> like the gyroscope's fall,
> truly unequivocal
> because trued by regnant certainty,
>
> it is a power of
> strong enchantment.
>   ("The Mind Is an Enchanting Thing")

Moore's object, beyond the object itself, making what is visible more visible, is to "make visible, mentality" ("Arthur Mitchell"). In his *Notebooks* Samuel Taylor Coleridge presents "thinking" as letting the mind construct its figures and, at the same time, watching the construction of those figures. Marianne

Moore is always thinking, and she gives us the pleasure of watching while she sees and simultaneously thinks about what she sees. She makes her own mentality visible, first of all, and then that of her subject; they often turn out to be indistinguishable.

She offers us details and intimates the process of her thoughts not only in the poems, but in the appended notes, for those who won't be offended by them. "Perhaps," she says in "A Note on the Notes" (in *Complete Poems*), "those who aren't annoyed by provisos, detainments, and postscripts could be persuaded to take probity on faith and disregard the notes." "Probity" in the sense she means it here, with respect to getting the facts and sources of inspiration out on the table, is not something we materially demand from a poet, although we do demand emotional truth from poems. It is emotionally true of Marianne Moore that fact and technique are the only acceptable grounds and vehicle of one's emotional life, and of one's style. She is in complete agreement with Ezra Pound's conviction that technique is a measure of sincerity in poetry, and that "the touchstone of an art is its precision." She is in agreement also with his injunction to critics (Moore is as critical of life and art in her verse as in her prose) that "every critic should give indication of the sources and limits of his knowledge."[10] For an artist or critic to take these maxims as seriously as Moore took them, and to act on them as consistently as she did, is not commonplace. Spiritual accuracy, leading to the highest truths, must acknowledge its sources in such places as Richard Baxter's *The Saint's Everlasting Rest,* of course, but also in such places as *Sports Illustrated,* Hutton and Drummond's *Animals of New Zealand, Illustrated London News,* and documentary films about India. Abstraction is earned in Moore's poetry and her inspirations are owed to accumulations of detailed intricacy rather than to a *coup de main* by some muse of universals. Her imagery is not a "correlative" for feeling in the sense that Eliot's imagery is. In her poetry the correspondences between psychological and rhetorical, between obvious and hidden, or between things and their emotive possibilities are the products of an "unconscious fastidiousness." "The hero does not like some things," and she does like others. She has general feelings about the things she sees, but the things themselves, especially the "rock-crystal" things, always precede the poet's state of mind. They are there to be responded to, gifts; they are responsible; they represent the choices of responsibility.

Consider Moore's eccentrically heroic response to the buffalo:

> Black in blazonry means
> prudence; and niger, unpropitious. Might
> hematite—
>   black, compactly incurved horns on bison
>   have significance? The
> soot-brown tail-tuft on
>   a kind of lion
>   tail; what would that express?
>
>   ("The Buffalo")

"What would that express?" she asks, not "what would express me?" or "*would* that express me?" or even "would that fact express the bison?" though this last is the closest to her meaning. Here we have a fact, a color; does it *signify* anything? This attitude is scientistic and not particularly poetic except in the larger sense that science is also poetic and self-creative. Marianne Moore would agree with Elizabeth Sewell's observation that

> For poetry, all objects and happenings in the universe are for thinking with, and phenomena or events are always available as objects of contemplation. Poems are often verifiable, in human terms, in what they say, their inherent insight and wisdom concerning the human situation in general. Their more essential verification or justification, however, lies, I believe, in their continuing energy as instruments for divination, that is to say, as method.[11]

The objective of a poetry that would possess the power of divination is to find subjects, or images, which are complete in themselves, or which have the power of continuing in themselves *as* units of thought, and *as* vision, not as mere illustrations or "objective correlatives"; they are *evidence,* not truths imagined incarnate. They are, in a way, miracles.

Marianne Moore ends her poem "Saint Valentine" with the line, "Might verse not best confuse itself with fate?" Both verse and fate are interwoven with chance and choice. Verse is something given, as fate seems to be; both contain within themselves, completed and yet-to-be-completed, seeds of motivation, of "personal liking," and of attitudes toward the world which describe a personal destiny. "We prove, we do not explain our birth," Moore says in "The Monkey Puzzle"; it would be presumptuous to try to explain. "The Gordian knot need not be cut" ("Charity Overcoming Envy") and "We have to trust this art—/ this mastery which none/ can understand" ("Melchior

Vulpius"). "This mastery" is both our own skill and accuracy aimed at truth, and it is something which has power over us, something which makes us observe certain *certain* rules, that "regnant certainty" which is "a power of strong enchantment" in itself. This mastery is equally of verse and of fate and of the conversations between them. "Mysteries expound mysteries" ("By Disposition of Angels").

Our fate is not to become able to explain everything, but to become able to see, with a literalness of imagination. To see in this way requires, as Novalis has reckoned, "long and tireless practicing, a way of looking at things that is both untrammeled and ingenious, sharp eyes for slight indications and marks of significance, an inner poetic life, well-trained senses, a simple and god-fearing spirit."[12] It is difficult to imagine a better description of Marianne Moore's "hero" or of herself. Her self examining the icosasphere, for instance:

> in which at last we have steel-cutting at its summit of economy,
>   since twenty triangles conjoined, can wrap one
> ball or double-rounded shell
>   with almost no waste, so geometrically
>   neat, it's an icosahedron. Would the engineers making one,
>   or Mr. J. O. Jackson tell us
> how the Eygyptians could have set up seventy-eight-foot solid
>   granite vertically?
>   We should like to know how that was done.
>
>   ("The Icosasphere")

Looking at the icosasphere, or at an obelisk, or at Roy Campanella leaping high, or at a basilisk, the poet is "not out/ seeing a sight but the rock/ crystal thing to see." She has a humble and persuasive curiosity, and although there is something childlike and innocent about it, we feel at the same time (and this is also childlike, but perhaps not innocent), that she is inquiring after what she feels to be an almost magical power of knowledge. She would like to know *how* a thing was done, how was it brought to birth. This is the power and the glory, to imagine the making of a thing.

In an essay entitled "Edith Sitwell, Virtuoso," Marianne Moore reflects upon the relationship between poetry and the world outside:

In his introduction to Paul Valéry's *The Art of Poetry*, Mr. Eliot
includes a postscriptlike speculation: "How poetry is related to
life, Valéry does not say"—connected in my own mind with Edith
Sitwell's self-descriptive comment: "The behavior of the world af-
fects our beliefs and incites the mind to tumult to speak as a Cassandra or as an elegist." Reflecting current preoccupation, Robert
Frost answers the query, why write: "It is what every poem is
about—how the spirit is to surmount the pressure upon us of the
material world."[13]

Before we consider the content of this passage, we might look at its presentation. The only words which belong to the writer herself, aside from her identification of the material quoted, are "connected in my own mind with . . . ,"
the adjective *self-descriptive* applied to Miss Sitwell's comment, and the "reflecting current preoccupation" applied to Mr. Frost's comment. The question suggested by Mr. Eliot is connected in Marianne Moore's mind with a
particular answer: that is, that poetry's relationship with life is a responsive
one—to prophesy or to memorialize—and both responses, that of a Cassandra
and that of an elegist, are incited by visions, to come or accomplished, of
death rather than of life. The relation of poetry to life is a relation of life to
death, a relation of the visible to the invisible. Moore's method of presenting
her own answer in another's words is as self-descriptive as the sentence she
quotes. Like the fate behind poetry, she is the inaudible arranger of the audible. Robert Frost's observation reflects "current preoccupation" but she does
not specify whose; through a current preoccupation which is particularly her
own, she has transformed Eliot's implied question about the relationship of
poetry and life into an entirely different question: why write at all? To
prophesy or memorialize, of course; but why? To surmount the pressure of
the material world. It is the matter and manner of survival.

Both the style and the content (if we may be allowed for an instant to
make this questionable distinction) of the passage under discussion "are connected in my own mind with" a "self-descriptive" recurrent preoccupation
of Marianne "Jonah" Moore's "Sojourn in the Whale":

[You] have heard men say:
"There is a feminine temperament in direct contrast to ours

which makes her do these things. Circumscribed by a
    heritage of blindness and native
    incompetence, she will become wise and will be forced to give in.
Compelled by experience, she will turn back;

water seeks its own level":
    and you have smiled. "Water in motion is far
    from level." You have seen it, when obstacles happened to bar
the path, rise automatically.

The self, the "you" addressed, is represented in the poem by Ireland (a country with which Moore identifies herself in several places), and the pressures whose force makes her do the things she does are the obstacles of a material world. The style of the water, rising and joining, is automatic and ongoing, a kind of conversation. In "Melanchthon" the poet writes

    openly, yes
    with the naturalness
        of the hippopotamus or the alligator
        when it climbs out on the bank to experience the

    sun, I do these
    things which I do, which please
        no one but myself. Now I breathe and now I am sub-
        merged.

"To experience the sun" she is not only "sub-" but "merged." It is the object she looks toward, modestly enough, and the self that she sees; it is verse describing fate, where fate is in verse, a random and natural felicity.

    There are two predilections pervading and informing Marianne Moore's work at every level. One is poetic wonder, the need for a near-magical communication with the objects and objectives of nature, and the other is a detached curiosity which demands precise and intelligent observation of these. It is important to see how her subjective enchantment and her objective devotion to facts work together to produce those particular celebrations that we recognize immediately as those of Marianne Moore. They are the elements of her style. If the ways of making poetry can be divided into the way of the self and the way of the not-self,[14] we may say that in her poetry these ways are not only identifiable, but often identical.

    The poet sees herself as moving between the poles of attachment to and detachment from the things of the world. One of "The Labors of Hercules" is

    to teach the bard with too elastic a selectiveness
    that one detects creative power by its capacity to conquer
        one's detachment,

that while it may have more elasticity than logic,
it flies along in a straight line like electricity.

We may talk about style in terms of the creative power of selectivity—i.e.,
picking and choosing among the general lexicon of words and images according to personal liking—but this alone does not always lead to the most generous of communications. With respect to the latter one must consider the logic
of order, syntax, the way in which the selected items touch upon each other.
One mode of style is the result of personal liking directed inward, the other
implies personal liking directed outward; one mode frees one to deviate from
the norm, and the other preserves respect for the norm. To conquer one's detachment is to allow oneself to be diverted from one's private path; the pure
illuminations of electricity flying along in a straight line have no particular
forms in themselves, but are given form by certain obstacles of attachment.
Hence the bard taught by Marianne "Hercules" Moore will be aware of the
dangers of self-consuming detachment and will make considerable "efforts of
affection" to atone for it, to correct it, and to make it of use. These efforts,
too, are the efforts of style.

"The mind," especially a mind like Marianne Moore's that "make[s]
visible, mentality," "is an enchanting thing."

> It tears off the veil; tears
>   the temptation, the
> mist the heart wears,
>   from its eyes—if the heart
>   has a face; it takes apart
> dejection. It's fire in the dove-neck's
>
> irridescence; in the
>   inconsistencies
> of Scarlatti.
>   ("The Mind Is an Enchanting Thing")

"It's conscientious inconsistency," or precision of the most respectful and
respectable kind, that is not avoided even at the risk of diminishing an accuracy in general. It is revealing, uplifting; in her essay, "A Burning Desire To

Be Explicit" (in *Tell Me, Tell Me*), the poet says, "Writing is a fascinating business. 'And what should it do?' William Faulkner asked. 'It should help a man endure by lifting up his heart.' [Admitting that his might not always have done that] It *should.*"

According to Marianne Moore "the mind/ feeling its way though blind, walks along with its eyes on the ground" ("The Mind Is . . ."). The mind has adapted to feeling its way—tapping, tapping—from one edge of the path to the other, each tap a syllable, in necessary explorations not only of the premises we stand on, but of the grounds of our being. Moore knows how to follow her own blind leads, building from the ground up, starting with pedestrian observations which, taken together as they are given, bespeak the immense peregrination through the dark and toward the dark wherein each feeling mind is humbly bound to uplift and to enchant. "Where there is personal liking we go."

STYLING STYLE

MIRROR-OF-STEEL UNINSISTENCE

A mirror-of-steel uninsistence should countenance
continence,

> *objectified and not by chance*
> *there in its frame of circumstance*
> *of innocence and altitude*
> *in an unhackneyed solitude.*
> *There is the tarnish, and there, the imperishable wish.*

THE FACE AND FAVOR of a responsible knight in armor are given to self-restraint which is embodied in unbreakable images "objectified and not by chance." This is one conception of style: the wish for integrity that shows on the surface, the solitary expression of a self-contained person. Considering silence, Marianne Moore momentarily decides that "the deepest feeling always shows itself in silence," correcting this in the following line, which reads "not in silence, but restraint" ("Silence"). Silence is not ideal, but "light is speech" (the title of another poem) only when it is not lightly given. Silence is an important prerogative and part of character, as with the cat described in the poem "Peter" who "can talk but insolently says nothing," and silence signifies with people as well, who can "be robbed of speech by speech that has delighted them." The choice to speak rather than to be silent is the first stylistic choice. It may be a matter of survival on a most primative level, premeditated somatically, and involving no conscious choice, if any, beyond that of pitch, duration, and intensity. At the beginning it is not a matter of truth at all; a child can cry for one thing fictively, consciously or unconsciously, in order to get something else. Still, it is a matter of style in origin if not in originality. It establishes the grounds of separate being on which later self-restraint and the choosing of words can have specific meaning.

The farther away a person is from the primal scream, the more complex and conscious the decisions she has to make about silence and its opposite. One searches for that opposite in language. Words begin to suggest themselves for contradictions, music for purer contradictions; potencies replace latencies, affirmations denials, knowledge in-comprehensions; in short, complexity replaces simplicity, and a revealed chaos a concealed one. This is obvious. Style is *how* this thing is done, and *that* is not always obvious.

There is no absolutely precise negation of silence, and perhaps there is no imaginable silence either. Style is precisely the cumulative product of all our attempts to contradict permanent silence as we try to imagine it. Any style, therefore, of any animal, is a sign of nothing less than survival, and written literature is nothing more than an attempt to prolong it. It is a certain mode of contradiction, a pretended comprehension, and a near-revelation of "the principle that is hid" that Marianne Moore admires in the grace of a snail ("To a Snail"). And it is "compression" that she admires as "the first grace of style" in this animal. In denying, compressing, and revealing only as much of the world as the unsilence of the world permits, an individual denies, compresses, and reveals himself as a *survivor*—an utterly unique thing, an unimaginable being playing at imagining himself, so to speak.

One way to distinguish oneself as a survivor is to make a sound or to hear a music that no one else can make or hear. Mallarmé, in a letter to Gustave Kahn (June 8, 1887), expresses great excitement over "a new view of poetry":

> anyone who has a sense of musical structure can listen to his own particular and inward arabesque of sound; and if he succeeds in transcribing it, he can create his own prosody, apart from the general type which is a sort of public monument in the city of art. What splendid freedom! . . . What you have done is open a path which is your own. And, what is equally important, you have shown that such paths can be innumerable. The laws you have found in our language are very precise and immediately apparent upon a reading of your work. And they *do exist,* as must countless others which other ears may hear.[1]

The newness of the view for Mallarmé is the emphasis upon the individual, specifically upon care for an individual as part of care for language in general. Freedom is to be found in the infinitely complex laws of language insofar as the poet can see or hear them infinitely. Marianne Moore would have liked the term "inner arabesque" because it suggests the possibility of translating the outer ornaments of style into inner ornaments, those that are hid. Nothing that is inner, exact, and invisible can be charged either with excess or with lack of being. For each inner shape an outer one exactly matching it is ideal. Style is one's failure to reach that ideal, and a perfect style would be perfectly inapparent in its naturalness. This is the style of music Marianne Moore admires in "Propriety":

> a not long
> sparrow-song
>   of hayseed
>   magnitude—
> a tuned reticence with rigor
> from strength at the source. Propriety is . . .

> The fish-spine
> on firs, on
>   somber trees
>   by the sea's
> walls of wave-worn rock.

Style for Marianne Moore is most proper when "uncursed by self-inspection"; she finds herself near the ideal in the simple recitation of dancers' proper names in the poem "Style," in her absolutely direct report of the accuracies of "Four Quartz Crystal Clocks," in the useful expressiveness of "A Carriage from Sweden," and in the resigned calmness of an Indian elephant. Marianne Moore's own style of presenting the styles of objects varies so greatly between the poems in matters of lexical and formal choice, and her dedication to the objects themselves seems so free of self-inspection, that her work approaches the "propriety" of music or quartz in its own right. This is a "mirror-of-steel uninsistence," a kind of negative capability, not of a dramatic sort, like Shakespeare's or Dickens', but of a more modest and objective sort, wholly Moore's own.

The struggle for survival may be identified with the struggle for a style that recognizes both inner and outer exigencies. In "Critics and Connoisseurs" Marianne Moore announces at the outset, "There is a great amount of poetry in unconscious/ fastidiousness." Both conscious fastidiousness and unconscious fastidiousness are expressions of moral choice, and both of them are what make up a personal style, or, in general, "People's Surroundings" from strategy to ornament:

In these noncommittal, personal-impersonal expressions of
     appearance,
the eye knows what to skip;
the physiognomy of conduct must not reveal the skeleton;
"a setting must not appear to be one,"
yet with x-ray-like inquisitive intensity upon it, the surfaces go
     back;
the interfering fringes of expression are but a stain on what stands
     out,
there is neither up or down to it;
we see the exterior and the fundamental structure.

The eye knowing what to skip is an expression of unconscious fastidiousness; it is a more or less corporeal intuition. The eye has a style with regard to "people's surroundings," a biological style of openings, closings, seriatim impressions, clockwork focus, and adjustments to light. The eye in the poem just quoted is an eye for style, but it does not consciously make a style of its own. It is too unconsciously fastidious for that, too near the pure stylistic impossibility of silence.

The eye itself functions in its choosing according to biological judgment, the eye of style according to contextual judgment, while the I of the individual struggles against all sorts of judgments, denying them, compressing them, discovering them, and so on. Conscious fastidiousness, precedent to conscious evaluation, leads to the declaration of moral attitudes, mottoes and paradoxes. Marianne Moore tells us, over and over, that Surface is Depth, that Opposition breeds Unity, that we should be kind to animals, that Humility is Power, and that faith is indispensable. The "Labors of Hercules" are all rhetorical and didactic, though Moore admits in "Snakes" that "the passion for setting people right is an afflictive disease." She judges according to an ideal community where "blessed is the man who 'takes the risk of a decision'—asks/ himself the question: 'Would it solve the problem?/ Is it right as I see it? Is it in the best interests of all?'" Marianne Moore's style is made up of innumerable patterns of such distinctions, and there is a great amount of prose in it.

One can distinguish style in the smallest phonological and grammatical units as well as in the largest registers of meanings. All useful descriptions of style must deal with the particulars of choice on a phenomenological level and, if they are to be worth anything with respect to literature, with evaluation on the moral level. Leo Spitzer, one of the most suggestive of critics who have applied themselves to stylistics, recommends that the scholar

work from the surface to the "inward life-center" of the work of
art: first observing details about the superficial appearance of the
particular work (and the "ideas" expressed by a poet are, also,
only one of the superficial traits in a work of art); then, grouping
these details and seeking to integrate them into a creative principle which may have been present in the soul of the artist; and
finally, making the return trip to all the other groups of observations in order to find whether the "inward form" one has tenta-
tively constructed gives an account of the whole. . . . Our to-and-
fro voyage from certain outward details to the inner circle and
back again to other series of details is only an application of the
principle of the "philological circle."[2]

This method predisposes one to accept the individuality of style and the
necessities of secret centers, "a web of interrelations between language and
the soul of the speaker" (Spitzer).

Roland Barthes, on the other hand, sees style as "a citational process, a
body of formulae, a memory, a cultural and not an expressive inheritance."
Whereas Spitzer asks us to regard style as a sphere with a center, like an apricot or peach, Barthes asks us to regard style as having no center, like an onion
—"no kernel, no secret, no irreducible principle, nothing except the infinity
of its own envelopes—which envelop nothing other than the unity of its own
surfaces."[3] These two models do not necessarily present mutually exclusive
approaches to style. Both visions—one of personal codes, one of personal
transformations of collective formulae—are useful with regard to the style of
Marianne Moore, sometimes styling herself as knight, enveloped in armor, or
lizard hidden in foliage; other times offering us old adages and guided tours of
word-museums and alphabetistic zoos. Sometimes it is useful to imagine a
single center which goes to extremes to protect itself and its centrality, and
sometimes it is more useful to see the center dispersed in proliferations and
attachments. To have it both ways is not necessarily to dodge the important
difference between the two views, and one need not dilute the force of either
conviction by the sort of inane critical tolerance that says there is *some* truth
in the one and *some* truth in the other way of looking at style. To have it
both ways rather requires the critic to have a "negative capability" which
complements the artist's own as nearly as possible, the negative capability
that Keats defines as the state of mind "when man is capable of being in un-
certainties, Mysteries, doubts, without any irritable reaching after fact &
reason."[4] If we can distinguish between a *critical* negative capability, one
which loses itself in the act of complementing the object looked at according
to the object's own mysteries, and a *creative* negative capability, belonging

to a consciousness which is prone to lose itself insofar as it actually assumes identity with the object looked at, we may say that Moore's poetry belongs in the critical category. Her poems apply the critical values that are best applied to themselves: personal liking that does not apologize for itself, "mirror-of-steel uninsistence," and a faithful ease with contradiction and paradox.

The ideal and the apparent are frequently at odds in any critical approach to the world. The poet-critic may ask, "Does the universe have a center or doesn't it?" The answers may be: ideally, yes; apparently, no. The critic-poet then must be aware of whether she is making her judgments in terms of the *ideal,* that everything eventually converges toward some "secret center" whether it looks that way or not at first (Spitzer), or in terms of the *apparent,* where layers and layers of meaning can coexist like free-flying galaxies with no provable reference to one provable center (Barthes). We frequently feel that Marianne Moore is saying both yes and no to such basic questions and meaning both most sincerely and consciously. This response to the world of forms is one which lies easily with paradox, and Marianne Moore does this with splendid sensitivity to her own and others' "conscientious inconsistency" ("The Mind Is an Enchanting Thing"). The ability to have equal faith in subjective centers and objective appearances, a faith that the same truths about survival, or about personal or collective style, are finally to be revealed and are to be equally true despite the differing premises they might have started from, is what for Marianne Moore makes the mind "an enchanting thing." It is worthwhile to make this mentality visible.

In an essay called "Edith Sitwell, Virtuoso," Marianne Moore remarks that it often happens that what one says of another is true of oneself, and in another place she admits

> one of New York's more painstaking magazines asked me, at the suggestion of a contributor, to analyze my sentence structure, and my instinctive reply might have seemed dictatorial: you don't devise a rhythm, the rhythm is the person, and the sentence but a radiograph of personality.[5]

Language by its nature is bound to describe language, and style is bound to describe itself by being and its author by image or, vice versa, its author by being and itself by image. The enclosing and entangling act of writing is, like a knight's self-sacrificing acts of faith, in need of armor, a "mirror-of-steel uninsistence" that can both reflect and deflect the attack from without on one's personal integrity. The armor is also an emblem of one's cultural belonging, heritage, and hope. Its reflections are all on the surface, yet the surface is dis-

torted precisely according to the shape of the wearer's own body. Belonging
both to the specific individual and to the species *homo sapiens,* this distortion
is a silently accurate simile for style, but it is not the only one. There are as
many similes for aspects of style as there are for near-oppositions to silence:
     Style is, for instance, like "Those Various Scalpels,"

> those
> various sounds consistently indistinct, like intermingled echoes
>   struck from thin glasses successively at random—
>   the inflection disguised:

or like "A Jellyfish":

> Visible, invisible
>   a fluctuating charm . . .

or a "Marriage":

> This institution
> perhaps one should say enterprise . . .
> requiring public promises
> of one's intention
> to fulfil a private obligation . . .
> a striking grasp of opposites . . .

or like love in "Melchior Vulpius":

> slowly building
> from miniature thunder,
>   crescendos antidoting death—
>   love's signature cementing faith. . . .

or "An Octopus" of "relentless accuracy"

> with its capacity for fact.
> "Creeping slowly as with premeditated stealth,
> its arms seeming to approach from all directions."

To play with such images is instructive as they are nearer silence than any un-metaphorical definition, and hence nearer to "the principle that is hid" in style.

We have considered two plausible images so far for the whole of style, the apricot á la Spitzer and the onion á la Barthes. "The Staff of Aesculapius," a late poem by Marianne Moore, suggests another image which seems to describe the complexity of style more accurately than either fruit or vegetable. It is a process as well as a product of precision, and life depends on it.

> Now, after lung resection, the surgeon fills space.
> To sponge implanted, cells following
> fluid, adhere and what
> was inert becomes living—
> that was framework.

The framework of a once-live animal cures the living loss of another; the inert structure fills an empty space and attracts life into it, providing for health and survival. Marianne Moore often refers to writing as a kind of surgery (perhaps taking a cue from Emily Dickinson). She ascribes to precision in writing "both impact and exactitude, as with surgery," elsewhere calling attention to the necessity for an "uninsisted-on surgery of exposition." According to her, apparently mindless people are "like those who see nothing the matter with bad surgery," and she admires La Fontaine for his "surgical kind of courtesy," an incisive style whose aim is not to please so much as it is to heal.

The sponge presents an accurate image for style, as it works both phenomenologically and structurally. This animal is unique in origin and appearance without being original, and it has its own niche in the pattern of the universe we know. If we take the sea for an image of language, the sea which Marianne Moore likens to a grave "in which dropped things sink—/ in which if they turn or twist it is neither with volition nor consciousness" ("A Grave"), an animal grown from that appalling and nutritive randomness, that hypnotic babble and dance into which whole bodies can disappear, will be a miracle of survival. It is clearly separable from its background, yet made by it; it is culminative, resembling and differing from others more or less like it; it is able to change according to the environmental currents running through it and able to retain its structure after death, to absorb new currents imposed on it and to attract new life and adapt to new uses. In Moore's poem it is an expression of the tiniest hugest moment when "what was inert becomes living."

A sponge, or a style, can be identical only with itself and is responsible for its own survival by selectively submitting to the anomalous "oceanic feeling." For a long time sponges were thought to be clusters of individual and independent cells, and though this is not strictly true biologically, it is still one way of regarding the organism imaginatively. Whether we approach style as a cluster of self-contained units, syllables or sentences, describe the exterior as arbitrary or symmetrical, or examine a cross section which will show us, deeply and perhaps randomly, a new surface and angle, we must keep all three in mind to keep the animal imaginatively whole. Imaginative wholes are for healing.

Thus wholeness—

wholesomeness? best say efforts of affection—
attain integration to tough for infraction.

("Efforts of Affection")

Intuition is imprecise no matter how biologically precise the eye. Marianne Moore asks, "What is more precise than precision?" and answers, "Illusion" ("Armor's Undermining Modesty"). It is for the sake of illusion that we entertain intuition, the illusion of a wholeness in or of the world, which sometimes seems broken or at least very breakable—words into syllables and atoms into even crazier particles. A style that comes from the depths of a person, as a sponge from its particular depths, almost inevitably attaches itself to something sunk and starts making a life-structure of its own, one and whole. But "we prove we do not explain our birth" ("The Monkey Puzzle") and all the completion of style proves, without explaining anything, is its own relative wholeness and its most general understated history. One can conceivably break language down to its individual cells—phonemes or letters. One can indicate it visually or spell a poem aloud. Marianne Moore says of E. E. Cummings' version of the mimetic, "the dislocating of letters that are usually conjoined in a syllable or word is not a madness of the printer but impassioned feeling that hazards its life for the sake of emphasis." Style is a matter of such "impassioned feeling" and a matter of life and death as well; it is sufficiently modest only when made natural by necessity, and it is natural insofar as "The physiognomy of conduct must not reveal the skeleton;/ 'a setting must not appear to be one.'" ("People's Surroundings"). Any organism—sponge, pangolin, pine tree, or poem—reveals only as much of its skeleton as can be seen on the surface. That its inner nature is not seriously discontinuous, more random or less genuine (though it may possess its own shades of difference) is, at first, a matter of faith:

We have to trust this art—
                              this mastery which none
        can understand.

We need not know that these words from "Melchior Vulpius" are part of a
syllabic pattern which looks like this:

                        667788
                        668888
                        669788

with subtle variation in the middle couplets building a "miniature thunder,"
or that the last words of each of the stanzas, if read in order, are meaningfully
symmetrical: faith/ death . . . breath/ saith . . . death—/ faith. Such form, in-
cremented by a pattern of indentation, is not a matter of choice alone, but reveals, as surely as the gestures of a body, a multi-determined attitude toward
the world. It is an attitude of the combined body and soul. M. Merleau-Ponty
suggests that language in itself is a person's "taking up of a position in the
world of his meanings," and his description of this process is pertinent to our
understanding of the development of style, where

> the phonetic "gesture" brings about, both for the speaking sub-
> ject and for his hearers, a certain structural co-ordination of ex-
> perience, a certain modulation of existence, exactly as a pattern
> of my bodily behavior endows the objects around me with a cer-
> tain significance. . . . the human body is defined in terms of its
> property of appropriating, in an indefinite series of discontinuous
> acts, significant cores which transcend and transfigure its natural
> powers.[6]

We may see each poem, then, in its "taking up of a position in the
world of [its] meanings," as a representative in some sense of the body of the
poet. We may see Marianne Moore's animal poems especially, in their great
attention to the movement and design of the animals' bodies where their
means of moving and their special "armor" seem to have moral significance,
as imaginative extensions of her own body and attitudes. As Leo Spitzer
observes,

just *which* phenomena the literary artist will choose for the embodiment of his meaning is arbitrary from the point of view of the "user" of the work of art. To overcome the impression of an arbitrary association in the work of art, the reader must seek to place himself in the creative center of the artist himself—and re-create the artistic organism.[7]

A text that is ideal defines its own ideal reader, the one that can share the knowledge of how a thing was done. Whether one needs to be at a felt "center" or not in order to begin the re-creation is a matter of opinion. The main task of the reader-writer is to learn to participate in the creation of the poem-world. Roland Barthes does not believe we can reach a single creative center, but he comes to a conclusion very similar to Spitzer's about the reader's role:

> To read is to find meanings, and to find meanings is to name them; but these named meanings are swept toward other names; names call to each other, reassemble, and their grouping calls for further naming: I name, I unname, I rename: so the text passes: it is a nomination in the course of becoming, a tireless approximation, a metonymic labor.

> Why is the writerly our value? Because the goal of literary work (of literature as work) is to make the reader no longer a consumer, but a producer of the text.[8]

To the extent that a critic cannot re-create or produce a text herself, like the poet who cannot *actually* create a pangolin (live and breathe as it may in her poem) that will eat the actual ants in her kitchen, she must have faith in the goodness of the mystery of the thing.

The world is a medievally manifest text to Marianne Moore, and its pressures on her as its interpreter create her ideal readership of it; she stands as close as possible to the "creative center" of this text, and she names and renames it in the course of its becoming, re-creating in small, and with trusting diligence, her own ideal world. Every text is dependent this way on another text. Marianne Moore trusts not only the art she does not understand, but she trusts the art of her readers to value her elaborate constructions, sometimes all but imperceptible in their modesty; she would pass on to us her understanding of freedom in creation, which is the freedom to set "personal-impersonal" and arbitrary-correlative limitations on the self.

It is a dangerous world. The proof of our survival despite all its dangers
—mortal and moral—is in the survival of language that connects us with past
and future. Lives are lost to the material world but are preserved in words as
in fossils, partially but importantly and lastingly. Species of animals from the
extinct *Dodo ineptus* to the mythological unicorn disappear from nature and
belief but are put back in their niches by poets like Moore who grieve over
such losses as representative of loss in general. Language, the most radically
conservative of living systems, is also most amenable to radical change, but
neither its most self-protective gestures nor its most experimental ones—
though both risk loss of meaning through obscurity and eccentricity—are a
serious threat to the protoplastic and self-perpetuating core. It is the ideal
substance in which to style survival. Language is a principle of life rather than
life itself; it cannot be killed in principle. Style, on the other hand, is a single
embodiment; it "risks its life for the sake of emphasis," risks understanding
for the sake of ornament, risks continuity for the sake of ingenuity, and risks
detachment for the sake of affection. It must be careful.

The wonder of a child and the discipline of a mothering tongue enact or
"act out" the bonds necessary for survival within the bonds necessary for
style. And this bondage, as Moore will tell us again and again, is freedom: "a
freedom to toil/ with a feel for the tool" ("In the Public Garden"), a power
that "in its surrendering/ finds its continuing" ("What Are Years?"). Every
poem, as a living organism, survives partly by what it has inherited and partly
by its individual adjustments to its environment. For every word we might
say the same. Marianne Moore's art of survival is mimetic, directed nominally
toward the world, prescribing imitation of artifact, animal, or artifice for the
survival of art. Her style is what it does, filling space so that what was inert
may become living. "That was framework." But for style, "There is no suitable simile," she says, having uninsisted on various ones in the poem called
"Style." And in a review of Pound's *Cantos* she reminds us that "to cite passages is to pull one quill from a porcupine." Nevertheless, there is no better
way to conclude the styling of Moore's "mirror-of-steel uninsistence" than to
pull one more quill of her "Style" which moves

> as though
> the equidistant three tiny arcs of seeds in a banana
> had been conjoined by Palestrina.

SURVIVAL

"If compression is the first grace of style," Marianne Moore says to a snail, "you have it." To a steamroller, on the other hand, she complains, "You crush all the particles down/ into close conformity, and then walk back and forth on them." Language shares the natures of both snail and steamroller; its self-generated pressures may be directed inward for the purpose of compressing a poetic self, or outward for the purpose of crushing and obliterating the critical differences between others. At one extreme language responds to the exigencies of the environment with exaggerated individual sensitivity, even "in the absence of feet"; at another extreme it behaves as a machine, a system of arbitrary sounds, an expedient that can break all senses and forms into patterns of black on white or of waves in air. Marianne Moore is a student of styles—from the jerboa's flagolet-like leaps to the fugues of Bach—and she submits her own inner necessities of ex(com)pression to the exigencies of com(ex)pression around her.

If Barthes is right, that there are infinite structures underlying and surrounding other structures of language, each with its own surface and center in necessary relation, then one could, in terms of style, regard each poem, each paragraph, each sentence, each line, and each paraphrase or permutation or "translation" of these as possibly enriching insights into the nature of language and the writer's human needs. With tact this sort of dissection and reassemblage should not kill.

Style is the offspring of machine and wishing-cap, the general thrust of life made specific. In Marianne Moore's work one may discern four types of this general thrust of life or style: one to be identified with survival, on the premise that expressing is being; one to be identified with conversation—persuasion or exchange, on the premise that individual moral choice and differentiation (sometimes opposition) are essential to expression; one to be identified with discovery, on the premise that deep silence, in the shape of a question mark, asks creation continually to find new forms for the obliteration of that particular silence; and one to be identified with selfhood as a process of vision and revision, on the premise that words are not simply identified with life, but with its uniquest reincarnations. Style stresses what words simply express. Expansion and reduction alternate as its natural tendencies. Turning toward the second of these, for example, words can, at bottom or at best, express only two states, presence and absence. Style stresses these.

Human survival depends on both the personal and the impersonal as-

pects of culture, and of language in particular. Where personal passion, "unnerved by the nightingale/ and dazzled by the apple" ("Marriage"), or just
"efforts of affection," come together with the "not unchain-like machine-
like/ form and frictionless creep of a thing/ made graceful by adversities"
("The Pangolin"), we can speak of style as a form of survival: the individual
expressing a private fate conjoined by tradition, the fatal limitations of a culture. Style as survival is phenomenal. It is unique to the individual, but not
necessarily a form of "originality." It is pre-moral in itself but may use or
depend on moral formulas that are inherited. As an extension of the body, it
gives form to space and time, and as an extension of the psyche, it armors
itself in image and all manners of lexical disguise.

   Style as survival's evidence has the grace of the given—the dog's individu-
alized triple turn before lying down, the bird's intuition about when to flap
and when to coast a current, a man easily laughing where other men are laughing, even having missed the joke. Buffon's famous *"Le style c'est l'homme
même"* can be understood in different ways: that a particular man's idiosyncrasies are embodied in the idiosyncrasies of his style; or, what is probably
more accurate, that style is the uninsisting result of a human and artificial
order of things, belonging to each individual man, but "good" only insofar as
it serves the material it presents.[9] It is Buffon's conviction, furthermore, that
only works which are well-written (that is, in a "good" style) will be handed
down through time, as ideas and discoveries are separable from style and can
be handed down without the impression of their author if the impression
happens not to be striking.

   This conception of style and its survival *as* style *in* style is a major concern of Marianne Moore, who is careful to preserve in inverted commas any
stylistically striking agglomeration of words, strikingly resetting them herself
like gems in her own stylistic framework. Reaching farther back, she integrates the unsigned masterpieces of style preserved as proverbs and mottoes
into her own style as well, often imitating their aphoristic succinctness to
halt and/or regenerate a flow of less concision. On a purely lexical level
Moore takes pains to admit the playful music of polysyllables little used in
the lyric poetry of her time, and she encourages words to flower by attending
to their roots. She has a special affection for proper names, as the most accurate of designations, and she arranges these to set off their precise music
much as she arranges her eccentrically gathered quotations and other verbal
memorabilia. She enacts Buffon's ideal of style in submitting her own use of
language to a proper (proper in the sense of personal as well as appropriate)
ordering of the subject at hand, the subject most often being how to survive
along with a particular means to that end, a protective and submissive style.
In short, she uses with good grace what is given.

Marianne Moore's attitude toward the language she has inherited in both cultural and individual forms is chiefly a protective one. The paper nautilus "constructs her thin glass shell" not for a commercial audience, but for the sake of survival; for this "the watchful maker of [the shell] guards it day and night; she scarcely eats until the eggs are hatched" ("The Paper Nautilus"). Certain words—some more than others—are treasures to be protectively displayed; their spirits must not be injured and their new poem-bodies must be sufficient armor against natural enemies—time and iconoclasm. Both versatility and specialization are essential as each word-as-survivor, each germinal phrase, each animal, and each artifact in Moore's poetry is uniquely co-responsible with the poetic environment. Padraic Colum has said of Marianne Moore that she "can place a word in a way that gives it the effect of a rarity."[10] Consider, for instance, the brief poem "'He Wrote the History Book'":

> There! You shed a ray
>   of whimsicality on a mask of profundity so
>   terrific, that I have been dumbfounded by
> it oftener than I care to say.
>   *The* book? Titles are chaff.
>
> Authentically
>   brief and full of energy, you contribute to your father's
>   legibility and are sufficiently
> synthetic. Thank you for showing me
>   your father's autograph.

The title of the poem is the spontaneous remark of a child, definitive (for him) of his father and his own relationship to that origin. Marianne Moore pounces on the *the* and begins her response "There!" for the thereness of history, the thereness of the father (for the child), and the thereness of the child himself whose very being there defines his father's creative efforts quite effortlessly and without any title. Dispense with his words and the poem has no title, but the child is *there* to begin with. "Titles are chaff." "Whimsicality" occurs where we expect "light," but illuminates the "mask of profundity so/ terrific" better than "light," making light of the professorial disguise and restoring the terror to "terrific" only, once more, to make light of it. The sound and root relationships of "profundity" and "dumbfounded" are put together out of innocence and into silence. Between the profound effusions one expects from *the* history book and the dumbfounded reaction they are perhaps meant to silence a reader with, is the perfectly natural not-too-informed or informative and not over-impressed statement of the child. It is not rare, but it has an effect of rarity on the poet, an effect which she means to pass on to us, giving us her own effects of rarity as she goes. The words "authentically," "legibility," "synthetic," and "autograph" as she uses them in this particular poem are all examples of this. The placement of them, at the beginnings of lines and at the end of the poem, add to the effectiveness. The poem is an excellent treatise on the proper-to-the-self use of words, the poet's own autograph reflected in another.

While we are considering Moore's penchant for rare placement we might think, in a lighter vein, of the sputtering invective directed at the escaped butterfly in "Half-Deity." It is made up of ordinary enough words, placed and tensed together however to give a rare sense of anger:

> Equine irascible
> unwormlike untouchable butterfly-
> zebra!

It is especially the "-zebra!", given the slight delay of the line break and the shock of its conjunction with "butterfly" that is the crowning humiliation for the recipient of the epithet, the words having accumulated before it to give a sense of endless resources of insult. It is practically Irish.

Another characteristic of Moore's style is her placement of modifying words between an article and its noun to give the sense of a situation rather than a simple object, a little story or a process contained within an object and even protected by it rather than a possibility or quality attached to it that might be broken off or lost. This is true of "a not long/ sparrow-song" ("Propriety") or the elephant's trunk that is "an at will heavy thing" ("Melanchthon"). The effect is always to heighten complexity, to add the dimension of action outside of verbal action,[11] at the same time that the verbal action is increased. Consider "the Coliseum/ meet-me-alone-by-moonlight maudlin troubador" ("The Labors of Hercules," 1951 version) or "an able sting-ray-hampered pioneer" ("Virginia Britannia"). The actions or situations implied, by virtue of a kind of musical-phrase unity of internal rhymes and rhythmic echoes, are inseparable from the thing acting. In "Granite and Steel" we find the phrase "affirming inter-acting harmony," in which "affirming" can be read as an adjective modifying "harmony," and here it helps enclose the sense of "inter-acting." Or it may be read as a verb, as the action of the bridge upon harmony rather than the effect of harmony itself. "Inter-acting" is hyphenated to emphasize the *acting* and to give depth to the last word of the poem, the last word upon the bridge—"an actuality"—which *ergo* has more than passive existence. A bridge is an act as language is an act.

Occasionally in the exertions of active play in Moore's poems a central word is almost lost, like the pansies (pensées too?) in "Virginia Britannia":

> Narrow herringbone-laid bricks,
>   a dusty pink beside the dwarf box-
> bordered pansies, share the ivy-arbor shade
>   with cemetery lace settees, one at each side,
>   and with the bird: box-bordered tide-
>   water gigantic jet black pansies—splendor; pride—
> not for a decade
>   dressed, but for a day, in overpowering velvet; and
>   gray-blue-Andalusian-cock-feather pale ones,
>   ink-lined on the edge, fur-
>   eyed, with ochre
> on the cheek.

Or words may be rendered (temporarily or permanently) incommunicado by a well-meant abbreviation, as in the poet's comments on the patch-box inscription in "Smooth Gnarled Crape Myrtle":

>   "Joined in
>   friendship, crowned by love."
> An aspect may deceive; as the
> elephant's columbine-tubed trunk
> held waveringly out—
> an at will heavy thing—is
>   delicate.
>   Art is unfortunate.
>
>   . . .
>
>   And what of
> our clasped hands that swear, "By Peace
>   Plenty; as
>   by Wisdom Peace." Alas!

One feels sure that there is some best solution for putting all the patches of sentiment in the patch-box together, but one wishes also that the poet who presumably knows what she is doing in thus putting them together in one place would explain a little more. Still, "contractility is a virtue as modesty is a virtue" ("To a Snail"). Trust is imperative in the end. "We have to trust this art—/ this mastery which none/ can understand" ("Melchior Vulpius").

In "An Octopus" the poet's eye is attracted to the "spotted ponies with glass eyes,/ brought up on frosty grass and flowers/ and rapid draughts of ice water" who seem to be cousins of Marianne Moore herself, with her impenetrable penetrating eye, and with her identification with whoever has "lived on all kinds of shortages" ("Sojourn in the Whale"). "These conspicuously spotted little horses" are virtually invisible in the following scene:

> . . . among the birch trees, ferns, and lily pads,
> avalanche lilies, Indian paintbrushes,
> bear's ears and kittentails,
> and miniature cavalcades of chlorophylless fungi
> magnified in profile on the moss-beds like moonstones in the water;
> the cavalcade of calico competing
> with the original American menagerie of styles
> among the white flowers of the rhododendron surmounting rigid leaves
> upon which moisture works its alchemy,
> transmuting verdure into onyx.

The ponies may be "conspicuously spotted," but they are not conspicuous as very much more than part of a pattern, the pattern of "cavalcades of chlorophylless fungi/ magnified in profile . . . moss-beds . . . moonstones . . . cavalcade of calico competing," the pattern of c and i and f and m, of strongly accented two- and three-syllabled words. Often we suspect that the object is purposely lost in its swaddling of syllables, as if exposure might be dangerous. Even a paperweight "of three-ore-d/ fishscale-burnished antimony-/ lead-and-tin smoky water-drop type-metal/ smoothness emery-armored/ against rust" is thus protected.

We have seen Marianne Moore to be amply protective of her various verbal inheritances ("In the short-legged, fit-/ ful advance, the gurgling and all the/ minutiae—we have the classic/ multitude of feet" ("In the Days of Prismatic Color"), and inventive in devising new forms in which they can develop. She is just as amply protective of her own self. It is her style to assign to style a maternally fussy overdressing of her "child" or her self and an ingenious scattering of red herrings in the form of ellipses and tropes meant to distract any casual predator from his tender prey. Of the artist Leonardo she says "Height deterred from his verdure, any polecat or snake . . . it kept them away." And in "The Frigate Pelican" it is the bird-artist's magnificent ability to fly that foils "the weight of the python that crushes to powder."

But the artist does not only take what is given in her medium in order to nourish and protect herself; she takes so that she can give in return, by example and suggestion, revivification and decision. In his interview with Marianne Moore, Donald Hall asked, "What effect does poetry have on living language? What's the mechanics of it?" Her answer: "You accept certain modes of saying a thing. Or strongly repudiate things. You do something of your own, you modify, invent a variant or revive a root meaning. Any doubt about that?" It is obvious, of course; but the "mechanics" of it are set to work on a much subtler level of style than are intention or preference. In the essay "Idiosyncrasy and Technique" Marianne Moore points out that technique comes from *"tekto—to* produce or bring forth—as art, especially the useful arts." To a large extent, specifically technical care gives an art its usefulness. And if art is not useful, in Moore's mythology of morals, it is not justifiable. It is most evident in the case of buildings and bridges, or gadgets where shabby workmanship undermines use; but it is true of poetry that it loses its usefulness, its power to bring forth its object, when the "mechanics" on the most detailed levels of style are not realized in the finished article. Sound in itself can be logical and mimetic, in agreement with its "meaning" on other levels, or it can be counterlogical and ironic, denying (or at least altering) the meaning of which it is a part.

"From plosives and fricatives to the frictions and explosions of mankind and the universe," Josephine Miles points out, "is not an impossible way, though never a way to be assumed."[12] And so we do not assume that [y]→/i/, [e]→/i/, and [i]→/e/ are to be, respectively, associated with tenderness, indifference, and hatred; and we do not assume that every glottal stop indicates a readiness for combat—to strangle or be strangled.[13] We do assume however that a poet can be unconsciously fastidious with phonemes, requiring them to help bear tones of invective, hesitation, confusion, or affection. Is "the pale ale-eyed look the sales placard gives the bock beer buck" ("Armor's Undermining Modesty") made up of wails or chuckles? Is the "pent by power . . . paradox. Pent. Hard pressed" pattern of the first two lines of "Like a Bulwark" a hint of its explosive potential, the "foiled explosiveness" of "Then the Ermine" that is said to be "a kind of prophet?" The "Mouse-skin-bellows'-breath/ expanding into rapture saith// 'Hallelujah'" in the transformation of its panting to praise with slowing $\bar{a}$'s to $\breve{a}h$, the throat relaxing in a summary and somatic openness.

Such analysis might suggest to us that style may contain catharses of no semantic description, depending on the availability of subversive phonemes to

the fastidious unconscious. Or we could project, on a phonemic level, a magical style where non-sense syllables hidden in sense make a supernatural sort of
sense, peculiar to the individual superstitions and fears of the author. Or we
might imagine a hungry style where pure orality gives itself the illusion (in
analogues to that of form and content) that by moving the mouth the stom-
ach is filled. All these hypothetical sound-dependent aspects of style have un-
doubtedly to do with survival of both language and man, but they are, as
hypotheses, no more provable than an afterlife. It has been suggested that our
psychic equilibrium depends as much on the sorts of "acting out" that happen in giving voice to phonemes, apart from logical meaning, as it does on
REM sleep.[13] All we can say is that it is a not impossible assumption.
    In "His Shield":

        The pin-swin or spine-swine
            (the edgehog miscalled hedgehog) with all his edges out,
            echidna and echinoderm in distressed-
        pin-cushion thorn-fur coats, the spiny pig or porcupine,
            the rhino with horned snout—
        everything is battle-dressed.

The poem too is battle-dressed, not only in its sounds but in the histories of
its sounds and in their future echoes. The poem is dressed to battle silence in
general and the silence or absence of a listener in particular. It battles absent-
mindedness with presence of mind in the naming of things. In addition to the
particularity of naming, however, this sort of sound-sequence eases the imagination or prepares its receptivity with an abstract musical play—a sophisticated version of a small child's self-entertaining repetitions of sounds, the
babble that that confirms the translatability of his play, its symbolic nature.
In the above example we feel a prickly-ness and rejection in the syllables
apart from their semantic meanings. *Edg—edg—edg—ech—ech:* one does not
want to keep the words in one's mouth; they move out and determine each
other as musical combinations do. (In this case we think of a nervous kind
of music, say, a Bartók string quartet.) In another poem, "Dream," Moore
invokes Bach:

        For his methodic unmetronomic melodic diversity
        contrapuntally appointedly persistently
            irresistibly Fate-like Bach—find me words.

It runs on like a sterile allemande. Once the sounds start—the *od*'s, *-ic*'s and *-ly*'s—they are, like the *—edge, -ech, -in,* and *-ess* sounds of the previous example, irresistible (in the sense that they cannot be fought off as well as in the sense that they are compulsive and attractive); they are also seemingly self-determining, as Fate is. "Fate-like Bach—find me words"; deference is all.

It is hard to draw a line between consciously and unconsciously motivated sound-patterns, yet both, including the blur between them, may be regarded as "stylistic." Insofar as style is survival, the elusive "content" of sound in itself, aside from its formal properties, must be regarded as a human inheritance—the ability to make highly distinguished and articulate sounds—and a necessary nourishment. It is possible that our purest idiolectal utterances are on this primitive level. The use of sound for aesthetic purposes implies a different sort of survival—that of art. So one might say that the "content" of sound is a relatively unspecialized collective phenomenon, necessary to the survival of language in general, and that the forms sound takes to celebrate itself and the play of its agent are necessary to the survival of every individual tongue. Both general and particular aspects of language have style as the stars have style. Speaking of constellations, what good is one without the diversity of the others?

The mechanics involved in reviving root meanings of words are various, and giving examples from the poetry of Marianne Moore is difficult, not because their occurrence is rare or over-subtle, but because in reading a poet that has such care for the nature and precision of words as they stand alone (Wallace Stevens is another such poet), one tends to get in the habit of reading each word to its depths (or its alternate surfaces, depending on what sort of structuralist you are). Each word automatically takes revelation on itself, unlike words that are legally precise or merely practical. It is arguable, though, that the attitude is entirely the responsibility of the reader, and that Marianne Moore read everything, practical or fantastic—witness the notes—with the special alertness she charms us into sharing. We become so used to taking into consideration, say, the root-connections between affect, affection, and affectation, that history is no longer quite separable from their present use. Usefulness, past usage and new, is all.

The way we are drawn into this mode of reading words according to all their uses is, to some extent, mechanical or technical. For instance, a word may simply be used in an unusual context to force us to remember a neglected meaning. Thus "the plastic animal all of a piece from nose to tail" ("Snakes, Mongooses . . .") reminds us that "plastic" is ancient Greek as well as modern. We know the animal is a living snake, or the word "plastic" might not be forced back to its plasm-nature. In this case Moore is not necessarily making a double comment on the pagan-charmed snake by using a word that is itself plastic in sense. Yet she *could* be. She could be saying on some level that the snake made to "stand up in his travelling basket" becomes as artificial and commercial as a plastic toy and undignified by such malleability. It is just as well, for the sake of survival, that such lexical questions remain open to various interpretations. The ultimate indeterminability of word usage is in some ways analogous to adaptability in evolution. Because the revival of root meanings may revive obscurity as well, a poet and critic both may be blamed for indefinition that does not help understanding . . . or shall we say *cannot* help understanding?

In the above example the word "plastic" calls attention to itself but does not particularly or immediately illuminate the snake. In "The Hero" Moore speaks of "snakes' hypodermic teeth," reviving the graphic image of something inserted under the skin as well as the hollow-needle-injecting nature of the teeth themselves. The emphasis here is on the teeth and not the adjective. It is an example of perfect cooperation between root meaning and flowered meaning. It goes to seed in the mind.

"He 'Digesteth Harde Yron'" speaks, in the first and last stanzas, of the ostrich as "sparrow-camel." Here the poet is reviving and translating an earlier and more descriptive name for an animal that—judging from the fate of its close relatives—may be in danger of extinction. In the notes to the poem we are given the Greek word στρουθιοκαμηλοζ, and it does have a direct bearing on the poem and on the poet's style of survival because it makes clear to us in what is Greek to us (possibly), that this is an animal with a history, an animal that, no matter what its other creative properties, inspired a new word that is now an old one, but not less valid. The word *ostrich* comes from the same root, through Latin *struthio* (sparrow) prefixed by *avis* (bird). But the word *ostrich* certainly denies the bird a great deal the wonder conferred on it, if not all, by the description "sparrow-camel," the highly unlikely combination, fit for any mythical bestiary, of small bird with imposing beast of burden. Not just the word, but the wonder must be revived; not only the history and appearance of the bird, but its future survival must be attended to. Faith that the revival of such a root name can aid the survival of the named is a magical faith. It is neither beneath or beyond the child in the poet, however Presbyterian.

We recall that the poem "'He Wrote the History Book'" begins and ends with words foregrounded not just by position but by relation to each other through root meanings. A small boy announces to the poet, "My name is John Andrews; my father wrote the history book." Charmed, she replies, "Authentically/ brief and full of energy, you contribute to your father's/

legibility and are sufficiently/ synthetic." "Authentically" connects the child
with the authority of his own origin, which is the same as that of the history
book, his father. He is like a footnote underlining the genuine source of what
his father has created, in a word. In this he performs the same function with
respect to his father's history book as the notes behind Moore's poems do
with respect to her creations. They do not explain but substantiate a circumstance; they contribute to the "legibility" of her motivations and extend our
sense of the author's relation to the world outside her written world. This is
what the child's proclamation does, "putting together" two sorts of authority,
two sorts of history—personal and suprapersonal. He is synthetic as any genuine article is synthetic, comprising the authorities of self (being) and other
(history), immediacy and continuity.

Sometimes the use of two words that contain the same root emphasize
the root by reflecting each other, as in "An Egyptian Pulled Glass Bottle in
the Shape of a Fish," which speaks of "the spectrum,/ that spectacular . . .
fish." The spectrum is an image of radiant energy, essentially bodiless, but
visible. The root *spect-* emphasizes the visibility—that anything can be literally
spectacular if we realize that "the power of the visible is the invisible." In
"The Jerboa," describing "an elegance/ ignored by one's ignorance," the
sense that "ignorance" is something that actively acts is made explicit. Sometimes two words seem to share a root but don't, the distinction between them
thematic, as in "Elephants," which speaks of a "pattern of revery not reverence." The distinction between the root meaning "to dream" and the one
meaning "to revere" is essential to the poem because the poet, celebrating the
dreamlike quality of Buddhist ceremony and the verb *bŭd,* meaning "know,"
does not want her meditation to be interpreted as a form of worship. The
"echidna and echinoderm" in "His Shield" do get their names from the same
source, but they are as different as mammal and starfish, the point being that
the porcupine ("pin-swin or spine-swine") combines their natures, pointing
out the spines of the root they share.

In "Light Is Speech" we are sunstruck with etymologies. We are told
that "the word France means/ enfranchisement" and that "French" is "that
still unextirpated [literally, *un-pulled-up-by-the-root*] adjective," related to
light because light is "free frank . . . language." A philologist named Littré
is described as a "man of fire, scientist of freedoms," relating him through
fire—*feu*—*feu-de-bord*—lighthouse to the lighthouses already mentioned in the
poem, and through freedom to the French word-cluster. Montaigne enters the
poem, and the notes tell us that he was once freed from bandits because his
speech impressed them. In "Light Is Speech" it is his speech that "lit remorse's saving spark," again connecting fire and words and perhaps—no,

certainly—suggesting the value of literacy and a possible illumination of the name Littré.

Marianne Moore does not write for the sake of etymological meditation, nor does she often insist on the history of words as in the example above, so frankly obsessed. To characterize her style as, so to speak, rooted in words themselves would be a mistake; still our consciousness of her consciousness of words as beings with histories and families helps us understand the precise nature of her private lexicon. Truth depends on the smallest accuracies added up. So we must be sure of a word's character before we put it to work: "—polo// Restating it:/ *pelo*, I turn,/ on *polos*, a pivot" ("Blue Bug"). It must be made clear that "the musk ox/ has no musk and is not an ox—/ illiterate epithet" (where epithet is used *as* epithet, the perfect identification the musk-ox does not have with his name, pointing out, perhaps, that a word is best identified with itself and not with something it is not). In "Four Quartz Crystal Clocks" we are reminded that Jupiter is *jour pater,* and that glass eyes are not eyeglasses; and we are entreated to sympathize with the incongruity of the "bell-boy with the bouy-ball/ endeavoring to pass hotel patronesses."

Moore's use of the negative can reflect both economy and duality. She favors the negative prefixes especially, so we can have "uninsistence," "unvenomous," and "unself-righteousness" demonstrating not only themselves but their most *exact* opposites. One is made to feel that the exact opposite of a word is presented more exactly by the full presence of what it stands *against,* what is absent in its very presence, the absence being effected by the simplest of prefixes. This persistent phenomenon of Moore's style indicates a struggle on the lexical level, where "unconfusion submits its confusion to proof" ("The Mind Is an Enchanting Thing"), and it opens the gate to the central paradoxes of this poet's vision.

The range of possible tones, or the total register of thematic expectancies with regard to lexical choice (to use a choice jargon) in Moore's poems is very broad. Each word is so much itself that they all seem to escape system and to prepare us for the unpredictable. It is "conscientious inconsistency" ("The Mind Is . . .") or well-tempered versatility that characterizes Moore's idiolect, one that can, without seeming strange or unconversational to us, use words like "mechanicked," "griffons" (writes), "betokens," and "discommodity." And she can make use of idiomatic phrases—the mind "with its own ax to grind," "put the wood to that one," or "as the crow flies"—without a sense of straining after the common in an eccentric context.

Moore's flashes of verbal virtuosity are, though not in quotation marks, often set off by prosaic transitions, like several lines of a text spontaneously quoted in conversation, like a knickknack suddenly noticed, picked up, and put down again to get on with the business at hand. Consider "the at first slow, saddle-horse quick cavalcade// of buck-eye burnished jumpers/ and five-gaited mounts, the work-mule and/ show-mule and witch-cross door and 'strong sweet prison'/ are a part of what has come about—in the Black/ idiom —from 'advancin' backwards in a circle.'" "The [at first slow, saddle-horse quick] cavalcade// of [buck-eye burnished] jumpers" stands out in its bric-a-brac of adjectives and provides a slow start by the insertion of many quick syllables. So much energy expended on a luxury is a luxury. But it never lasts. The next lines catalog in stressed syllables—every one working, none excess—the "show-mule," "witch-cross," and "strong sweet" which are rhythmically equal, though not morally so, literally and strikingly contrasted to luxury. The awkwardness of "are a part of what has come about" introduces yet another lexical field—the academic use of little functional words leading up to a quoted phrase which, in this inconsistent text calls up two very different "fields" of meaning, one of idiom and one of abstraction. History, voluntarily blind to what is ahead, repeats itself. The next sentence of the poem comes back to using words as ornament and luxury: "Rare/ unscent-/ed, provident-/ ly hot, too sweet, inconsistent flower bed!" But ironically it does not strike us as inconsistent because there is behind Marianne Moore's lexicon, for any one poem, as well as for the poems taken together, not a single, very broad register of possible words, but a register of small distinct registers, any one of which can be called up at any point without marring the felt coherence of a poem. It is this very "conscientious inconsistency" that allows the poet to follow "my wish . . . O to be a dragon" with "Felicitous phenomenon" instead of simply "happy thing." The wish, apparently, is strong enough to eject the poet's vocabulary out of the expected verbal orbit into one more highly energized, more complexly musical, more whimsical. In other words, Marianne Moore establishes her lexical norm *in other words*, i.e., words as *other*, to be used as textures in a collage, illuminating each other by tactile difference. Her style presents us with a jumbled thesaurus of tones which are made to cohere by a grammar of detachments, a sort of counterlogical logic of associations.

Marianne Moore's style is, largely speaking, nominal as opposed to verbal; proper names, as the crème de la crème of denominations, are prominent in the poems as well as the notes to the poems. In "The Steeple-Jack" she describes two signs, one reading "C. J. Poole," the other "Danger." The most specific of designations is featured with the least specific. In another poem she reminds us of "a too often forgotten surely relevant thing, that Roebling cable/ was invented by John A. Roebling." The more specific the name the better; the second time Émile Littré is mentioned in "Light Is Speech," he is called "Hippocrates-charmed . . . Maximilien Paul Émile Littré." And when, in the notes, she gives the author of *Sentir avec ardeur* as "Madame Boufflers

—Marie-Françoise-Catherine de Beauveau, Marquise de Boufflers (1711-1786)" with obvious relish for the precision and illusion that such a naming implies. "Every name is a tune" she sings in "Spenser's Ireland." Thus, "Rinaldo/ Caramonica's the cobbler's, Frank Sblendorio's/ and Dominick Angelastro's country" is the way one weaves the web one weaves of Italy (in "Keeping Their World Large"). Precision of sound complements precision of designation in such things as "Wo-re-wo-/ co-mo-co's fur crown," "the fragile grace of the Thomas-/ of-Leighton Buzzard Westminster Abbey wrought-iron vine," and the jazz of "Fats Waller, Ozzie Smith, Eubie Blake and Ted Atkinson charging by on Tiger Skin." The essence of the "poetry" in "'He Wrote the History Book,'" discussed above, is in the child's announcement, reported in the notes, of his proper name, properly linked with his origin. It is the last stanza of "Style" that is, importantly, crammed with proper names to the near-exclusion of everything else. It is the triumph of individual style, a celebration and memorial of the style of others;

> it is like the eyes,
> or say the face, of Palestrina by El Greco,
> O Escudero, Soledad,
> Rosario Escudero, Etchebaster!

Not only are the names more precise than precision, but the syllable-count in each line made up of such names matches those established in earlier stanzas. There is no proper name that does not qualify as a tune in qualifying as style. Marianne Moore could imagine calling a car (the then-unnamed Edsel which the Ford Motor Company had invited her to name) "Mongoose Civique" as well as "Utopian Turtletop" or "Andante con moto." One of her letters to the Ford Company concerning the naming of the car reveals her persistence and serious playfulness in the matter; it ends with a parenthetical "(I cannot resist the temptation to disobey my brother and submit TURCOTINGO)." The name, she believed, was intimately concerned with appearance, performance, and fate; even a car must have a properly descriptive one if it is going to survive. Proper names are, in a way, the opposite of chaos in making distinct what otherwise might have no distinction. The propriety of the name Edsel (*not* one of Marianne Moore's suggestions) could not save the car itself, yet the name survives as a watchword for failed enterprise. It would be even harder to discard a Utopian Turtletop.

There is another lexical feature of Marianne Moore's style that implies order, and that is the use of motto or the tone of mottoes and proverbs. They doctor disorder: "Physicians are not so often poets as poets are physicians, but may we not assert that oppositions of science are not oppositions to poetry but oppositions to falseness?"[14] Mottoes and proverbs may be seen to do for language what scientific paradigms do for scientific exploration. They are handed down as discoveries, as sums and sine qua nons of wisdom. And "if compression is the first grace of style . . ."; "Make hay"; *Il faut dire en deux mots/ Ce qu'on veut dire.*" "Make hay" is one of three clustered abbreviations of mottoes in "The Frigate Pelican." Their function is traditional—to point a moral and adorn a tale—but in a countertraditional way. That is, they come in the middle of a descriptive passage only very indirectly related to them. The very emblems of human continuity become agents of discontinuity. Moore invokes "an apple a day" in describing a china plate—no, not the plate but the nectarines painted on it: "the peach Yu, the red-/ cheeked peach which cannot aid the dead,/ but eaten in time prevents death."

"People's Surroundings" quotes Poor Richard "so to speak" and tells us also that "a good brake is as important as a good motor." "Smooth Gnarled Crape Myrtle" describes the painting of birds on a box lid under which is inscribed the motto "Joined in friendship, crowned by love." The poem ends, not without a certain obscurity, with a motto from the title page of Lodge's *Rosalynde:* "By Peace/ Plenty; as by Wisdom Peace." This certainly has the air of summing up; it is an obvious ending; but it seems to have no profound meaning with regard to the text adorned with a "Rosalindless redbird," or to the other motto, similarly reverently irrelevant. This often seems to be the case in Moore's use of motto, by allusion or quotation, and her own aphoristic statements. There is a hint, in a note to "Smooth Gnarled Crape Myrtle," of one of the stylistic uses of motto and aphorism. Here someone points out that the "speech of man changes and coarsens" while the bird still sings the pure heroic Sanskrit of the ancient poets. We recognize the motto as condensed poetry of very ancient source—yes, this is how poet's ideally talk—but it is a language that is used mainly for the beauty of its syntactical brevity and for its air of truth in itself, apart from the relative chaos of the text. The use of a motto might be to us as obscure as Sanskrit, yet we can tell that something important survives in it. It is in the style of what Northrop Frye calls "high hieratic,"[15] though it may originate in the low demotic, or anywhere. The high hieratic is indicated by "momentary co-ordination of vision," "a passage that stands out"; it is more individual than social. By making the most idiosyncratic use of the most "social" forms of literature, mottoes and proverbs, the poet makes the point that generalities may be taken personally, that "Art, admired in general,/ is always actually personal" ("In the Public Garden"). Or art, begot by continuity, is expressed most strikingly in the unique, the self-contained, and the discontinuous. The motto (or mottoid), as summation, pause in sense, or culmination, may be regarded as a sort of superpunctuation. It is a sign of confidence in the true-sounding order of things. If absolute truth, as we suspect, is attainable only in absolute silence, true-*sounding* may be the best we can hope to offer, or a sounding of truth by hypotheses that are well-grounded.

Marianne Moore's prose, as well as her poems, tend to get gnomic or obscure with compression (one is reminded of the letters of Emily Dickinson) when she feels very strongly. Explicitness, she tells us in *Predilections,* is the "enemy" of brevity, and the victory of brevity, however tense with restraint, is a victory of goodness. The business of writing requires constant moral awareness of the battle against self-indulgence. Often the feeling underlying the gnomic statement in her work is one of dislike or anger, as in her review of Ezra Pound's *Cantos* where, after reasonably fluent paragraphs of practically unqualified praise, she confronts Cantos XIV and XV, both brilliantly offensive and scatological. "Petty annoyances are magnified," she states; "when one is a beginner, tribulation worketh impatience."[16] Her use of the archaic form of the verb is meant to add to our sense that her objections to these Cantos, not explicitly stated, have an ancient and proverbial authority.

Roland Barthes points out that "literary expression harks back, by transformation, to another syntactic structure" and that a certain style comes from exercising transformations not of "idea" but of form, and he mentions the proverb as one of the principal such stereotypes from which literary language is generated.[17] If it is the nature of a literary expression to "hark back" in some way to the most compact forms of verbal expression to be found in the history of language in general, it seems very possible that the literary expression we come to think of as having a personal style also harks back to the language associated with an individual's childhood. Structures of the simplest kind yet compact with meaning necessarily make up the process of learning to talk. Aphorism rediscovers words on a sophisticated level which may be felt to hark back not only to the origins of literary language in general but also to the child's first feeling power in the original naming of things.

Quotations are, like mottoes or new-coined aphorisms (or aphoroids?) used in Marianne Moore's poetry as units, as found poetry — some pleasantly vague, some distinct as graffiti. Their use, however, is almost always in the service of continuity, not discontinuity. The technical feat involved is like that of setting a jewel into a piece of metal that is precisely suited to the stone and that will, if the technique is successful, appear to honor the stone. It is a matter of arrangement and propriety:

in this dried bone of arrangement
one's "natural promptness" is compressed, not crowded out;
one's style is not lost in such simplicity.

("People's Surroundings")

There is a note on "natural promptness" that gives the full sentence from which it was taken: [of a poet] "Gifts of wit and natural promptness appear in him abundantly." "Natural promptness," like "natural piety" is a poetic "find." Design in poetry is a matter of timing considerably more than it is a matter of spacing, though they can be seen to work together.

An article in *Scientific American,* examining Galileo's notes, points out that he could have made highly accurate time-measurements involving the acceleration of falling bodies simply by singing and noting at certain points in the song the positions of a ball rolling down a plane. This method can be used to measure small fractions of seconds, smaller than those that could have been measured by any timing instrument that would have been available to Galileo.[18] The article points out that we can all tell if a musician is just slightly off the beat; a grace note just before the beat sounds vastly different from one played exactly on the beat. This sort of promptness is not learned but perfectly natural, and although it operates in spoken language on a grosser level, one can speak of "natural promptness" in poetry as a musical and technical effect, being there on time with precisely the right emphasis and intonation. The poet to whom natural promptness was first ascribed survives partly by virtue of it.

"Novices" is an explicitly enraged and purposely unsubtle but witty attack on those "supertadpoles of expression" who have no sense of natural promptness in poetry, who speak of "dracontine cockatrices" rather than confront true images of the "sea-serpented regions" in themselves. The novices do not understand the timing of the prophets, the power of prophetic speech, or the unconscious passion of the sea as an image natural to prophetic passion. There is another thing the novices do not understand, and that is that the power of language is such that one can move and be moved by words that one does not take credit for. The poem ends with a lesson in writing and submission, a collage of quotations from *The Decameron,* A. R. Gordon's *The Prophets of the Old Testament,* P. T. Forsyth's *Christ On Parnassus,* George Adam Smith's *Expositor's Bible,* and Leigh Hunt's *Autobiography:*

"split like a glass against a wall"
in this "precipitate of dazzling impressions,
the spontaneous unforced passion of the Hebrew language—
an abyss of verbs full of reverberations and tempestuous energy"
in which action perpetuates action and angle is at variance with
        angle
till submerged by the general action;
obscured by "fathomless suggestions of color,"
by incessantly panting lines of green, white with concussion,
in this drama of water against rocks—this "ocean of hurrying
        consonants"
with its "great livid stains like long slabs of green marble,"
its "flashing lances of perpendicular lightning" and "molten fires
        swallowed up,"
"with foam on its barriers,"
"crashing itself out in one long hiss of spray."

The passage presents prose recombined into poetry in an unself-conscious symbolic action. Something "other" speaks through the poet who takes credit for little but arrangement. Coping with all that has been written before one "in which action perpetuates action and angle is at variance with angle/ till submerged by the general action" is like coping with the ocean itself. The only way to represent the ocean "unlit by the half light of more conscious art" is by bringing to one's audience some literal souvenir of it. The language of the sea is perpetual; because it is in continual motion, rearranging itself with utmost unconscious precision as all natural things do, it can suggest to us a style of survival which does not, and cannot, be original in the literal sense, and cannot have the last word, either.

Marianne Moore developed what we might call her "quotational" style in order to get across the sort of message that leaves her speechless. The passage at the end of "Novices," quoted above, is mimetic, the lines building, getting heavier with accents and longer "till submerged"; then they build a second time, withdraw, and dissolve finally in the long hiss of spray. The poet takes on herself the syntagmatic burden of order-making and, remarkably, relinquishes credit for specific lexical or metaphoric choice. It is as if she is compensating for her rich nominal (as opposed to verbal) chatter, the "gray-blue-Andalusian-cock-feather pale ones ink-lined on the edge" and "wide-spaced great blunt alternating ostrich-skin warts that were thorns." Indulging in this sin of explicitness every so often is balanced by the sort of passage in which she allows herself no play at all. "Novices" is about submission to external as well as internal forces, about how to make them work together most naturally. As we read without the benefit of the notes, the sublimely latinate words are as if anonymous in their impersonality. Moore seems to remind herself and us that poetry is made, not named; that poetry is in proof—verbatim exactness, repeated evidence, and not sloppy or vague personal intuitions. "We prove, we do not explain our birth" ("The Monkey Puzzle"). Chosen silence and chosen speech are matters of fatal evidence and unparaphraseable waves. If they are not, then they are not very well chosen, and their chances for survival are impaired.

"By survival of this ancient punctilio," Moore says in "Bowls,"

> in the manner of Chinese lacquer carving,
> layer after layer exposed by certainty of touch and unhurried
>   incision
> so that only so much color shall be revealed as is necessary to the
>   picture,
> I learn that we are precisionists
> not citizens of Pompeii arrested in action
> as a cross section of one's correspondence would seem to imply.
> Renouncing a policy of boorish indifference
> to everything that has been said since the days of Matilda,
> I shall purchase an etymological dictionary of modern English
> that I may understand what is written.

Bits of life quick frozen into letters are tantalizing evidence of life, certain moments' expressions petrified, but a cross section, a random design revealed by slicing the organic whole of time, can only hint vaguely at the entire picture, the unified patterns of moment by moment choice, aim, and execution which the wholeness of life and games and art share. Reconstituted history does not share this wholeness. Style, a phenomenon which is parallel to life in games and art, unfolds its meaning as the lacquer carving does, "layer after layer exposed" in time and spatially, as related to the whole picture, the whole body of a poem or of a poet's work.

By studying the *process* of revelation we learn our human nature as precisionists, not by studying frozen moments; survival is a matter of contiguity, not simultaneity. The rules that govern the possibilities of moment succeeding moment without specificity of any one move or moment make up "the principle that is hid" in life or in style. In the latter, including games and arts of any sort, the rules are reduced and emphasized, made precise by concentration, and a good deal of the pleasure that is derived from the enactment of these specialized hidden principles is that they are to a great extent discover-able. It is in the process of discovering them, moreover, that we discover our own true nature as precisionists. A cross section of life may hint at, but can-not fulfil, our expectations in the way that continuous play can. This is the reason for preserving "ancient punctilio" and for observing the rules of style; without it we would still have precision, but it would be a chaos of precision —too much reality. Style, or punctilio, provides the illusion that is beyond the precision devoted to the individual moment. Illusion is more precise than precision because it is a function of continuity; pressed by time, it shuts out a fatal superfluity of information about the world at any one moment. Illusion is precisely the illusion of control that makes survival possible. For animals it is instinctual, but for man it is a saving artifice.

The poet, as precisionist *and* illusionist to a very conscious degree, can-not be indifferent to the history of revelation, in himself, in a particular work of art, or in a particular word. The etymological dictionary is a necessity because in containing the history of words it contains human precisionist history, and in containing the hidden principles of the survival and evolution of words and meanings, it contains the hidden principles of future verbal possibilities. The poem "Bowls" explains that the poet will purchase such a dictionary not only to understand what is written—a precisionist occupation—but to "answer the question/ 'Why do I like winter better than summer?'" That is to say, the history of changing definitions and the preservation of ancient punctilio contain enough information about ourselves that through them we can learn to answer, from the roots, questions of personal illusions and predilections as well as questions of precision. In both sorts of questions we are to assume that there is a "principle that is hid." Without it there would be no *point* in survival in general, or in the manifestations of personal style.

These considerations may seem abstruse at this point, but they are, I believe, essential to a full perception of Marianne Moore's own style of self-consciousness as it penetrates and influences every aspect of her poetry, in-cluding not least the technical aspects. Technique, as Pound says, is the mea-sure of sincerity. Morality in writing is not a matter of hazy intuitions about good and evil but a matter of continuous, minute, and informed judgments. It is a matter of conscience and the arrangement of perceptions that, shared by a community, determines spiritual survival. It parallels the structures of na-ture that, shared by all matter, determine biological survival. The spiritual value of technique in art is stressed in the essay "Idiosyncrasy and Tech-nique," where Moore states that "structural infirmity truly has, under sur-realism, become a kind of verbal blight threatening firmness at the core." The artist is morally responsible for continuity and connection in art, as these are necessary for its survival. There is a mimetic bond between art and nature, such that the artist may arrange his art after the fashion of nature or arrange nature after the fashion of art, the object of both being mutual survival via the acknowledgment of mutual principles. "Nine Nectarines," a poem which describes a painted plate, begins "Arranged by two's as peaches are,/ at intervals that all may live"; the fruit is "arranged" *in order to live,* and we need not ask whether the "idea" occurred first in nature or in nature's human reflectors, because it is simply a fact and there is no honest way to distort it.

"The Steeple-Jack" shows the opposite phenomenon, just as necessary to survival, but to survival as an art rather than as a principle. This poem begins, "Dürer would have seen a reason for living/ in a town like this, with eight stranded whales/ to look at"; and it goes on to make a selective arrangement of the town's natural phenomena, adding a church steeple and a danger sign, all leading to the conclusion (a necessary one for art, a *raison d'être*) that "it could not be dangerous to be living/ in a town like this." Living is not easy; one has a moral obligation to make arrangements for it.

A poem becomes a fixture by being written down, and fixture is a paradox. It can mean death in its changelessness and a lasting part of life in its presence. The last stanza of "The Fish" is a fixture of technique that does not compromise the paradox, but rather illuminates it and makes it applicable beyond itself. It makes it live, although the subject, a chasm, is

> dead.
> Repeated
> > evidence has proved that it can live
> > on what cannot revive
> > > its youth. The sea grows old in it.

Repetition, compulsive or not, contains both death and immortality. The suggestion of possible infinite repetition, as in the form of a poem where one stanza-form is repeated again and again, arbitrarily begun, arbitrarily clung to, and at last arbitrarily abandoned in favor of silence, also suggests death, the final fixture that gives value to a whole process. The rhyme of "dead" and "repeated" is technical affirmation of the paradox; even the punctuation makes a mimetic point. The next rhyme, "live" with "-not revive," emphasize a different but related aspect of both nature and art, that life is given, and the entropic gift cannot be repeated, only extended by replacing what is necessarily lost through time. "Repeated evidence" of life is formal and "what cannot revive" is the specific content that flows through the form. Youth and growing old occupy the same last line; the form is no more than a vehicle for framing what is lost. Death and repetition, living on the condition of losing, and time captured long enough to be named either youth or age—the close relation of these is constantly demonstrated in the artistic process, no matter what the specific content, and threatening as the paradoxes are, the artist must have a moral as well as technical obligation to observe them. Marianne Moore ends her essay "Feeling and Precision" with this connection:

> Professor Maritain, when lecturing on scholasticism and immortality, spoke of those suffering in concentration camps, "unseen by any star, unheard by any ear," and the almost terrifying solicitude with which he spoke made one know that belief is stronger even than the struggle to survive. And what he said so unconsciously was poetry. So art is but an expression of our needs; is feeling, modified by the writer's moral and technical insights.

Technique is a matter of *insight,* not of information or of any superficial appearance. For Marianne Moore it is a matter of faith in the invisible laws that determine structure. She was most conscientious about the spiritual origin of technique, both in its individuality and in its generality, and about the material origin of illusion, including that of moral responsibility. This conscientiousness, and this consciousness of the needs both of the self and of the other, penetrates every aspect of the construction of her poems. There is absurdity in it, naturally, as it displays the profundity of superficiality in everything.

THE SYLLABIFICATION OF SURVIVAL

Marianne Moore wrote with the subject of survival constantly on her mind, not her own survival particularly, but that of the words she used, the forms they gave and took, and the subjects they celebrated. It is interesting to investigate one specific aspect of her style, her use of "syllabic" or "isosyllabic" verse, to see just how intimately it is connected with one of the more general preoccupations of her sensibility, the preservation of living forms.

Syllabification is the basis of all metric structures, but the "metric stretch," or "foot," is determined by the syllabic stress or pulse, the culmination and delimitation of the metric stretch by a certain pattern of stress. Marianne Moore writes what is technically known as "isosyllabic" verse, meaning that the metric stretch is one syllable long regardless of the variations in stress or duration of the different syllables. The special ingeniousness of Marianne Moore's preference for this "meter" which, in effect, discounts itself by counting as equal syllables that are unequal, is basic to "the principle that is hid" in her style. It is playful, absurd, and profound.

The form of a syllabic poem such as Marianne Moore is famous for writing can begin totally arbitrarily. The following might be a recipe: take a stretch of verbal expression not necessarily written as verse but preferably a prose that is concentrated and whole; divide it according to whim into lines of varying or equal numbers of syllables; indent to taste; and set aside as a model stanza. Repeat the procedure of this model stanza using any leftovers from the content along with new materials until enough identical stanzas have been put by to satisfy one's hunger for meaning as well as for form. The end of the set of stanzas and the end of the last sentence should coincide. There should be no waste. Marianne Moore was not a slave to these formal stipulations and at times felt perfectly free to write "free" verse, but it is the isosyllabic form, determined by number of syllables, ignoring stresses, for which she is best known. As a stylistic element this form carries far more of her unique vision than is generally credited to it.

The first thing to notice about Moore's syllabic method is that all syllables are created equal in the metric eye. Examples of elision can be found, but they are few; by and large, each syllable is treated as an individual. This of course has nothing to do with the context directly—the syllables are no more created or creative in equal measure than men are, but the fact that each is numbered as "one" on some level of the universal scheme of things is significant, if only for its inherent craziness.

No art form can avoid all aspects of mimesis, as all are doomed to reflect and reveal some aspect of the creative process that is responsible for their being. Likewise, no art form can present a perfect mimesis—absolute identification with its precedent form or image—without the sameness approaching, if not achieving, meaninglessness. Meaning, in a fallen world, always derives from discrepancy, and the most meaningful choices of the artist have to do with the presentation of conflict—between the work of art and himself, the work of art and the "real" world, between aspects of "content," between aspects of "form," between "form" and "content," and so on. (I choose to protect certain words with quotation marks, not to suggest the allegedness or indefensibility of their undressed applications, but to preserve a necessary ambiguity.) The dominant feeling about "free verse" (if that association of words is not anomalous) is that the form should follow the individual content, lines breaking at breathing points, at the poet's whim, or upon a stressed word, syntax dispensable in imitation of thought, punctuation replaceable by space or grace or used inventively in the service of idio-syncrasy. All these things may be seen as urging the recognition of a conflict between the individual artist and his collective audience, the tradition-makers and/or trend-recognizers. Stylisticians choose to talk about the phenomenon in terms of "norm" and "deviance," deviance being a measure of style's in-dividuality. Marianne Moore has managed, without violating the collective norms of expression, to present the conflict of individual and collective en-tirely within the frame of her work and within herself, and has succeeded better than most poets of her period in escaping critical antagonisms from without. Her primary violation or deviance, if there must be one, is with respect to the modern norm that form-and-content express an original unity. In her isosyllabic stanzas the content of the form is in subtle, unreasonable, and unresolvable conflict with the form of the content. That is, the practice of reducing all syllables to the same quantitative value is theoretically contra-dictory to the fine discrepancies of musical pulse that must be made between those same syllables. It is like music written with no specified time signature or bar delimitations (as in Lucien Berio's *Sequenza* for flute, for instance) with every note looking like an eighth note, the space between them the only indication of time. This may be regarded as "deviant" in some respect, but it is a reflection of the normal conflict between collective and individual inter-ests nonetheless.

The *syllables* themselves are collective property, and are counted as if the author had no favorites. The *stanzas* into which they are counted, how-ever, are an individual property, entirely dependent on the poet's whim. They may add up or not, multiply or divide among themselves, with no influence upon the sound or soundness of the syllables. The *syntax* of each sentence is in agreement with rules collectively formed, but the intersections of the *line breaks* are a property of the individual stanza; if these two happen to be on speaking terms, as when they coincide to end a poem or a sequence of stan-zas, the coincidence may be interpreted as specially significant, in conflict itself with the prime motives of the haphazard.

Character, style, and survival are interchangeable as subjects of the following predicate: *formed by the restrictive shaping of contingency and possibility*. The point is made again and again in Marianne Moore's verse, that that which is "hindered to succeed" ("The Paper Nautilus") does indeed, that "a tuned reticence with rigor" denotes "strength at the source" ("Propriety"), and that anything, like the sea, "struggling to be/ free and unable to be,/ in its surrendering/ finds its continuing" ("What Are Years?"). The emphasis in the versatile predicate above is on the restrictive, not the possibility; it is on willed control, not gratuitous contingencies. In "Tom Fool at Jamaica" (Tom

Fool is a race horse), "'Chance" by chance ends a stanza and begins a new sentence, to be continued in the next stanza: "[it]// is a regrettable impurity'; like Tom Fool's/ left white hind foot—an unconformity; though judging by/ results a kind of cottontail to give him confidence." Since one cannot control the element of chance in creation and cannot honestly pretend to, it is best regarded with a sort of superstitious faith. Faith, I believe, is the key to Marianne Moore's discovery of the mimetic usefulness of her syllabic forms.

It is important to note that Moore's choice of meter is not noticeable in an ordinary reading or hearing of the poem. The principle is invisible and inaudible, yet absolutely tyrannical as far as the maker of the poem is concerned. If noted, it is an accident unrelated to reading skills. In observing her syllable-by-syllable meter with such untiring accuracy, Marianne Moore is placing her faith in a naturally unmanifest yet totally rigorous form, "a tuned reticence with rigor from strength at the source." She trusts the integrity and dynamism of her words and syntax to the fracturing randomness of syllabic specifications. The decision to count is a decision which results in a personal moral obligation; it is moral because appointed as a principle of conduct, a principle of "propriety" in expression, and as a commitment that is personally adhered to regardless of any collective judgment. Choice, including specifically stylistic choice, lies between chance and faith. The faith that is originally significant is the creator's own faith in faith's significance. This is not offered as a conundrum, but as a principle of poetic operation. This faith, like that defended by Kierkegaard's "knight of faith," does not impose itself; it is an armor of "mirror-of-steel uninsistence . . . objectified and not by chance" ("Armor's Undermining Modesty"). It is mimetic with respect to a creation effected and governed by a "principle that is hid" ("To a Snail"), in which "the power of the visible is the invisible" ("He 'Digesteth Harde Yron'"). The paradox inherent in all this is that by investing a form of supremely uninsistent, unimposing, unrebuking modesty, Marianne Moore successfully suggests highest power. She displays the mimetic connection between artist and god no less firmly than James Joyce, but from virtually opposite moral premises.

"Blessed is the man," says Marianne Moore, "whose faith is different/ from possessiveness—of a kind not framed by 'things which do appear'—" ("Blessed Is the Man"). It may be true that William Carlos Williams found in Moore's poems the ideal of his "no ideas but in things" motto, and certainly she has been celebrated by those who celebrate Williams' famous maxim and objectivist aims in poetry, but to see the romance of *things* as central to her poetic motives is a mistake. The "rock crystal thing" that the "hero" sees

("The Hero") is a metaphysical thing, and it is essential to Moore that a work of art which moves us "acknowledge the spiritual forces which have made it" ("When I Buy Pictures"). Faith is not a matter for display, but a private confidence in the discipline, however unreasonable its reasons, of *the* creative force, of the absolute freedom of captivity and captivation by choice, "freedom to toil/ with a feel for the tool" ("In the Public Garden").

> So he who strongly feels,
> behaves. The very bird,
>   grown taller as he sings, steels
> his form straight up. Though he is captive,
> his mighty singing
> says, satisfaction is a lowly
> thing, how pure a thing is joy.
>   This is mortality,
>   this is eternity.

("What Are Years?")

Strong feeling in humans replaces the instincts lost in the fall from animal grace; it dictates our behavior and our "style" of being insofar as style is a matter of survival. That survival is limited by time and space is a notion unavailable to instinct but unavoidable in human feeling. It is the consciousness of this limitation that makes us consciously reproduce—reproduce ourselves in the act of reproducing ourselves in time and space that are specially concentrated and restricted, as in any art, so that we can see the event of limited existence in small. The choices involved in how to use a small space and time, how most effectively live and love and die in it, produce style. Human style as an expression of survival has as fulcra the means and the end, or, more consequently, sex and death. Every writer knows this in his bones, including the chaste lady who can tame the unicorn.

Ivan Fónagy, discussing verbal style in general, remarks that in the orchestration of all literary works there is dependence on two principles, recurrence and tension. He says further that these two depend in turn on "two forces whose interplay determines all human activity": (1) the play of tension and release as the sexual principle and (2) the metrical organization representing the presence of the death instinct.[19] For Marianne Moore, as we have seen, both eternity and mortality are manifest in the metrical cage; the living free power that escapes the cage is music, the seductive play of style no less important to survival than biological conjugation. Fónagy mentions also that style may be regarded as a necessary "acting out" of deep feeling, as neces-

sary to human equilibrium as the restorative dream. Having related the innocence of isosyllabics to acknowledgment of faith, absurdity, death, and eternity, it is time to look at the musical defiance of fate. (One may indeed see
"style" as protagonist in a linguistic family romance, the writer doomed to
rape his mother tongue in defiance of father time, tradition, and the com-
monalty of sense—a view suggested by the work of Otto Rank.)

It is a curious fact that in the alphabetical index to Marianne Moore's
Complete Poems, there are two minds suggestively coupled:

> Mind, Intractable Thing, The
> Mind Is an Enchanting Thing, The

Definite articles replaced, the two titles offer one intractable and one enchanting rhythm. Dogged vs. charming, persistent vs. heady: throughout all
the poems these two musics and these two qualities of mind are found together like

> the opposing opposed
> mouse-gray twined proboscises' trunk formed by two
> trunks, fight[ing] itself into a spiraled inter-nosed
> deadlock of dyke-enforced massiveness.
>
> ("Elephants")

Like the contrapuntal music celebrated in "Melchior Vulpius," it builds from
"miniature thunder" and depends on "conscientious inconsistency" ("The
Mind Is an Enchanting Thing"), as in the following blend of dense unexpected
stress and easily draped definition:

> black opal emerald opal
> emerald—the prompt-delayed loud-
> low chromatic listened-for down-
> scale which Swinburne called in prose, the
> noiseless music that hangs about
> the serpent when it stirs or springs.
>
> ("The Plumet Basilisk")

The striking quality of the passage is due largely to the "opposing opposed"
urgency and ease in its rhythmic poise. Each of the six lines contains exactly

eight syllables rhythmically falling into two sections, the break coming between "scale" and "which" in the fourth line. The first half of the passage
contains twenty-five syllables and is full of unprepared-for stress; the second,
containing twenty-three syllables, is full of grace. Scanned, the felt difference
between the first and second halves of the passage is made apparent:

```
' ' _ ' _ _ ' _ ' _ ' _ _ _ _ _ ' _ ' ' ' _ ' _ ' _ ' '
_ ' _ ' _ ' _ ' _ ' _ _ ' _ ' _ ' _ ' _ '
```

The first half of the passage consists of twelve words and thirteen stresses,
the second of eighteen words and eleven stresses. The first falls into two
parts, the division indicated by a dash. There are five stresses and eleven syllables in the first part, eight stresses and thirteen syllables in the second. The
second half is divided by an anapestic foot set into the exact center of the
group of sounds with ten syllables of perfect pentameter on either side. The
anapestic foot thus performs the function of the dash in the first group. In
the first three lines of the passage there is no perceivable regular metric
stretch; in the second the regular swing of iambics dominates. There is irony
in this use of prosody, too, as what is referred to as Swinburne's prose is associated with a traditional regular poetic meter, perfectly natural here in its
camouflaging eight-syllables-per-line habitat. The first three lines, however,
associated with the veil of forest trees where "minute noises swell and change"
earlier in the poem, and which, as we fail to find prose-prone syntax, we associate with "poetry," actually present the irregular rhythmic tortures usually
tolerated by the tensest prose. There is no better passage to illustrate the
diversity of texture that is allowed by counting syllables rather than feet;
music becomes entirely a matter of self-determination because a decided
meter does not determine it. This is true of free verse as well, but I can think
of no poet who handles so much diversity with so much regular authority as
Marianne Moore in her carefully counted stanzas. It is as if the stipulated line
lengths put supernatural pressure upon the musical content of each line. There
is no waste; every sound stands up to be counted and is held accountable.
      Clusters of stresses enforced with internal rhymed syllables that are
inter-determining are especially characteristic of Marianne Moore's "splendid
with splendor hid" ("Sun") verse, "like 'turns in an ancient Chinese/ melody,
a thirteen/ twisted silk-string three-finger solo'" ("Blue Bug"). That last was
music recalling a dancer compared to a polo pony, and here is a dream recalling music:

> For his methodic unmetronomic melodic diversity
> contrapuntally appointedly persistently
>   irresistably Fate-like Bach—find me words.

("Dream")

This collection of syllables would be outrageous as prose, and they are equally outrageous judged from the poetic tradition. We might say that their beauty is in that there is no excuse for them, prosaic or poetic. They are simply "all this fiddle" ("Poetry"). The sequence, like music, is only partially analyzable quantitatively, but such analysis confirms the baroque impression. The three lines each fall into three parts, the pattern looking like this:

```
     5              5              7
 _'_'_         _'_'_         _'__'__

     5              4              4
 '_'__         _'_'          _'__

     5              3              3
 '_'__          ' ' '          ' ' '
```

We notice the symmetry of the first two groups of syllables in the first line, and the fact that each of the three groups has two stresses. We note that the second line begins as the first with a group of five syllables, with two stresses, but that the pattern of stresses is subtly different, and that the next two groups, each of four syllables, exactly echo the pattern of stresses in the last four syllables of the last two groups of syllables in the line above, that between them they have three stresses. The third line begins by echoing the five syllables and stress-pattern of the line it follows, and the dominance of three asserts itself in the last two syllable groups, each composed of three syllables, all stressed. We may note also that the second and third groups of the second and third lines, added vertically, yield groups of seven syllables, the number in the last group of the first line. I do not want to suggest that Marianne Moore, or any poet, would diagram such a relationship of sounds before writing the words, but the fact that such patterns exist and definitely appeal to our ears in writing or reading them points to a "natural promptness" in verbal as well as nonverbal music that is part of our biological as well as cultural inheritance. We do not have to be counting to hear what counts. The pattern of sound in the example just discussed is, if anything, more intricate than my gobbledygook of analytical statements has indicated, and could take pages more perhaps in a fiddling exhibition.

Reading it, however, with a perfect contempt for it, one discovers in
it after all, a place for the genuine.

                                                              ("Poetry")

      The inturning and practically autistic chatter of Marianne Moore's
baroque style is self-fulfilling, something usually said of prophecy. Whether it
is "Fate-like Bach—find me words" or "Bach-like words—find me Fate," the
fatal-playful motives in the end are found to circumscribe no less than one's
individual survival. Marianne Moore is fond of biological analogues to her own
creative processes. For instance, her admission to Donald Hall: "I never plan
a stanza. Words cluster like chromosomes, determining the procedure."
Whether they are chromosomes or randomly compatible adjectives, they—the
genetic motes of any and all—epitomize the biological-theological paradox
that accident determines design. That design is an accident? The paradox is
only confirmed or broken by faith, "not framed by 'things which do appear'"
("Blessed Is the Man"). Chromosomes and words do their clustering and
breaking in secret, invisible to us without the help of microscopes. At the
same time they determine the visible, pull toward the light the finished animal. As Moore says, of both art and science, "The objective is fertile procedure. . . . it's evolving."[20]
      One reason for examining the minutest units of a poem is the same as
one reason for examining all matter at the level of its smallest particles. Marianne Moore tells us that her first stanza usually determines the rest of the
stanzas in her isosyllabic poems. It has, conjoined with some hidden power in
her mind, the power to reproduce itself, like DNA, and to make a finished
body. A certain consequence, the life of the poem, comes from invisibility
and necessarily goes back to it. It is "the principle that is hid" that we value
in style, and this principle is the one responsible for the very inception of the
poem. One way to share the secret of all beginnings is to have a secret. "The
secret," Ernest Becker observes, "implies, above all, power to control the
given by the hidden and thus power to transcend the given—nature, fate, animal destiny. . . . The secret is man's illusion par excellence, the denial of the
bodily reality of his destiny."[21]
      The only thing more precise than precision, says Moore, is illusion, and
the more precise the examination or creation of a thing, the closer we are to
the real secret and the real denial of it—namely life itself. Counting syllables,
like counting molecules, is, whether the counters see it in this way or not, a
religious gesture. When poetry and science were young together, they ex-
amined the stars; the Big Secret was supposed to be in the biggest thing imaginable, the sky. Alphabets and atoms have moved far apart in their respective

disciplines since, and the smallest particles have become the stars of each, yet
they are still connected and there is still a real sense in which the premise of
Marianne Moore's poem "Light Is Speech" is true. Hence:

> Verse—unabashedly bold—is appropriate;
>   and always it should be as neat
> as the most careful writer's "8." . . .
>   Might verse not best confuse itself with fate?
>
>   ("Saint Valentine")

Is it accident that the line ending with "8" has eight syllables? If so, then
accident is as good as design. And is it coincidence that "8" written side-
ways, ∞, is the sign of infinity? The fact that Marianne Moore creates, or
finds, designs inaudible to the human ear and not visible to the prosaic eye
is cabbalistic in spirit. Only the initiated will know the secret of counting
syllables. "Syllable" comes from the Greek *syllabē*, "that which is held together." Surely anything held together is a miracle, and not least the letters
and the waves of sound held together by pronunciation.

The smallest particles are responsible for holding everything together
somehow, and this is the mystery and illusion that poets and scientists are
both after. Meanwhile we have to have faith that electrons can tell us of life
on Mars, if there is life there, and that quarks will yield the secret of pyramids, if there are quarks. We see in Marianne Moore's poems the important
notion that one needs the same kind of faith in matter that one has in spirit
because both ultimately originate in invisible force forced into visibility, or
inaudible strains made audible. It is to be expected that verse confuse itself
with fate, that the opening and closing of utterance confuse itself with an
aspect shared by 8 and ∞.

Only truth is beyond both illusion and precision and therefore beyond
the animal of style and that animal's precarious survival, where

> in the short-legged, fit-
> ful advance, the gurgling and all the minutiae—we have the classic
> multitude of feet. To what purpose! Truth is no Apollo
> Belvedere, no formal thing.
>
>   ("In the Days of Prismatic Color")

CONVERSATION

There are those who will talk for an hour
without telling you why they have
*   come. And I? This is no madrigal—*
*   no medieval gradual.*
*   It is a grateful tale—*
without that radiance which poets
are supposed to have—
*   unofficial, unprofessional.*

("In the Public Garden")

Style as survival may result in self-addressed soliloquies or artistic reveries that imply no expected response from an audience; its survival value is individual rather than social. This is only one aspect of Marianne Moore's style, however, another being her definite intention to exchange and instruct and delight, and this intention is embodied in style as conversation. It involves personal, syntactical, rhetorical, and moral principles, principles of style that are not meant to be hid. M. A. K. Halliday, in an essay called "Linguistic Function and Literary Style," divides linguistic functions into three categories—textual, interpersonal, and ideational. The "interpersonal" function he describes is both interactional and personal; "there is, in other words, a component in language which serves at one and the same time to express both the inner and the outer surfaces of the individual, as a single undifferentiated area of meaning potential that is personal in the broadest sense."[22] In the work of Marianne Moore we are reminded again and again that the abilities to communicate, to listen, to be interesting, to learn, and to be generally socially acceptable are moral abilities that show themselves nowhere as clearly as in one's conversation. For the poet who can say, offhand and sincerely, of poetry, "I, too, dislike it" ("Poetry"), style must aspire to the conversational state to be of use. This notion stands out in the essay "Henry James as a Characteristic American," where Moore claims, "Education for him, in a large sense, was conversation."[23] She goes on to praise his qualities (certainly conversational ones) of "good-nature" and "reciprocity" as characteristic American traits, and she quotes this hero in saying, "We need never fear not to be good enough if only we were social enough." Conversation analyzed may at first reveal itself as certain patterns of reciprocal syntax or as variously affected rhetorical patterns of address or answer; but ultimately, in the poetry and prose of Marianne Moore, conversation will be seen as a moral fabric of personal persuasions and eccentric yarns. Education, goodness, and reciprocity are, all of them, moral affairs and all of them are displayed in "conversation" in its largest sense, including its archaic meanings as "an abiding" or "a manner of living or conduct" as well as its most common meanings as social intercourse or just friendly talk. Marianne Moore means highest praise when she says of T. S. Eliot's prose, "I detect no difference between it and conversation."24

Conversation may be regarded as a hybrid of in-formations and conversions, its purpose being to convert to one's own opinions, or conversely, to be converted to another's; to be in good form, socially speaking, or to be informed. In a review of Pound's *Cantos,* Marianne Moore approvingly requotes Kung of Canto XIII, saying, "If a man have not order within him/ He cannot spread order about him." The function of style as survival is to maintain the order of one's own existence in oneself; the function of style as conversation is to spread that order outside. Both the personal expression and the interpersonal expression depend on a mixture of suggestive and precise statements, but one might say that for purposes of survival it is precision of response and expression that insure the continuation of the individual process of style, but for the purposes of conversation it is suggestiveness, or the precisely suggestive comment which insures the continuation of the mutual and moral process of style. This latter process suggests possibilities of parallel, tangential, and opposing constructions that may be openly stated or simply understood within a given work regarded as "conversation." It is in this way that a text can be said to create or to contain its own ideal reader.

In speaking of style as survival, we necessarily speak of recurrent rhythms and sounds that are obligatory in the survival of most living things, poetry being a special case of this necessity. One suspects that one reason why Marianne Moore disliked having to categorize her writing as "poetry" (for lack of a better term), and the reason that she could claim in a poem called "Poetry" that she disliked the genre in general, is that she perceived, rightly, the narcissistic properties in all heavily emphasized phonological and metrical patterns. At the end of her career she restates a sentiment regarding "poetry" that one can trace back through her work from the beginning. "Tell Me, Tell Me," she says,

> where might there be a refuge for me
> from egocentricity
> and its propensity to bisect,
> mis-state, misunderstand
> and obliterate continuity?

The autistic involvement of rhythm and sound for their own sakes, creating their own world in verse, does cut and garble continuous sense in many of Moore's poems. It is childlike in terms of an individual and primitive in terms of culture in general, yet it is necessary for survival. What must temper the primitive and self-indulgent aspects of verse is decidedly prosaic: syntactical relations leading to rhetorical and moral choices. Some choices are necessarily made at an autistic level, but choices at the social level are realistically limited —decided punctuation must defend against wishful timelessness to favor moral ends.

Northrop Frye, in *The Well-Tempered Critic,* opts for a *tertium quid* between the rhythms of verse and prose. What usually passes for "prose" in conversation, he argues, is ordered not by studied and literary prose rhythms but by an "associative rhythm" that falls short of conversation, being more like a "distributed monologue."[25] At her most self-satisfactory best Marianne Moore achieves what Frye calls "conversational style," an unobtrusive literary imitation of ordinary associative speech. Again, like goodness that is social, it is wholly American and addressed particularly to America

> where there are no proofreaders, no silkworms, no digressions;
> ... languageless country in which letters are written
> not in Spanish, not in Greek, not in Latin, not in shorthand,
> but in plain American which cats and dogs can read!
>
> ("England")

The observation just made comes not from a bona fide sentence but from a bona fide catalogue—an American and capitalist habit of possession turned "poetic" tradition via Whitman. So the syntax, rhetoric, and moral quality of style as conversation may not be those of strictly literary prose, but of a social and associative verbal medium the purpose of which is to spread one's personal order outside of one.

It is not just syntactical relations and the phenomenon of being in touch that qualify a conversational style, but also a degree of intensity. In her essay, "The Dial: A Retrospect," Marianne Moore quotes Mrs. Watson describing Padriac Colum: "He is so intense, you don't know whether he's talking or listening."[26] This sort of intensity must be present in style if it is to earn the goodness of sociability. One justification, and by no means the least important one, for Marianne Moore's extensive use of quotations in her poems and essays and reviews is that both listening and talking are implicit in them. Quotations are the fruit of audition and the seed of further talk. People "can be robbed of speech/ by speech which has delighted them" ("Silence"), but only temporarily. The more intense a statement is the more the abilities of listening and talking are simultaneously exalted. Writing, says Moore in the essay "Idiosyncrasy and Technique," "should at least have the air of having meant something to the person that wrote it."[27] It should have a "private air of interest" by which genuineness is distinguished from fraud. The qualities of the Duke of Windsor's prose, in his book, *My Garden*, are recognized by Marianne Moore in the same essay for their "impression of individuality, conviction, and verbal selectiveness." It is these that give one the air of intensity necessary for any aspect of style, but indispensable to the successful conversational style, one which converts as it converses.

Of Anna Pavlova, Moore observes that "humor, esprit, a sense of style— also a moral quality—made it impossible for her to show off, to be hard, to be dull." Style in this sense is a code of propriety; it is a "conversation" in the root sense of turning toward or coming together. In speaking of "revisions" of the Bible, meaning retranslations of key words, Marianne Moore points out that Philippians 3:20 is variously translated: "For our conversation is in Heaven," "We are a heavenly body," and "We are a colony of heaven." The Greek word in question literally means "citizenship" or "commonwealth," but the variations in its translation are not so important as the way this illustration comes together with the point of Moore's essay, which is that people should be bound not only by idiosyncrasy and technique but also by mutual agreement and mutual obligations to a collective body, a technical congregation, a conversational propriety. It is only after we have solved the moral quandries of remoteness and tact, idiosyncrasy and technique, that we can openly approach truth and have a truly heavenly conversation.

In style as conversation we are more concerned with conscious than with unconscious fastidiousness. The conversational elements of Moore's poems give them the movement of responsible prose and the freedom, within the readily acknowledged bonds of grammar and social habit, of the occasional poetic deviation from these bonds that is a part of personal survival. Whereas style as survival deals with freedom despite inevitable psychological and/or physical obstacles, style as conversation goes on to choose to obey or to choose to play against certain socially determined rules for expression.

Style necessarily incorporates survival; it less-than-necessarily sets up the conditions of conversation. When it does, the syntax is more or less normally constructed, the presence of argument or generosity of comment (the explicitness that is "the enemy of brevity") is felt as rhetorical, and this rhetoric tends to create its own reader by suggestion. We are made aware that certain choices have been made and are continuously being made with respect to the poem and its imagined reader according to some moral conformation that goes well beyond both poem and reader.

In style as conversation the smallest unit of analysis is not word, phrase, or syllable, but the sentence, associatively if not prosaically whole. In her interview with Donald Hall, Marianne Moore says, of her style, "I am governed by the pull of the sentence as the pull of a fabric is governed by gravity."[28] By "I" is meant poetic structure and workmanship, to correspond with the purely physical "fabric" governed by gravity. (One might note that the word "fabric" is sometimes used to refer specifically to the construction and maintenance of a church building, as it is unlikely that Marianne Moore is thinking simply of a cloth fabric.) The "pull of the sentence," likened to gravity, suggests that it has a power according to rules of its own. It is the pull of convention, the desire not merely to *be* in a certain way, but to *be understood* in a certain way. In style as conversation, forms can become moral regardless of content; forms are less a matter of fact, as they are in poetry, more a matter of fiction. (That is, forms are *assumed* as fiction in poetry, but not in conversation.)

In *Predilections,* Marianne Moore praises T. S. Eliot's "order without pedantry" and "terseness that is synonymous with hatred of sham." Such concerns take into consideration the presence and intelligence of an addressee; they are the concerns of a conversationalist, not necessarily a professor, poet, or preacher, though their styles may include, as Moore's does, conversational obligations and conventional obligatos. "Originality is . . . a by-product of sincerity; that is to say, of feeling that is honest and accordingly rejects anything that would cloud the impression, such as unnecessary commas, modifying clauses, or delayed predicates."[29] Style which for survival's sake must indulge the self must atone by indulging the sense of others for morality's sake. One speaks, insofar as one can, in tones and forms in which one might conceivably be answered. Conversational qualities in poetry should promote dialogue, or invoke it, not just with itself but in general, as an educational force. The most direct way of doing this will originate a natural originality, will not "put off" chronologically or metaphorically, the point to be made from its personal source. The point is to be attractive, as in gravitation.

The poem "To a Snail," which celebrates the survival of individuality in the "curious phenomenon" of the snail's occipital horn, also celebrates the power that goes beyond the ability to stay alive, the ability to convey particular meanings with that aliveness. "Contractility" is not just a biological device for avoiding predators, but "contractility is a virtue/ as modesty is a virtue." When contractility ceases to be necessary for survival and becomes symbolic of self-discipline and deference, the snail admits himself to a larger house than the one on his back. He attains, even "in the absence of feet," which is to say the absence of poetic convention, "'a method of conclusions.'" A body which determines its conclusions with reference to something independent of conventional stylistic indulgences and consistent with "'a knowledge of principles,'/ in the curious phenomenon" or a way of explaining an oddity with reference to symbolic wholes, is an ideal social body.

"The poem is a system," concludes Hugh Kenner with respect to the work of Marianne Moore, "not an utterance, though one can trace an utterance through it."[30] Insofar as the "system" is devised for social and moral expediency and is a system of communication of opinion, news of individuals and matters of fact that invite further comment—that is, insofar as the "system" bears a relation to the conglomerate of conversation—this is true, and Moore's poems might reasonably be described as systems of utterances with a social and moral purpose. They are not, however, as Mr. Kenner thinks, "oddly depersonalized system[s] of analogies" or, quoting Williams, "thing[s] made, not said." Marianne Moore's poems *are* said, are full of sayings and personal quirks, quandries and informations in the manner of superior conversation, not neatly programmed machinery.

Many of Marianne Moore's poems, or parts of them, are framed by conversational anecdote, or turn on some point in a remembered conversation. In "The Rigorists," for example, "'We saw reindeer/ browsing,' a friend who'd been in Lapland, said" begins a little revery on the virtues of being able to live on scant nourishment. "The Past Is the Present" is substantially dependent on remembering what "he said—and I think I repeat his exact words—." The poem "Spenser's Ireland" is a good example of an associative conversational style, the situation's being one person's rather impressionistically ordered statements of affection for an unseen country. Ireland is imagined as a poetic place, and it is a place where "it is torture . . . to not be spoken to," a place where an informally split infinitive is operative, and a place to quote one's grandmother concerning marriage, anonymous parties concerning fortitude, and much hearsay. The poem is punctuated in several places with short questions of itself, as if a reader's expressions of incredulity could be seen or heard between the lines.

If there is any sense in which Marianne Moore's poems are "depersonalized," it is in the process of translating over-condensed, inarticulate, deep feelings into a more public form of less affect than we know is there. Even so, and with her "burning desire to be explicit," she is often to be regarded as "enigmatic or disobliging or arrogant," three qualities she warns against in her essay "Feeling and Precision," though she well knows that writers can be successful in their own communities without regarding these as treacheries. For Marianne Moore poetry demands at least the courtesy of conversational accessibility. "'Superiority' is at the opposite pole from insight," she says in the essay "If I Were Sixteen Today,"[31] and the purpose of poetry is a "conversation in Heaven," a means of coming together, making a common wealth not less than common.

In the essay "Feeling and Precision," Marianne Moore offers the following "aids to composition": "if a long sentence with dependent clauses seems obscure, one can break it into shorter units by imagining into what phrases it would fall as conversation; in the second place expanded explanation tends to spoil the lion's leap—an awkwardness which is surely brought home to one in conversation; and in the third place, we must be as clear as our natural reticence allows us to be." It is one's "natural reticence" that disallows clarity, like the hypothetical censor between the id and the ego that determines which condensations or displacements may pass as proxies for the chaos behind them. Paul Ricoeur has referred to condensation and displacement as "operations comparable to rhetorical procedures."[32] If they do work rhetorically on the artist herself with respect to her mode of expression, they may work similarly on her audience. Frye notes that the associative language of informal conversation is used in literature for rhetorical purposes in dream poems and religious poems, and one might include poems of a more or less public contemplation, a certain degree of discontinuity prodding the lyric rumination.

"Not that intentional ambiguity cannot be an art," Moore assures us in "Idiosyncrasy and Technique." And she quotes a definition of literature which claims it to be what we have "when we impart distinctiveness to ordinary talk and make it still seem ordinary."[33] She agrees that writers may justifiably have a "willingness to baffle the crass reader," but objects that it can sometimes baffle the right reader as well. All in all, she is the manifest enemy of

> complexity,
> moreover, that has been committed to darkness, instead of
>
> granting itself to be the pestilence that it is, moving all a-
> bout as if to bewilder us with the dismal

fallacy that insistence
      is the measure of achievement and that all
truth must be dark.

                 ("In the Days of Prismatic Color")

On the other hand, the extreme protectiveness and economy Marianne Moore sees as necessary to art often lead to obscurities that are impenetrable as they are unintentional. Consider this passage from "Smooth Gnarled Crape Myrtle":

              It was artifice saw,
on a patch-box pigeon-egg, room for
fervent script, and wrote as with a bird's claw
under the pair on the
hyacinth-blue lid—"Joined in
friendship, crowned by love":
An aspect may deceive; as the
elephant's columbine-tubed trunk
held waveringly out—
an at will heavy thing—is
delicate.
Art is unfortunate.

We may be suspicious of "strangeness" which can "produce an aesthetic effect . . . qualitatively the same as that of serious poetry,"[34] but we cannot believe that the oddness of this passage of Moore's is contrived, as she herself is always telling us that "one should not be consciously obscure at all."[35] In the passage quoted above "it was artifice," not spontaneity, that saw an opportunity and space to write and that suited the size of the words to the smallness of the object written upon. Just as the small inscription, or the greatly compressed poem, may have heavy affective meaning, the heaviness of the elephant's trunk may express, at will, great delicacy. Art is unfortunate because it necessarily deceives by its appearance, by having sometimes to give us illusions without their complementary precisions and complexity for simplicity.

The fastidious use of conscious rhetoric, as opposed to unconscious fastidiousness, whether it contains obscurities of association or excess brevity, consists always of series of moral choices. Marianne Moore admires T. S. Eliot's "combative sincerity" in prose and in his verse "judgement [that] remains awake," and in his collected work, simply "conscience."[36] She quotes his self-satire, "Lines for Cuscuscaraway," as a compliment on his own

> conversation, so nicely
> Restricted to What Precisely
> And If and Perhaps and But.

Restricted or not, a useful conversational style must be rhetorically alive, the opposite of that "moribund talk/ half limping and half ladyfied," that "death mask" that Moore excoriates in "To Statecraft Embalmed." Precisions, conditionals, and suggestions must represent lively submission if they are to have power. For Marianne Moore deference and humility are weapons and "Nonchalance Is Good and":

> "Taller by the length of
>   a conversation of five hundred years than all
>   the others," there was one whose tales
>   of what could never have been actual—
> were better than the haggish, uncompanionable drawl
>
> of certitude; his by-
>   play was more terrible in its effectiveness
>   than the fiercest frontal attack.
>   The staff, the bag, the feigned inconsequence
> of manner, best bespeak that weapon, self-protectiveness.
>
>   ("In This Age of Hard Trying, Nonchalance Is Good and")

Courtesy and aggression are not mutually exclusive, and it is often Marianne Moore's explicit purpose in a poem to display the possible unities between opposed parties. This is true in "Combat Cultural" for instance, where "battlers, dressed identically—/ just one person—may, by seeming twins,/ point a moral," or in the "striking grasp of opposites" displayed in "Marriage," or in "Sea Unicorns and Land Unicorns," where

> . . . personalities much opposed,
> can be combined in such a way
> that when they do agree, their unanimity is great,
> "in politics, in trade, law, sport, religion,
> china-collecting, tennis, and church-going."

Riddles are a natural and affectionate form of artificial conversation, coming as they do in conversities and in-formations, and Marianne Moore seems to take great pleasure in this comparatively nontoxic form of bafflement. She does this in "An Octopus" for instance, where we are made to guess that the "octopus" is really a national park, or in "Those Various Scalpels," where she builds the image of a woman out of murderously hinting materials. "The Monkey Puzzle," especially if one does not recognize in the title the popular name of a sort of pine tree, is a superlative example of Moore's tendency to make metaphors work explicitly as riddles. Here is the entire poem:

> A kind of monkey or pine lemur
> not of interest to the monkey,
> in a kind of Flaubert's Carthage, it defies one—
> this "Paduan cat with lizard," this "tiger in a bamboo thicket."
> "An interwoven somewhat," it will not come out.
> Ignore the Foo dog and it is forthwith more than a dog,
> its tail superimposed upon itself in a complacent half spiral,
> this pine tree—this pine tiger, is a tiger, not a dog.
> It knows that if a nomad may have dignity,
> Gibraltar has had more—
> that "it is better to be lonely than unhappy."
> A conifer contrived in imitation of the glyptic work of jade and
>   hard-stone cutters,
> a true curio in this bypath of curio-collecting,
> it is worth its weight in gold, but no one takes it
> from these woods in which society's not knowing is colossal,
> the lion's ferocious chrysanthemum head seeming kind by com-
>   parison.
> This porcupine-quilled, complicated starkness—
> this is beauty—"a certain proportion in the skeleton which gives
>   the best results."
> One is at a loss, however, to know why it should be here,
> in this morose part of the earth—
> to account for its origin at all;
> but we prove, we do not explain our birth.

This poem is remarkable for its hesitance, its lack of commitment to animal or vegetable. It is *about* a tree, but more animals are assembled to describe it than anyone has reason to expect: the monkey; the lemur, by evolutionary association; the "Paduan cat with lizard" and tiger by no such clear

association; the Foo dog, utterly inexplicable; the lion, the porcupine, and
finally ourselves. The tree is associated also with art: with "Flaubert's Car-
thage"; with "an interwoven somewhat"; with a "glyptic work of jade" or cut
stone; it is a "curio" worth collecting. As both animal and art, the tree has "a
certain proportion of the skeleton which gives the best results" (a quotation
from Lafcadio Hearn's *Talks to Writers*). In short, as animal and art and
puzzle, all interwoven, this pine tree has an associative style. It has particularity as well as personal peculiarity and a "complicated starkness" that force us
to respect it as well as wonder at it.

"The Monkey Puzzle" lives like a saint, by paradox and denial; through
what it is said not to be in the poem, it gathers positive associations around it
that give it a spiritual being. A heretofore unnoticed tree becomes, suddenly,
exotic treasure; and, paradoxically, this happens by virtue of certain nega-
tions. It is "a kind of monkey . . . not of interest to the monkey." "It defies
one." "It will not come out." "This pine tiger, is a tiger, not a dog" (but not
a tiger, either). "Contrived in imitation," "no one takes it." "Not knowing
is colossal" and "one is at a loss . . . to know" and "we do not explain."
What is the power of the negative? In "Walking-Sticks and Paper-Weights and
Water Marks" Moore notices:

> Little
> scars on churchbell-
>   tongues, put there by the Devil's claws,
>   and other forms of negativeness need but
> be expressed and visible,
>   to prove their unauthority.

If, as she tells us elsewhere, the power of the visible is the invisible, then perhaps the rhetorical power of the positive is in the negative; by extension, the
power of advance may be in retreat—a survival technique elaborately noted
by Moore with respect to the sparrow-camel, the jerboa, the pangolin, and the
poet herself. She practices the uninsistence she preaches and makes her point
(most of the time) and disappears, like the mercurial chameleon, into un-
assuming shades of mauve and amethyst.

"Forms of negativeness": the "I, too, dislike it" of "Poetry," the mind
that is "not a Herod's oath that cannot change" ("The Mind Is an Enchanting
Thing"), and all the momentary retreats, reversals, and stylistic obstacles of
poems purposely "hindered to succeed" ("The Paper Nautilus") are, in Marianne Moore's poetry, forms of positiveness. They are forms of honesty and
precision that watch the mind and eye at work while keeping the reader in

mind with an eye to moral improvement. The tendency of Moore's verse to puzzle her readers despite her protestations of a "burning desire to be explicit," is also a form of negativeness that may not be intended but which, like the scars on the churchbell, cannot harm the essential ring of truth.

As for "The Monkey Puzzle," and other conundrums of style in Moore's work, we might say, as is claimed in "The Steeple-Jack," that "it is a privilege to see so/ much confusion." Confusion may be read here as con-fusion, a fusing-with as well as a disorder, the sort of con-fusion we find in Wallace Stevens' "Snowman," beholding "nothing that is not there, and the nothing that is." Moore's riddling anti-definitions of the monkey-pine create distinctions at the same time as distinctions are blurred; in this poem, as in many of her poems, "unconfusion submits/ its confusion to proof" ("The Mind Is an Enchanting Thing"). The real puzzle of the strange Chilean pine of "The Monkey Puzzle" is how we can "account for its origin at all; but we prove, we do not explain our birth." We prove it, in part, by conversing (as it is our nature to do when we want to prove something), and by a shared concern about our own and others' origins; the most superficial and profound forms of social discourse require addresses on some level to the most conventional question, where do you come from? Wallace Stevens says of the poet, and it is an apt statement to apply to Marianne Moore, "He shares the confusions of intelligence" ("Reply to Papini"). In the essay "Humility, Concentration, and Gusto," Moore warns that we can not "dignify confusion by calling it baroque." She goes on to admit, "I am preaching to myself, since, when I am as complete as I like to be, I seem unable to get an effect plain enough."[37] Would the monkey puzzle be a puzzle to us if Marianne Moore had not made it one? It is personality that is the real puzzle, and it is one of the joys of conversation in general that puzzles—made by another from another's world—are offered to us, puzzles we may not have seen for ourselves, but once answered, even if only partially, unite us in a sort of discovery. If we are lucky, it is self-discovery.

"The passion for setting people right is itself an afflictive disease" ("Snakes, Mongooses . . ."). Marianne Moore makes this comment without claiming to be cured. One of the things that identifies her poetry for us is the felt moral force behind it, one of the forces that impels her particular style. Morals that are not truly felt make for colorless writing and boring conversation that obliterate personality, but this is not true of Moore's style. Her "passion for setting people right" admits a live concern, and the trick of making it interesting naturally follows, according to Moore, the writer's genuine interest. Essentially, a moral style can come only from a moral person. "Must a man be good to write good poems?" Marianne Moore's answer is that "rectitude *has* a ring that is implicative . . . And with *no* integrity, a man is not like-ly to write the kind of book I read."[38]

Moral wholeness and integrity are assets for a writer in Moore's estima-tion and these personal qualities pervade every aspect of one's art. In admir-ing E. E. Cummings she notes "the wholesomeness of the uncapitalized begin-nings of lines," a trait of her own work too. In another essay, she remarks that nothing can be more "stultifying" than a needlessly emphasized pause (a sin of punctuation). To stultify a reader is surely to be avoided by a moral—i.e., community-minded and conversationally courteous—artist. "As for indignities—if one may ask admiration consciously to ignore and unconscious-ly to admire—":[39] this preface to an unexplicit objection to Cummings' work lets her admit the underside of personality while trusting her "unconscious fastidiousness" with the critical work of keeping certain unconscious admira-tions separate from her conscious moral convictions. "Distaste which takes no credit to itself is best" ("Snakes, Mongooses . . .").

In "Spenser's Ireland," "Denunciations do not affect/ the culprit, nor blows, but it/ is torture to him to not be spoken to." People need to talk, to be conversed with; an "emotionally-tied-in-knots animal" cannot be expected to be unconversational like the giraffe ("To a Giraffe"), and the poet has a moral responsibility to speak to this person who may be tortured by silence. Marianne Moore would "like to have a talk" with the lonesome hero "about excess,/ and armor's undermining modesty/ instead of innocent depravity" ("Armor's Undermining Modesty"), because moral hierarchies are best illus-trated in choosing to whom and of what one talks. But they are also dis-played in *how* one talks. Marianne Moore is pleased when she finds a biologist digressing, with a shade of outrage, to deplore untidiness in the use of terms, yet she might hesitate to digress this way herself, finding "denigration" so "disaffecting" that "I should not let my sense of incapacity as an orator hinder me from saying what I feel about the mildew of disrespect."[40] And so she might digress for all that. It is a complicated affair, balancing one's dis-affection for denigration with the sometimes justified "passion for setting people right." One cannot accept the demoralization of a sloppy address, but one should not be overbearing in trying to cure it. One must make constant self-searching choices that disregard the essential amorality of the language machine. Moore agrees with Auden's emphasis on the choice of moral respon-sibility in literature and says of his work, "the thought of choice is central to everything he writes"; quoting Auden himself, "the will, decision, and the consequences—there is no separating them."[41] The consequences, for such artists are, ideally, as much social as they are aesthetic.

Conversation as one possible characterization of style implies a personal sort of communication, but is not to be confused with communion. Anna Pavlova's relationship with her dancers and audience is a good model for the conversational performance of a poet who, like Marianne Moore, wishes to make her efforts of affection vitalize art without undermining its firmness. "'At even her first motion,' " wrote René Jean, "'she seems about to embrace the whole world'"; world being a term precise in more than the immediate sense, for in her dancing with persons remoteness marked her every attitude."[42] Marianne Moore may seem at first to give us "the pale-ale-eyed impersonal look/ which the sales-placard gives the bock beer buck" ("Armor's Undermining Modesty"), yet such self-advertisement—cool to frozen and almost too buccally calculated—is deceptive. We have to remember that "an aspect may deceive" and that "art is unfortunate" ("Smooth Gnarled . . .") if it is not realized that beneath the surface are "sea-serpented regions 'unlit by the half-lights of more conscious art'" ("Novices"). The notion that an artist can have a more intimate conversation with the "world" than with specified persons in it, is attested by many published "confessions," the force of which, more often than not, is moral. To actually change the world is too grandiose an ambition perhaps, but simply to embrace it, to have a "continual conversation with a silent man" is ideal, where on the deepest level

> it is not speech, the sound we hear
>
> In this conversation, but the sound
> Of things and their motion: the other man,
> A turquoise monster moving round.
>
> (Wallace Stevens, "Continual Conversation
> With a Silent Man")

DISCOVERY

Besides the use of words as self-expressive noise and news of survival, and besides the persuadings and informings by words that are conversational, both of which as "styles" are subject to change in means and ends, there is the use of words to discover—by experience or by accident—momentary or lasting truths. When we speak of "stylistics," of sounds and structures, we try to sound sophisticated, but

> principally throat, sophistication is as it al-
> ways has been—at the antipodes from the init-
> ial great truths.
>
> ("In the Days of Prismatic Color")

Like the need to survive and converse, the need for discoveries motivates
Marianne Moore's verse, provides subjects for it, and gives its character to her
style. The discovery, and the rediscovery in poetry, of the four quartz crystal
clocks, the icosasphere, a technique of surgery, the sadness of Leonardo, the
Brooklyn Bridge, or a synthetic cloth—"taslon, the drip-dry fruit/ of research
second to none" ("Saint Nicholas")—these in themselves are not important so
much as the discovery of being able to see them in a particular way and of
being able to use the instrument and the scope of one's style to celebrate
them. Discovery is a by-product of caring about a thing. One might say of
Marianne Moore's prose and poetry what she says of Abraham Lincoln's
writings, that "diligence underlay the verbal expedients—one can scarcely
call them devices—so rapt Lincoln was in what he cared about."[43] Superficial caring can produce no more than "the satire upon curiosity in which no
more is discernible/ than the intensity of the mood" ("When I Buy Pictures"),
but caring that is persistent and of "x-ray-like intensity" ("People's Surroundings") will discover the real objects of curiosity, the self and the source of
things. "Discovery, in science and poetry," remarks Elizabeth Sewell, "is a
mythological situation in which the mind unites with a figure of its own devising as a means toward understanding the world. That figure always takes
the form of some kind of language, and that is why we have to go more
deeply into language instead of trying to escape from it."[44]

We may see style as matter no less than manner, as affect *cum* effect, an
instrument conceived and developed for the purpose of exploration, as the
elephant's trunk is seen in Moore's "Melanchthon":

> the I of each is to
>
> the I of each
> a kind of fretful speech
>   which sets a limit on itself; the elephant is
>   black earth preceded by a tendril?

The tendril expresses the tentativeness of language or of a person exploring
something seen or sensed but not quite understood. The word *explore* derives

from a word meaning "to cry out" as at a discovery; the act of this word in particular contains its goal in its origin and regular use. It is a vehicle of exploration, as is any "fretful speech" which is intimate with its matter. "I" to "I" is almost certainly, in the lines quoted above, "eye" to "eye," as the elephant's trunk reaches its sensitive tip far beyond the face of the elephant, reaches out—a kind of "fretful speech" solidified into delicate elephantine investigation. "Through-/ out childhood to the present time," says "Melanchthon," "the unity of/ life and death has been expressed by the circumference// described by my trunk." This is something that the body and language do together. The choice of what particular language—flowers, radar, mathematics, music, or touching words—immediately involves, and is, style.

"'Great poets,' Mr. Pound says, 'seldom make bricks without straw. They pile up all the excellences they can beg, borrow, or steal from their predecessors and contemporaries and set their own inimitable light atop the mountain.'"[45] Marianne Moore chooses to quote this observation of Pound's because it claims for the writer the blessing of his connection with tradition and claims it with the modesty of one who remembers the scrounging appropriations of his noviceship. At the same time it does not underestimate the uniqueness of a style comprised of such borrowings. The emphasis should be on choice, on style as a process of choosing the best of former discoveries and the best of previously gathered evidence on which to base one's own experiment. "Jacob Bronowski says," notes Moore, "that science is not a mere collection of discoveries, but that science is the process of discovering. It's not established once and for all; it's evolving."[46] Probably all knowledge, including that of poetry, comes in the form of the process of discovering, and the ability to repeat the process. "Repetition, with/ the scientist, should be synonymous with accuracy," claims Moore in "Four Quartz Crystal Clocks." And discovering the ability to repeat one's self is tantamount to discovering one's self and source of style.

The conviction that "all artists who discover anything . . . must, in the course of things, . . . push certain experiments beyond the right curve of their art," another observation of Pound's that appealed to Marianne Moore, pertains especially to style. The scientist who discovers a law of behavior or a possibility of effect in matters that are beyond the sense of sight—literally "out of sight," from quarks to remote galaxies—is bound to have pushed inquiry beyond "the right curve," the anticipated limit. Always, the poet or scientist who is bent on discovery must make proposals in the dark, marry and fumble until the dark conceives, both itself and them. It is the process of discovering the ability to repeat one's self.

A certain technical finesse is not amiss, but to discover a language in which the poet can express things she does not consciously know requires the admission that the medium—words in this case, but it is equally true of paint or clay or flesh—is allowed consciousness and an activity of its own, as fastidious as is the activity of its unconscious. This consciousness of word and image, which may best correspond to our own unconscious, can effect the dream that leads to the discovery of the carbon ring or to the personal discovery that the dark couple, the Ken and Ida that come to call in the dream, stand for knowledge and the id. Awake, a word can awake another word with minimal participation from the writer's consciousness. Intuition is imperative. Kenneth Burke notes that "sensitivity in the selection of words resides in the ability, or necessity, to feel behind the given word a history—not a past history but a future one. Within the word, collapsed into its simultaneous oneness, there is implicit a sequence, a complexity of possible narratives that could be drawn from it."[47] Appositely, we may invoke the observation of Henry James, who, in his preface to *The Princess Casimassima,* says, "What a man thinks and what he feels are the history and character of what he does." Thus history and character, in one who expresses herself and in that by which she is expressed, perhaps together embody "the principle that is hid" in style, discovered in the gracefulness of the snail as well as in the construction of the icosasphere and the puzzle of the monkey puzzle.

Every word has its own "associative field," its *arbitraire du signe,* through which word can discover word by derivation, similarity, opposition, homonymy, idiomatic occurrence, or rhythmic stress. Anyone who writes at all self-consciously knows that this is true and that this process leads to non-technical as well as technical discoveries. One such discovery is the discovery of "a place for the genuine," assuming that one has something genuine to put into it. In Marianne Moore's amputated version of the poem called "Poetry," this is the only thing that justifies the genre; the entirety of what she will admit to its definition is that

> I, too, dislike it.
>   Reading it, however, with a perfect contempt for it, one discovers in
>   it, after all, a place for the genuine.

This "poem" has the power to wound, as the sharpness of the word "contempt" cannot be dulled by trick definition by the critic, and one must feel that she means precisely "contempt," that she does feel she should scorn her work (knowing that other people call it "poetry" even if she does not like to call it that herself).

Contempt is the precisely appropriate response to what is perceived as mean, vile, and worthless. To prove the truth of her contempt for "poetry," Marianne Moore excised virtually all of the widely admired and quoted original version(s), abandoning what must have seemed to her to be a malinspiration—at its best rather disaffecting evidence of her care for the "genuine." Yet there is one way for a critic to accept this evidence of uncharacteristic scorn, and that is to assume that *perfect* is as important and unlikely in the vocabulary of this particular poet as *contempt*. Another poem points out that the light of a star is "perfected" by darkness ("Disposition By Angels"), and we can postulate that contempt is perfected by awe. A perfect contempt realizes that the body of a poem, like the famous gun that Emily Dickinson discovers in the poem beginning "My Life had stood—a Loaded Gun," has the "power to kill/ without the power to die." Put more appositely to Marianne Moore's discovered contempt, it has the power to contain and dispense fate without the power to join fate. The fate or death is genuine and is not less genuine in being contemned by the supernal and awe-ful witness, the reader.

If this reasoning, this attempt to heal a disparity in what we perceive to be the character of the poet, is valid, it might as well serve as an example of style as discovery, or at least style as leading to discovery. It may be applied in elucidating one of the overriding questions of all our essays into Moore's work, that is: how is verse to be *confused* with fate? They are to be confused only in the style of *perfect contempt*—the words themselves contemning and convicting themselves: style plus afterthought.

Sincerity or genuineness in life are not the same as sincerity or genuineness in poetry. In the everyday life of language one merely has to say what one knows or thinks to be true, and one is not responsible for not saying what one does not know. There is a romantic notion, however, and maybe it is true, that poets write true things without consciously knowing them. They are, as Louise Bogan has put it, "prey to an end not evident to craft." If we believe this, then craft can only sharpen the tone of oracle, not contribute to its inherent genuineness. There is no way to measure the sincerity of intuition except by intuition; the more aphoristic, gnomic, or Delphic the utterance, the more credence it begs for. Summaries, like proverbs or mottoes, are honored for their graspability and comprehension. Truth can even be defined as a certain *sort* of comprehensiveness in the acknowledged absence of omniscience. This sort of truth is, to no small degree, and as any prophet will be reluctant to tell you, a discovery of the "right" style.

In a sweetly grandmotherly yet uncondescending essay called "If I Were Sixteen Today," Marianne Moore quotes Martin Buber's assertion that "the free man believes in destiny and that it has need of him."[48] She follows this statement immediately with her own distinction and emphasis: *"Destiny, not fate."* To most of us, including the lexicographers, destiny and fate are about as interchangeable as two differently derived words can be. One can only guess what Marianne Moore's idea of distinction between them was, and it cannot be too trivial to bother with, as the concept of fate is crucial to several poems and a key to technical as well as spiritual aspects of her style in all the poems.

"Those Various Scalpels" asks an important question about the relationship of destiny to words:

> those
> various sounds consistently indistinct, like intermingled echoes . . .
>   Are they weapons or scalpels?

That is to ask, are the aggressive words of the woman described meant to injure or to explore and heal an injury? The answer:

> these things are rich instruments with which to experiment.
>   But why dissect destiny with instruments
>   more highly specialized than the components of destiny itself?

"The components of destiny" are not as specialized as the sophisticated words and embattled imagery that are the poem's subject, and in the end the poet despairs of finding out the true, unspecialized, necessarily abstract features of one's ultimate condition. Destiny is the same for everyone and need not be particularized. Fate, however, at least in Marianne Moore's poems, may be confused with verse. The word *fate* derives from the Latin *fatum* which meant, literally, "that which has been spoken," usually meaning a sentence spoken by the gods to an individual. In one poem of Moore's Bach is described as "fate-like": "Fate-like Bach—find me words" ("Dream"). The title poem of the collection called *Like a Bulwark* says of its unnamed subject that it is "compressed; firmed by the thrust of the blast/ till compact, like a bulwark against fate." The poem is a riddle and contains, under great pressure, "pent by power that holds it fast—/ a paradox." The paradox is obviously that the greatest constraint allows the greatest freedom—one of Marianne Moore's very favorite paradoxes—and it could reasonably be applied to personality, integrity, poetry, faith, truth, and silence—all abstract components of destiny and components, as we have noticed, of Marianne Moore's style as well. The compression of destiny and the "hard pressed" style of the poem, which is in the end "as though flying Old Glory full mast," are a "bulwark against fate"; the unspoken is a bulwark against the spoken, as limitation forces expression into significance. Louise Bogan may have been right for only the majority of poets; perhaps some poets are "prey to an end" that is all too evident to craft.

Style may contain or conform to the components of destiny, but it *enacts* fate. Fate may be predicted by its partial enactment, as style as a means of discovery or revelation must move at the pace of its medium. In literary style, this usually means the pace of the sentence. "In the Days of Prismatic Color" contains a quoted translation of the *Greek Anthology*'s description of a dragon setting out for a drink of water: "part of it was crawling, part of it was about to crawl, and the rest was still torpid in its lair." It is a good description of the felt movement of revelation in Moore's style, the aptest part, as a metaphor for both fate and style, being the observation that some of the animal (or poem) is latent, but not unattached. The still and yet-to-be-mobilized part is not separable from the moving and visible part of the whole organism; the fate of the tail is determined far in advance by the head and the desire that has presented itself to the head.

Style is fated, at least to a certain extent, by "the pull of the sentence," its direction becoming clear as the words are put down one by one. Fate, like verse, is a process, a process undertaken by each person as an individual, self-sentenced, idiolectal; destiny is a predetermined condition of life. There may be no *real* distinction between destiny and fate as the words are used by most people. But Marianne Moore did make an emphatic distinction. Far from wanting to confuse things further, I have only tried to elaborate on what distinction there *might* be in terms of the poems and the question: "Might verse not best confuse itself with fate?" Criticism perhaps is bound to confuse itself with art. "Art is unfortunate."

Discovery in any analysis is participatory insofar as the scientist or artist or sensitive reader must intuit the process and be able to reconstruct materially or imaginatively the original conception. M. Merleau-Ponty, in his *Phenomenology of Perception,* pertinently describes the process of style as a mode of discovery:". . . an as yet imperfectly understood piece of philosophical writing discloses to me at least a certain 'style' . . . which is a first draft of its meaning. I begin to understand a philosophy by *feeling my way* into its existential manner, *by reproducing* the tone and accent of the philosopher (emphasis mine)."[49] Reproducing is a form of understanding. Survival depends on it in more ways than one, as do friendship, marriage, and conversation; as does any invention; as does any new light on the mountain. The creative urge and the mimetic urge come together—whether it is the urge for self-reproduction or world-reproduction.

Marianne Moore is excited about the icosasphere. She wants to describe it minutely, wants to discover how it was done, and how the pyramids were created, and how food-grapes are grown, and how the ostrich manages to survive. Children, poets, and scientists have particular curiosities in common: they want to know *how*. "A child is a 'portent'; a poet is a portent," Moore remarks in a review; and, we might add, anyone armed with real or metaphoric telescopes and microscopes is a portent. Of what? Of the near-simultaneity of creation and destruction, between which is all our temporal existence, the whole, manifestations and latencies.

> And therefore I have sailed the seas and come
> To the holy city of Byzantium.
>
>   . . . to sing
> To lords and ladies of Byzantium
> Of what is past, or passing, or to come.
>   (Yeats, "Sailing To Byzantium")

Style as discovery is intimate with style as masquerade; these two aspects of style each depend on the other's finesse to determine their own real value. It is only worth discovering something well disguised, and it is only worth disguising something temptingly revelatory. After all, "the power of the visible is the invisible" ("He 'Digesteth Harde Yron'"). "Concealed rhyme and the interiorized climax usually please me better than the open rhyme and the insisted-on climax," says Marianne Moore in the essay "Feeling and Precision," probably not thinking of the precisely feminine biology of the statement which fatefully underlies it. Because concealment is precedent to revelation and, in addition, a formal predilection of the poet under consideration, we should consider her style as concealing and interiorizing as much self as it can. As the only way to reveal "the principle that is hid" in style is to approach the phenomenon directly, we must keep in mind that:

> Literature is a phase of life. If one is afraid of it,
> the situation is irremediable; if one approaches it familiarly,
> what one says of it is worthless.
>   ("Picking and Choosing")

Style, representing the personality of a literary product, formal or informal, requires an etiquette of circumspection and a reciprocal style; style is the trading ground for the values of artist and critic. The over-familiar approach destroys the purpose of style in the first place, which is to enclose and protect and withhold for discriminating release the secrets—not of the poet's everyday life particularly—but the secrets of creativeness in general.

> Creative secrets, are they secrets? Impassioned interest in life, that burns bridges behind it and will not contemplate defeat, is one, I would say. . . . Tyrone Guthrie sums up what I have been trying to say about idiosyncrasy and technique: "It is one of the paradoxes of art that a work can only be universal if it is rooted in a part of its creator which is most privately and particularly himself."[50]

"Discoveries in art, certainly, are personal before they are general," claims Moore in the same essay. Style, developed as a sort of greatly embellished personal signature, is, like the person, a result of combined fortuity and choice. By setting up certain forms according to taste, experience, and expedience, style prods both conscious and unconscious fastidiousness to join like halves of a dialectic intent on giving life to a necessary, if not superior, tertium quid. In the process of making this sort of personal discovery general, style acquires its character and proves that the impulse to name is equal to the impulse to see. In a review of Sir George Sitwell's book on gardens, Marianne Moore relates the garden to language through "engineering zeal":

> Engineering zeal in any case is seen to have its verbal prototype. . . . The secret of burnished writing is strong intention. The man is the style.[51]

It is interesting that she puts the man before the style, as the old cliché derived from Buffon puts style first in the statement. But to consider style before the man is to put the vehicle before the tenor—not a swift way to arrive anyplace. No, the writer comes before what is written, before his fate if not before his destiny, and "the writer should have 'a sense of upthrusting vitality and self-discovery' without thinking about the impression made, except as one needs to make oneself understood."[52]

One wants to make oneself understood, but one does not want necessarily to bare one's soul. The thick-skinned elephant Melanchthon boasts, "My soul shall never/ be cut into/ by a wooden spear" ("Melanchthon"). The superficial and civilized aspects of Marianne Moore's poetry, their thick though sensitive skin and the self-assurance warily bespoken by them, should be emphasized. Through the wrinkles in this skin and, occasionally, the penetrating of it—not by the wooden spear of the pencil but by the metaphoric "x-ray-like intensity" advised in "People's Surroundings"—the underlying primal feelings are freed to be acknowledged. From motivation to formal completion, art stipulates a process of stylistic discovery by both poet and critic, both of whom may inhabit the same body, for instance in the event of a revision. The passion with which an artist protects herself against discovery by the critic within or without is a clue to her struggle against *all* invasions, those of affect as well as those of apathetic enmity.

Occasionally pain comes to the surface, or near to it, in Marianne Moore's poems. The following sort of lyrical cries are not ordinarily dealt with by critics because they do not predominate or in any way supercede the praiseful content of most of Moore's work, but it is important to note within the cloak of her style that

> we do not like some things . . .
>   suffering and not
> saying so; standing and listening where something
> is hiding.
>   ("The Hero")

>   Could
> not all personal upheaval in
> the name of freedom, be tabooed?
>   ("Is Your Town Nineveh?")

> reef, wreck, lost lad, and "sea foundered bell"—
> as near a thing as we have to a king—
> craft with which I don't know how to deal.
>   ("The Mind, Intractable Thing")

As if, as if, it is all ifs; we are at
much unease. . . .
                    equanimity's contrived
by the elephant.

                              ("Elephants")

an arrow turned inward has
      no chance of peace.

                    ("See in the Midst of Fair Leaves")

                  you'll see the wrenched distortion
        of suicidal dreams
                  go
staggering toward itself and with its bill
attack its own identity.

                    ("To Statecraft Embalmed")

Marianne Moore sometimes seems to be like the carrot she describes in
"Radical," "everything crammed belligerently inside itself," and often perhaps her own "equanimity's contrived," as she says the elephant's is. Though
Moore is, undisputably and foremost, "a literalist of the imagination," she is
not unrelated to the "pedantic literalist," unmercifully caricatured in the
following poem:

            Prince Rupert's drop, paper muslin ghost,
                white torch—"with power to say unkind
            things with kindness, and the most
                irritating things in the midst of love and
                    tears," you invite destruction.

            You are like the meditative man
                with the perfunctory heart; its
            carved cordiality ran
                to and fro at first like an inlaid and royal
                    immutable production;

then afterward "neglected to be
    painful, deluding him with
loitering formality,"
    "doing its duty as if it did it not,"
        presenting an obstruction

to the motive that it served. What stood
    erect in you has withered. A
little "palm tree of turned wood"
    informs your once spontaneous core in its
        immutable production.

                            ("Pedantic Literalist")

The "pedantic literalist" is discovered: pale, thin, and breakable, he is dis-covered in his style of hard impenetrability and sham-full "production." It is not clear whether it is his vulnerability or his tendency to say irritating things at inappropriate times that invites his destruction, but it is clear that Mari-anne Moore is willing to undertake the task. The art of caricature itself can be an art of destruction, of setting up a particular figure with intent to destroy by comic exaggeration any threat the figure may present in reality. It is destruction through recreation, through mastery and disclosure of character.

The pedantic literalist serves as scapegoat for a poet's anger at unspon-taneous art in general and at her own tendencies toward unspontaneity. Kenneth Burke's observation concerning literary scapegoats aptly describes one aspect of Moore's caricature:

> the delegation of one's burden to the sacrificial vessel of the
> scapegoat is a giving, a socialization, albeit the socialization of a
> loss, a transference of something, deeply within, devoutly a part
> of one's own self. . . . It delegates the personal burden to an ex-
> ternal bearer, yet the receiver of this burden possesses consub-
> stantiality with the giver, a pontification that is contrived . . . by
> objectively attributing one's own vices or temptations to the dele-
> gated vessel.[53]

The wit of caricature is found halfway between pleasure and the negation of pain, and that is where Moore's "pedantic literalist" is found, double-edged because vulnerability to the saying of unkind things and the need to destroy or to sacrifice a scapegoat by saying unkind things are characteristics of the caricaturist as well as the caricatured.

The heart of the pedantic literalist is simultaneously superficial and profound; the "carved cordiality" that is "inlaid and royal" suggests the care and great expense undertaken in order to insure primary interest in the surface. The artist whose spontaneity must have at one time gone into the craftsmanship of such a heart has long disappeared. There is no pain left to be discovered, only a "loitering formality," as in Emily Dickinson's famed and familiar lines:

> After great pain, a formal feeling comes—
> The Nerves sit ceremonious, like Tombs—
>
> . . .
>
> A Wooden way
> Regardless grown,
> A Quartz contentment, like a stone.
>
> (#341)

The heart in Moore's poem becomes an "obstruction/ to the motive it served." the motive of life itself, presumably. "What stood/ erect in you has withered"; the climax of inspiration has long since passed and been obscurely buried; the only art is art of concealment. Destruction and obstruction lead to an immutable production, a dead art. This is the art Moore's poem describes, but in describing it there is a lively relish for the destructive power of words as presently used, and in the appositeness of the form; the poem itself, about dead art, is not itself dead; it is simply deadly.

"There is nothing to be said for you," Marianne Moore says to a figure of stone, "Guard/ your secret. Conceal it under your hard plumage, necromancer" ("To Statecraft Embalmed"). It is a strange thing to say under any circumstances, but no more strange than what she says of the woman caricatured in "Those Various Scalpels," whose hair is like

> the tails of two
> fighting-cocks head to head in stone like sculptured scimitars re-
> peating the curve of your ears in reverse order,

and whose cheeks are seen as

> those rosettes
> of blood on the stone floors of French chateaux.

The stone surface, with its undertones of aggression and the petrification of feeling, is sinister and betrays the consciousness of death as well as of dead affect that might detrimentally be enlivened by a "necromancer" if not guarded by stone. The hero of "The Hero" does not like "deviating head-stones," the epitaphs, perhaps, that reveal something unexpected or eccentrically personal, that bring the anonymous loss too close to curious life. Not even stone can prevent the discovery of fate and human fraility as sometimes even

> the rock seems frail . . .
> its vermilion and onyx and manganese-blue interior expensiveness
> left at the mercy of the weather.
>
> ("An Octopus")

In "The Monkeys" the cat who has the last word objects to regarding art

> as symmet-
> rically frigid as if it had been carved out of chrysoprase
> or marble—strict with tension, malignant
> in its power over us and deeper
> than the sea.

Marianne Moore's armored verse often has this appearance, its armor being specially designed not only for defense, but for offense as well.

A malignant and restraining tension in art is related to the power of the sea, the sea "in which dropped things are bound to sink—/ in which if they turn and twist, it is neither with volition nor consciousness" ("A Grave"). This is the sea that "drives a wedge/ of iron through the iron edge/ of the cliff" ("The Fish"). In "Spenser's Ireland" the Irish gather magic fern seed to forfend against "giants all covered with iron," and Marianne Moore asks for a metaphoric equivalent for embattled poetry:

> might
> there be fern seed for unlearn-
> ing obduracy and for reinstating
> the enchantment?

The seed required is to be gathered from the stylistic motifs that for the in-dividual poet grow to accommodate innocence and faith, change, death, and ecstasy; and the principles that feed their roots are all usefully hid.

As for reinstating the enchantment beyond this, there is one other thing: the ability to repeat one's self. Essentially, there is only one discovery, and that is the discovery of creation, of the primal scene, of the desire in one's self to know how a thing was made and how to do it oneself. This is, in a sense, to say that all curiosity is sexual curiosity, but that is an oversimplifi-cation. So much depends upon the control of the word-experiment, the flesh-experiment, the choice and choice and choice. "We must have the courage of our peculiarities," says Marianne Moore, and, in another place, she admits her admiration of William Carlos Williams for being "reckless" with words: "if you can't be that, what's the point of the whole thing?"[54] The point is to discover the point, of returns, of no returns. The point is to discover.

SELFHOOD

The discovery of the ability to repeat one's self, the discovery of conjugations and a style, the discovery that style reflects what is loved. . . . Words can trap one in narcissism much as the body can. In a late poem, reflecting on this as-pect of her own involvement with words and word-sounds, Marianne Moore's response is to parody herself:

> I've escaped?
> am still trapped
>
> by these
> word diseases.
>
> No pauses—
> the phrases
>
> lack lyric
> force; sound capric-

> like Attic
> capric-Alcaic,
>
> or freak
> calico-Greek.
>
>   ("I've Been Thinking")

The capric- . . . capric-," choking as it does over the word "capricious," adequately sums up the *ich ich ich* barrier to sense which is here both medium and message. Nevertheless, it is a skillful self-parody—high grade calico, if not silk—informed by the self and by a real felt danger as much as her more serious or ambitious poems; in *that* sense it is serious.

The constant informing of the self by the self and the self-conscious hesitance of Moore's style are important to the defeat of the egocentricity from which refuge is sought in "Tell Me, Tell Me":

> where might there be a refuge for me
> from egocentricity
> and its propensity to bisect,
> mis-state, misunderstand
> and obliterate continuity?

She would discover a selfhood in style that is beyond self-enclosed choppy reiterations. Mirror, mirror on the wall, she speaks into her poem "A Face":

> I am not treacherous, callous, jealous, superstitious,
> supercilious, venomous, or absolutely hideous:
> studying and studying its expression,
> exasperated desperation
> though at no real impasse,
> would gladly break the glass;
>
> when love of order, ardor, uncircuitous simplicity
> with an expression of inquiry, are all one needs to be!
> Certain faces, a few, one or two— or one
> face photographed by recollection—
> to my mind, to my sight,
> must remain a delight.

The first two lines of this poem are a desperate catalogue, informed by that self-mocking humor which is humorous simply because it is an evasion of the directness of suffering. In saying she is not treacherous, callous, jealous, or any of those things, she is telling us she has considered those possibilities; but, as she rightly sees, the problem goes beyond simple excuses for unhappiness. Having considered and discarded them, she is still "studying and studying" with "exasperated desperation" like somebody trying to revise a neatly finished but superficial poem in the direction of profundity without spoiling the form. There's "no real impasse," yet she is ready to efface the image of herself altogether, break the glass. The two tones of the first stanza—the first grievingly joking, the second puzzlingly grieving—give one the sense that the real block to feeling or knowing how to describe one's own face is self-consciousness supreme. The only way out is to remind oneself, after those "intermingled echoes" of adjectives mockingly listed in the first stanza, that "love of order, ardor, uncircuitous simplicity/ with an expression of inquiry are all one needs to be!" Failing in depth, then, the revision is to be toward greater superficiality, pleasant to everyone. If one can accept plain and polite words, one need not need to be a complexly describable self at all, but simply to be, to love and inquire. On one level this is glib, but on another level, familiar to Marianne Moore, praising and questing are the only real substantiation of being. The face that is closed to itself, ignored in favor of other faces that are loved, or one other particular face, solves the critical problem of self-image with a sight-delight rhyme. The solution, as in many of Moore's poems, is part avoidance and part displacement to other issues, and it is, if technique is a true measure of sincerity, a heartfelt one. The poem does not, however, satisfy the appetite for phonological delicacies dressed with despair that the style of the first stanza arouses. It is as if we were offered a crazy salad only to have it puréed before our eyes.

"When plagued by the psychological," Moore says to a giraffe, "a creature can be unbearable." She intends to direct her own conversation toward the outside, toward the other face, toward the feats of the Gentlemen of the Feather Club, and toward the survival in the real world of peculiar creatures, only some of whom write poems, but all of whom merit them. Her preoccupation with the psychological always betrays itself, however, in coming to terms with words that have obvious psychological import even if they do not epitomize egocentricity as she fears they might. On one hand Moore knows that she must pay attention to her "inward arabesque of sound" if she is to have something to say and a way to say it; on the other hand she knows she suffers from "these word diseases" liable to obscure her clear intentions and confuse her readers. Nevertheless, the distinction of her style is partly to be found in this conflict between her eccentric self-definition and her centric efforts of affection and/or communication.

In *The Philosophy of Literary Form,* Kenneth Burke reminds us of the myth of Perseus who could not face the serpent-headed monster without being turned to stone, but who was immune to danger if he could arrange to see the monster in his magic mirror instead. Burke relates this myth to the function of poetry: that by seeing the dangerous thing in the mirror of art we somehow keep ourselves from being harmed by it.[55] If one can see one's own face in the glass and not smash it, one becomes able to face the world with its lost and fallen faces ("A Face"). The pangolin, one of Moore's shiest and most self-protective animals, is an "ant and stone-swallowing uninjurable artichoke." The ideal animal can swallow stones without becoming what he eats; an ideal art must have some of the enchantment of fern seed to keep it, not just safe from the "giants all covered with iron," but from *being* a giant all covered with iron.

Language is the protective mirror of Marianne Moore the dragon-killer. Her interest is in displacing the "monsters" of feeling to the surface of her art, and concurrently, attracting the reader's attention there. Norman Holland, in his book on the dynamics of literary response, speaks of the phenomenon of "displacement to language":

> That is, our conscious attention shifts (to some degree, at least) from the content of the utterance to its form. Attention, concern, if you will, psychic energy, are taken away from substance and given to language. In terms of our model, such a displacement weakens our involvement with the deeper, fantasy levels, fraught with fear and desire; instead, we concentrate our involvement on the verbal level. The words, themes, lines may introduce deep fantasies, but usually they will be "higher" and more neutral in the transformational process from unconscious fantasy to conscious meaning. . . .
>
> In theory, any atypical phrasing, any that differs from the way we would ourselves phrase the matter, shifts our attention to that extent from substance and onto form.[56]

In the poem "England" Marianne Moore seems to be saying almost the same thing when she notes (among the characteristics of France):

> the "chrysalis of the nocturnal butterfly,"
> in whose products mystery of construction
> diverts one from what was originally one's object—
> substance at the core.

The diversion, freely admitted to be just that by both poet and critic, need not postpone the original object indefinitely. In many cases, on the contrary, it is only an examination of the "mystery of construction" that can ultimately lead one to "substance at the core."

In saying certain things in a way that is peculiar to herself and calling attention to the construction rather than to the deep meaning, Moore means to divert us—to entertain with a purposeful distraction. She likes to incorporate phrases in quotation marks into her poems to convince us that her interest in what is being said is just as much in the *how* as in the *what*. Perhaps this is why the whole of the last part of "Novices"—about the terrible passion and force of the sea—is in sets of inverted commas. "The chrysalis of the nocturnal butterfly" has resonance with images of butterflies and nocturnal flying things in other of Moore's poems. We may be diverted from its intense personal meanings by the sense that its being in quotation marks gives us, that it was said by somebody else and picked up by a passing fancy. Far from it—this mention of the nocturnal butterfly is necessarily related to the courtship and loss of the strange butterfly in "Half-Deity," the spooky thing that flies out at night to frighten "The Hero," and the "pest" that alights on the poet's wrist to arouse wonder and anger in "Armor's Undermining Modesty." Quotation marks in Moore's work are an important gesture of modesty as well as a diversion. She is well aware of their protective use, and in her essay on the work of Sir Francis Bacon she comments on her own technique:[57] "The aphorisms and allusions to antiquity have an effect of formula; quoted wisdom from Greek, Roman, Hebrew, and Italian sages tending to excuse attention as much as to concentrate it."

One of the odd things about Marianne Moore's self-protective style is the aggressiveness she occasionally attributes to it, and the real though muted aggressiveness that we feel is behind it. "The staff, the bag, the feigned inconsequence/ of manner, best bespeak that weapon, self-protectiveness" ("In This Age of Hard Trying Nonchalance Is Good and"). The gods are accused of lack of humility, humility being "the polished wedge/ that might have split the firmament." ("In This Age of Hard Trying . . .") It is the *rhetoric* of humility that is the real wedge—between her and us, us and a deep understanding of her poems. In a rather funny but serious caricature (never reprinted by her after her friends brought it out in 1921) called "To Be Liked By You Would Be a Calamity," she says:

> "Attack is more piquant than concord" but when
>   You tell me frankly that you would like to feel

My flesh beneath your feet,
    I'm all abroad; I can but put my weapon up, and
    Bow you out.

"Attack is more piquant than concord," and to be preferred, but when feeling is too strong, we retreat. The situation called up by this poem is not very
clear—"to be *liked* by you would be a calamity"? Is to be liked in some way
to be stepped on? Randall Jarrell makes a parenthetical remark in his essay
on Moore, "Her Shield," that may be pertinent here in connection with
calamitous likings and aggressive retreats:

> (By being disarming we sometimes disarm others, but always dis-
> arm ourselves, lay ourselves open to rejection. But if we do not
> make ourselves disarming or appealing, everything can be a clear,
> creditable, take-it-or-leave-it affair, rejection is no longer re-
> jection. Who would be such a fool as to make advances to his
> reader, advances which might end in rejection, or worse still, in
> acceptance?)[58]

Marianne Moore obviously has mixed feelings about acceptance and
rejection, and also about the protectiveness of her language, which is seen by
her on one hand as an asset, and on the other as a liability insofar as "efforts
of affection" are involved. She concludes her essay on Ezra Pound with a
quotation from his poem "Salvationists":

Come, my songs, let us speak of perfection—
We shall get ourselves rather disliked.

And Moore comments: "We shall get ourselves disliked and very much liked,
because the zest for perfection communicates its excitement to others."[59]
Her own style strives for a precision or perfection of expression, and is like
the "fossil flower" found in "An Octopus":

                concise without a shiver,
    intact when it is cut,
    damned for its sacrosanct remoteness—
    like Henry James "Damned by the public for decorum;"
    not decorum, but restraint;
    it is the love of doing hard things
    that rebuffed and wore them out—a public out of sympathy
                        with neatness.

The "armor" of decorum and restraint may put off "a public out of sympathy with neatness," or it may attract them, to the extent that they find "perfection" exciting. Even the "perfect contempt" with which one is advised to regard poetry in the poem "Poetry" may be found to be exciting. Perhaps the verbal armor is put on specifically in the event of too much excitement, with the knowledge that its cumbrousness contains one's own excitement at the same time as it defends against the world's reciprocal attacks on that excitement.

Marianne Moore concludes "Armor's Undermining Modesty" with her ambivalence in the matter of armor:

> A mirror-of-steel uninsistence should countenance
> continence,
>
>> objectified and not by chance,
>> there in its frame of circumstance
>> of innocence and altitude
>> in an unhackneyed solitude.
> There is the tarnish; and there the imperishable wish.

With "a mirror-of-steel uninsistence . . . in an unhackneyed solitude," she is like the Lady of Shalott, a reclusive female Perseus, opposing with her weaving art a world of shadows in a mirror; she is a heroine whose Medusa is simple love in the real world. The mirror holds one's wishes as the armor contains and reflects and deflects desire. The modesty of the armor *should* countenance this sealing away of a part of the personality; yet it does tarnish, and it is the "tarnish" that calls attention to the mirror-of-steel, to the fact that it is merely a protective device.

"With what shall the artist arm himself save with his humility?" quoth Marianne Moore.[60] Moore's "humility" is protean; we have seen it in "the polished wedge that might have split the firmament," in self-abnegating obscurity, and in other "forms of negativeness" reducible to terms of language and its precisions. There is one form of protective language used by Moore, however, that is not visually precise, and that is her use of abstraction.

> "Diversity, controversy; tolerance"—in that "citadel
> of learning" we have a fort that ought to armor us well.
>> ("Blessed Is the Man")

> After all
> consolations of the metaphysical
> can be profound. In Homer, existence
>
> is flawed; transcendence, conditional;
> "the journey from sin to redemption, perpetual."
>
> ("To a Giraffe")

Marriage is defined in Moore's poem by that name as "this institution,/ perhaps one should say enterprise," and its first protagonist, Eve, is abstractly regarded as "the central flaw/ in that first crystal-fine experiment,/ this amalgamation which can never be more/ than an interesting impossibility."

There is a precision in poetry that is not concerned with detail, but has almost the same feeling as detail. Whole poems, as diverse and particular as their observations might be, sometimes leave one with the abstract-precise feeling of allegory. We may regard the tone of abstraction in Moore's poems as an aspect of her verbal armor in that it displaces our attention from the level of personal desires and quirks to a level of civilized, social, or religious aspiration. This is certainly one of the major techniques of "Marriage," taking its place alongside displacements to puzzling rhetoric and dazzling images.

Aneila Jaffé, in *The Myth of Meaning*, notes that "the tendency to abstraction can be taken as a symptom of a collective introversive movement originating in the unconscious, a turning to the inner world."[61] She regards this tendency as compensating for a tendency in the opposite direction, which, in the case of Moore's poetry, would be her efforts to see particularly and minutely. If in seeing so actually or literally "the eye is not innocent," as Moore somewhat strangely suggests "to a giraffe," then raising one's observations to expressions of abstraction would restore innocence and the modest armor of introversion.

> The Spectre is the Reasoning Power in Man; & when separated
> From Imagination, & closing itself as in steel, in a Ratio
> Of the Things of Memory, It thence frames Laws & Moralities
> To destroy Imagination. . . .
>
> (William Blake, *Jerusalem,* Chap. 3, plate 74)

Blake's Spectre claims earlier that he is the Rational Power of those men "who teach Humility to Man" (Chap. 3, plate 54). The rational power in man that is not balanced by irrational powers becomes a force of evil. Marianne Moore knows this and that she must fight the tendency in herself to become "an intellectual cautiously creeping cat" ("Bird-Witted"), to write poems that are like "giants all covered with iron" ("Spenser's Ireland"), or to be excessively preoccupied with any polished and abstract surface. To submit to these things exclusively is to be enclosed "in steel as in a Ratio" rather than in the more human "mirror-of-steel uninsistence" that allows poetry its freedom.

For Marianne Moore there would seem to be dangers on all sides without her armor of articulateness, but there is danger also within it. Sometimes it is a danger of hollowness, when the poet must fill up space with satisfactions of syllables; sometimes it is the danger of bursting with "efforts of affection" when the poet must "steel" herself "straight up" with abstract happiness like the little bird in "What Are Years?" "Though he is captive,/ his mighty singing/ says, satisfaction is a lowly/ thing, how pure a thing is joy."

At no time are we directly exposed to the deepest level of motivation in Moore's poetry, but are continually exposed to different *attitudes* of protectiveness which reveal it indirectly. Moore protects her readers from direct statements of her suffering, knowing that "when plagued by the psychological/ an animal can be unbearable" ("To a Giraffe"), and she withholds aggressiveness also—"everything crammed belligerent/ ly inside . . . a tail-like, wedge shaped engine" ("Radical"). There is danger in too much precision concerning feeling, but there is danger in illusion, also, and the poetry of Marianne Moore, taken all together, may be regarded as an illustration of the tension between two modes of confronting experience: a scientistic and particularized observation and an aesthetic, illusive fabrication of the human self drawn from observation. It is as if she admits, "I must look and be seen to be looking to be convincing at all, but I must be seen only indirectly, in the 'mirror-of-steel uninsistence' of my own vision."

Marianne Moore, "perceiving that in the masked ball/ attitude there is a hollowness/ that beauty's light momentum can't redeem" ("Nothing Will Cure the Sick Lion but to Eat an Ape"), considers the possibility that a displacement of curiosity and truthful passion to the surface might not be enough to satisfy the "hollowness"; "since disproportionate satisfaction anywhere/ lacks a proportionate air," we must be careful not to be satisfied with the easy "cure" for or by surfaces and their illusions of beauty. She finds stylistic tendencies in the fiction of Henry James that seem to match her own —tendencies to displace emotion to realms of style and observational "embroidery." But she excuses him.

Things for Henry James glow, flush, glimmer, vibrate, shine, hum, bristle, reverberate. Joy, bliss, ecstasies, intoxication, a sense of trembling in every limb, the heart-shaking first glimpse, a hanging on the prolonged silence of an editor . . . are too live to countenance his fear that he was giving us 'an inch of canvas and an acre of embroidery.'[62]

Moore might as well be saying this of herself, excusing her own similar fear that embroidery's excess is somehow superfluous. Consider, for instance,

> A brass-green bird with grass-
> green throat smooth as a nut spring[ing] from
>   twig to twig askew, copying the
> Chinese flower piece—business-like atom
>   in the stiff-leafed tree's blue-
> pink dregs-of-wine pyramids
>   of mathematic
>   circularity.
>
>   ("Smooth Gnarled Crape Myrtle")

Embroideries upon contained images, or images of containment, in James and Moore both, are images wanting to leap out of themselves, wanting to spring "from twig to twig askew" in mimetic flurries of involvement. The leaps of images and imagination are reenacted in proliferations of words and are symbolic of the visible-invisible contained energy of style. The amount of "embroidery," though it may sometimes smother a central image, may be regarded as an indication of the psychic energy of that image, the depth of feeling attached to it.

In "Then the Ermine:"

> Foiled explosiveness is yet
> a kind of prophet,
>
> a perfecter, and so a concealer—
>   with the power of implosion;
> like violets by Dürer
> even darker.

We come back to the question of how verse might best be confused with fate.

Exactly how is this "foiled explosiveness" "a kind of prophet?" We recall the
prophets of the Old Testament of whom Marianne Moore is so fond and their
ability to maintain poetic exuberance in the face of utter destruction; we recall that in spite of the prophets' cosmic messages, their personalities did not
dissolve. (Marianne Moore chides the "novices" for not being able to tell the
difference between Isaiah, Jeremiah, Ezekiel, and Daniel ("Novices"). Containment does not necessarily preclude fierce self-expression; on the contrary,
a "foiled explosiveness" "with the power of implosion" tends to sharpen the
poet's sense of herself, her personal isolation "of innocence and altitude/ in
an unhackneyed solitude" ("Armor's Undermining Modesty"). "Opposition
and the motive of self-defense," says Esther Harding,

> can thus furnish the impulse necessary to bring about a separation
> from the group and lead to the discovery of the uniqueness of the
> individual. Thereby the instinct of self-defense, which contains
> the seeds of war and potentialities for destruction of the whole
> human species, shows itself to be capable of functioning in a new
> realm, and now its power is transferred to the quest for the su-
> preme value within the human psyche.[63]

The consideration of war in Moore's well-known poem "In Distrust of Merits,"
turns her inward with the same force with which it lashes out at war:

> They're
> fighting in deserts and caves, one by
> one, in battalions and squadrons;
> they're fighting that I
> may yet recover from this disease, My
> Self; some have it lightly; some will die.
>
> . . . It cures me; or am I what
> I can't believe in? . . .
>
> There never was a war that was
> not inward; I must
> fight till I have conquered in myself what
> causes war, but I would not believe it.

This is an assertion of individuality at the same time as it is a condemnation
of the individual. It is poetry regarding itself with "perfect contempt," while

at the same time it seems to offer a cure for what is contemned. This poem is, ironically, one of the few poems in which Marianne Moore does not wear full armor; but the impulse to armor is there all the same, in cliché and abstraction. The explosiveness is foiled with a turning inward; the purpose of the external war is to expose an internal one. The turning inward is for the purpose of self-effacement at the same time as it is for the purpose of self-definition against a background of chaos. The freedom to do this is the freedom fought for.

"In Distrust of Merits" does, in distrust specifically of personal merits, give up some of the idiosyncrasy of style that marks Moore's other poems. It symbolizes in this, like some of her amputative revisions, a self-sacrifice. T. S. Eliot has remarked that "the progress of the artist is a continual extinction of personality."[64] This, to my mind, is a questionable statement, but Moore does seem to want to "progress" in this direction in "In Distrust of Merits." It is interesting to see the poem as an experiment in style that partakes of the prophecies of "foiled explosiveness" by sending the poet back to her self and her own comfortable armorings, because she never wrote another poem in exactly the style of "In Distrust of Merits" ("Keeping Their World Large" is the closest to it). Perhaps she distrusted its merits compared with the merits of her most natural self-expressions. Perhaps she decided that, as Jaffé puts it, "the conscious personality, obeying its individual destiny, is the only bulwark against the mass movements of modern society."[65] Marianne Moore wanted her poetry to be "Like a Bulwark":

> Affirmed. Pent by power that holds it fast—
> a paradox. Pent. Hard pressed,
>   you take the blame and are inviolate.
>   Abased at last?
>   Not the tempest-tossed.
> Compressed; firmed by the thrust of the blast
>   till compact, like a bulwark against fate;
>   lead-saluted,
>   saluted by lead?
> As though flying Old Glory full mast.

This poem may be seen as a definition of "the power of implosion" that prophesies a perfect and concealed fate. The bulwark *against* fate *is* fate. After all the compression and abasement and forced humility, even humiliation, there is relief, a sudden image of glory and freedom. It is "full mast"— the salute of lead not followed by a half-mast patriotic mourning. "For

mortal rage and immortal injury, are there or are there not medicines?"
Marianne Moore asks. "We need not be told that life is never going to be free
from trouble and that there are no substitutes for the dead; but it is a fact as
well as a mystery that weakness is power, that handicap is proficiency, that
the scar is a credential, that indignation is no adversary for gratitude, or heroism for joy. There are medicines."[66]

And there are preventions, protections, transformations. All a matter of
style. "There is a great amount of poetry in unconscious fastidiousness," and
in the fastidiousness that, "with the power of implosion," can transform the
weakness, handicaps, scars, and indignations of the poet into an individuality
that can claim, as Moore does in "Efforts of Affection," "vermin-proof and
pilfer-proof integration/ in which unself-righteousness humbles inspection."
An "integration too tough for infraction" is the armor, the fastidiously
"foiled explosiveness" that predicts, or predicates, the self. It is in the protectiveness of language that verse is to be particularly identified with fate, as
consciousness of fate protects us from a meaningless continuance. The fate
is twofold, multifold, paradoxical: it is to conquer one's separateness through
battle at the same time as one's separateness is insured by mirror-of-steel
armor. "There is the tarnish; and there, the imperishable wish." The tarnish
is part of the wish, for the substance at the core must be revealed by the
eventual breakdown of all such external constructions. At the core of the
earth metal is liquid with heat and compression, pure possibility. The substance at the core of poetry is the artist's self and the artist's wish to erupt
with the vitality of the earth itself. The wish is part of the tarnish.

TAMING ANIMALS

SUCH POWER AS ADAM HAD

"Like happy souls in Hell," enjoying mental difficulties,
the Greeks
amused themselves with delicate behavior
because it was "so noble and so fair":...
augmenting the assertion that, essentially humane,
"the forest affords wood for dwellings and by its beauty
stimulates the moral vigor of its citizens."
The Greeks liked smoothness, distrusting what was back
of what could not be clearly seen,
resolving with benevolent conclusiveness
"complexities which still will be complexities
as long as the world lasts";
ascribing what we clumsily call happiness,
to "an accident or a quality,
a spiritual substance or the soul itself,
an act, a disposition, or a habit,
or a habit infused, to which the soul has been persuaded,
or something distinct from habit, a power"—
such power as Adam had and we are still devoid of.

("An Octopus")

MUCH ATTENTION has been given to Marianne Moore's fascination with animals, because it is often in the poems where animals figure foremost that the precision of the poet and the precision of her subject most closely coincide. She describes the reindeer "with its firm face part brown, part white ... gray-/ brown fur with a neck like edelweiss or/ lion's foot—*leontopodium* to be exact"; and the jerboa with "fine hairs on the tail,/ repeating the other pale// markings, lengthen[ing] until/ at the tip they fill/ out in a tuft—black and white"; and the cat's eyebrow, "the small tuft of fronds/ or katydid-legs above each eye." Examples of close observations such as these abound. The particularity and peculiarity of her observations are not due only to love of animals, but to love of looking and naming, looking to control. Marianne Moore's menagerie serves the same purpose as her collection of *objets d'art,* her caricatures, and her collages of quotations (or "messes of mottage" to use an appropriate term of Joyce's). What she looks for is beyond the animal, beyond the art, beyond the telescopic or microscopic alphabet of characteristics; it is the "rock crystal" that the hero sees that she would ultimately see. The Greeks, she tells us in "An Octopus," "amused themselves with delicate behavior/ because it was 'so noble and so fair.'" "Delicate behavior" is what Marianne Moore finds attractive in all her animals; even the "elephant's columbine-tubed trunk/ held waveringly out—/ an at will heavy thing—is/ delicate." If the poet is primarily interested in art, delicacy, manners, and language, we may ask why she repeatedly turns to buffaloes, pigeons, arctic oxen, ostriches, snails, elephants, rats, race horses, lizards and porcupines to find and express those interests. Without human forms of art and precision, the randomness and wild complexity of the natural world is not wonderful, but threatening. On the other hand, animals may be seen as an antidote to the unspontaneity of the "pedantic literalist," an unspontaneity that Moore often finds tempting herself. For Marianne Moore, animals and animal nature, like certain qualities of human nature, present a definite threat to art unless understood by that art. Her carefully mimetic record of these animals is an "amusement," as it was for the purist ancient Greeks of whom Moore is fond, but it also involves an heroic, romantic task, that of purifying the world through vision.

The animals are tamed and brought into the orderly world of "benevolent conclusiveness" that Moore feels safest in. In her art, or rather by means of it, the animals become friends and magical protectors. Anna Freud calls attention to the fact that children invariably try to overcome their fear of certain animals by identifying with the feared animal and by making the animal a playmate and special protector.[1] Marianne Moore's ambivalence toward snakes and all relatives of snakes, as documented by her poems, suggest this sort of phenomenon. (Whether it is strictly autobiographical or not is another question, but that need not concern us at the moment.) The king referred to in "The Jerboa" "feared snakes, and tamed Pharaoh's rat" instead; "The Monkeys" "were afraid of snakes"; of the cat Peter, "demonstrate on him how the lady placed a forked stick/ on the innocuous neck-sides of the dangerous southern snake"; of Leonardo's habitat, "height deterred/ from his verdure, any polecat or snake"; in "Sea Unicorns and Land Unicorns" the rolling of sea lions "disperses . . . those sea snakes whose forms, looped/ in

the foam, 'disquiet shippers'"; "The Frigate Pelican" redeems the poet from
the "python that crushes to powder"; the town of "The Steeple-Jack" ap-
peals to the poet because "the climate is not right . . . for exotic serpent life";
Eve, in "Marriage," is "constrained in speaking of the serpent"; in "An
Octopus" the poet refers to "the concentric crushing rigor of the python."
Nevertheless, snakes are also associated in Moore's poetry with beauty and
majesty and magic, with the "something feline, something columbrine" of
Adam in "Marriage", and in "Snakes, Mongooses, Snake Charmers, And The
Like" the snake is

> thick, not heavy, it stands up from its travelling basket,
> the essentially Greek, the plastic animal all of a piece from nose
>   to tail;
> one is compelled to look at it. . . .

It is, like the elephant's trunk, an "at will heavy thing"; "thick, not heavy . . .
plastic," it is enchanted and enchanting. The snake, at least in one place, is
seen as "essentially Greek," and we must remember:

> The Greeks liked smoothness, distrusting what was back
> of what could not be clearly seen,
> resolving with benevolent conclusiveness
> "complexities which still will be complexities
> as long as the world lasts."
>
>   ("An Octopus")

The reptile is one of the complexities that must be resolved; one is compelled
to see it clearly. Thus Marianne Moore devotes one of her longest, most
magical and beautiful essays to the plumet basilisk and its relatives. She admires the chameleon who can "snap the spectrum up for food." And her
fondest wish is "O to Be a Dragon," a dragon that can, not accidentally, be
invisible at will.

Marianne Moore's response to the fearsomeness of snakes is to play at
being a magical relative, chameleon or dragon or basilisk. Her response to the
unwieldiness of elephants is to write two long poems—"Melanchthon" and
"Elephants"—in praise and understanding of the inner delicateness of elephants, of what it means to be an elephant, of how the elephant's being fits
into the being of the poet. The animal-as-protector theme is best seen in

"Leonardo Da Vinci's," a poem about a painting of St. Jerome and his lion where "the vindicated beast and/ saint somehow became twinned; and now, since they behaved and also looked alike, their lionship seems officialized."

It may be objected that this response to "beasts" in Moore's work, the childlike defense of transforming the beast into a friend, or oneself into the beast, does not apply to Moore's equally numerous poems about unaggressive animals, ones who hardly threaten. These include the pangolin, various birds, the jerboa, the cat, arctic ox, snail, skunk, paper nautilus, and others. Marianne Moore's desire to tame these unaggressive animals is not exactly the same as her need to tame dangerous animals. Nevertheless, the complexity presented by these animals' very existence, along with the fact that all of them have enemies, puts them in need of intense and almost magical control if they are to be part of the medieval wholeness that Marianne Moore demands from nature. She mothers them. Also, she can "demonstrate on [them]" the techniques she uses to tame more ferocious or unpredictable animals, just as she imagines demonstrating on the sleeping cat Peter the way the lady with a forked stick immobilizes the dangerous snake.

Every detail must be seen clearly to be accurately related to the other phenomena of the world and to the self. Marianne Moore is a high priestess of this clairvoyant activity; she is the defender and spiritual interpreter of her animals. They become supernaturally protected and protective as she does, by virtue of discovered tentacles of relationship with all other forms of life and of art. Thus the reindeer has a neck "like edelweiss or/ lion's foot—*leontopodium* to be exact" as well as being a "candelabrum-headed ornament." To be exact, this creature has connections with plant life, with its possible predator (Moore repeats this fact in two languages in case the scientists didn't get it the first time) and with art and light. The pangolin is, in its turn, related to the artichoke, snake, "furled fringed frill/ on the hat-brim of Gargallo's hollow iron head of a matador," machine, ant, plain man, sailboat, and visionary. The way to defend against those disturbing "complexities that will be complexities as long as the world lasts" is literally to embody those complexities.

In *The Human Metaphor*, Elizabeth Sewell considers "uses of the mind-body figure as an interpretive instrument in the great range of forms or figures which constitute the universe, and conversely, how those external figures may interpret happenings in the body-mind."[2] In Marianne Moore's poetry, and especially in her "animal poems," we see her developing various mind-body figures which do help to interpret the universe; they are explorative like the elephant's trunk "held waveringly out" or the pangolin's "exhausting solitary trips through unfamiliar ground at night." (It is surprising how many of her animals travel at night, considering what a "daytime" poet she is normally considered to be.) Her animals are self-defending and all manage to find a kind of self-sustaining power within their specific circumscriptions. They all have minds and morals as well as bodies, and the "mind" is also that of the interpretive poet

> ascribing what we clumsily call happiness,
> to "an accident or a quality,
> a spiritual substance or the soul itself,
> an act, a disposition, or a habit,
> or a habit infused, to which the soul has been persuaded,
> or something distinct from habit, a power."
>
> ("An Octopus")

The trademark of Marianne Moore's collective of animals is their "happy" habit of soul, their power. The jerboa, "not famous, that/ lives without water/ has happiness." All of her animals know how to deal with the world they find themselves in; they interpret it with their bodies and actions, encompass within their forms all forms in doing so, and thus protect themselves and anyone to whom they have taught the larger meanings of their existence, from chaos. Animals are instruments of precision, as the pigeon is "an instrument not just an instinctive individual" ("Pigeons"). The pigeon, like a sensitive artist, knows where he has been, where he must go:

> Mysterious animal with a magnetic
> feel by which he traces back-
> ward his transportation outward.
>
> ("Pigeons")

Each flight of bird or foraging forth of pangolin or jerboa is worthy of a poem. It transports the poet. It is an overture to the strange experience of beauty, a gesture of communication or affection toward the world. Marianne Moore's world is one of signatures and naturally derived meanings. She tames its wildness with praise as one tames the anger of a god; she tames it with benevolent conclusions, and with vigilance.

In subjectivating animal life and animal endurance in the way that she has, Marianne Moore not only describes her own life and means of endurance as an artist, but divines them, using the animals in her poems as explorative instruments of the "body-mind" or world-mind. T. S. Eliot, in his essay on Harry Crosby, remarks:

Crosby was right, very right, in looking for a set of symbols which should relate each of his poems to the others, to himself, rather than using in each poem symbols which should merely relate to other poems by other people. . . . his verse was consistently, I think, the result of an effort to record as exactly as possible to his own satisfaction a particular way of apprehending life.[3]

We might say the same of Marianne Moore. She sought and found those particular animals in which she could lose herself to find herself. Her poems are more illuminating in their relations to each other than they are in their relations to the poems of others. Her assessments of the way the world works, the way it expresses its moralities, beauty, and truth, are observations of the not-self from which, as one finds in the course of observation, one cannot wholly separate oneself. As Rilke says in the eighth of his *Duino Elegies:*

> . . . we, spectators always, everywhere,
> looking at, never out of, everything!
> It fills us. We arrange it. It decays.
> We re-arrange it, and decay ourselves.
>
> (translated by J. B. Leishman and Stephen Spender)

There are, roughly, five themes which bind Moore's animal poems together, all of which are related to those poems not centrally about animals and to her style in general. They are: *survival,* which may be seen as a metaphor for the survival of any individual in a world that conspires against one at the same time as it nourishes one; *"delicate behavior,"* an expression of integrity with regard to the world, an attitude for fitting conversation with it; *judgment* with regard to ethics and aesthetics; *art* devoted to animals and the turning of animals into art, a loving petrification; and *magic,* the discovery in animal nature and the self of the ability to enchant and protect a supernatural vision. All these themes are drawn together by the poet's pervasive interest in "capturing" them, saving them from the danger of extinction through ignorance, classifying and preserving them. It is a magical prevention against loss of life and art as well. Marianne Moore would save not only real but legendary creatures—the unicorn, for instance:

> Thus this strange animal with its miraculous elusiveness,
> has come to be unique,
> "impossible to take alive,"

tamed only by a lady inoffensive like itself—
as curiously wild and gentle.

                    ("Sea Unicorns and Land Unicorns")

Marianne Moore observes something about T. S. Eliot's *Book of Practical Cats* that directs us to something similar in her own attitude toward her animal friends and their amusing, serious, delicate behavior. She comments:

> yet does not Mr. Eliot appear to be, in discreet ways, a novelist? Observe in *The Naming Of Cats,* would-be familiarity at an impasse; the manoeuvre, 'O Cat'; the overture, Strassbourg Pie or potted grouse; the awaited denouement:
> And so in time you reach your aim
> And finally call him by his NAME.[4]

In the same essay, Moore calls Eliot "master of the anonymous," and "the cat who could never be caught." Of course, she is partly making fun, but she may also be referring, in a friendly way, to charges leveled at both Eliot and herself at the outset of their careers—charges of lack of emotion, annoying impersonality.[5] Marianne Moore, too, might in discreet ways appear to be a novelist at heart, as novelists are interested in peculiar habits, survival of families and races, ongoing critiques of life and manners, relationships discovered, and above all (but this they share with poets and magicians as well) the magical control gained by naming, by creating a meaning out of a mouthful of air. Marianne Moore engages in naming and remains all but anonymous; she would like to be like Adam, first namer and tamer of animals. She is amply aware, and makes us aware, of her reachings in her animal poems and all her poems, toward an Edenic power of innocence and fresh vision, "such power as Adam had and we are still devoid of."

A SYMBOL OF JUSTICE

*The power of the visible
is the invisible; as even where
no tree of freedom grows,
so-called brute courage knows.*

> *Heroism is exhausting, yet*
> *it contradicts a greed.*
>
> ("He 'Digesteth Harde Yron'")

Marianne Moore has deep respect for individuality, for the freedom and mystery that lets one be unique while bearing a web of relationships to other creatures and things of the world. In a poem written to celebrate a new breed of pigeon developed by the Gentlemen of the Feather Club, it is important to Moore to place the new bird in the context of its family tree:

> Older than the ancient Greeks, than
> Solomon, the pigeon family is a
> ramifying one, a
> banyan of banyans.
>
> ("Pigeons")

The poem goes on to distinguish many distinct survivals of different kinds of pigeons. They are meticulously described; for instance, one is "hid in unimag-/ inably weak lead-colored ostrich-/ plumes a third of an inch long, and needle-fine cat-whisker fibered battleship-/ gray lace." The bird would seem to deserve and derive protection by virtue of such workmanship lavished on its body. There is sadness in the poem because of the feeling that description and magical naming cannot save; the celebration of pigeons must include the fact that the dodo did not survive except in name: *"Didus ineptus;* man's remorse enshrines it now . . . A new pigeon cannot compensate."

The "Wood-Weasel" is a less comprehensive celebration, yet it too is a celebration of naming and toughness of species. A playful poem, the first letter of each line helps to spell backwards the name of Hildegarde Watson, and the animal himself (a skunk) is playful. He is also "determination's totem" and his special skin "smothers anything that stings." "The Rigorists" too are expressive of the ability to survive. They are the reindeer "adapted to scant *reino."* They share with the artist, that "rigorist of the imagination," her "tuned reticence with rigor at the source" ("Propriety"). And they share with many of Moore's animals—the jerboa, the paper nautilus, the giraffe living "on top leaves that are small"—the ability to be and to make do with little. The reindeer are rigorists despite a certain surrounding luxury:

> They are rigorists,
> however handsomely cutwork artists

                of Lapland and
            Siberia elaborate the trace
            or saddle girth with sawtooth leather lace,

and they are rigorists despite being

                candelabrum-headed ornament[s]
            in a place where ornaments are scarce.

    Art, whether one is surrounded by it or carries it around with one as
part of one's body, is not enough to live on. One must adapt, especially where
the weather (and not only the physical weather) is cold and inimicable to
growth. The reindeer with their talent for survival were, we are told at the
end of the poem, "a gift preventing the extinction of the Eskimo." All rigorists, who must fulfill some rigor of the imagination as well, have a purpose in
helping each other survive. There is an art that is not purely luxurious, and
that art, by example, should help us to go on living. Someone, a rigorist, who
has sojourned in the whale, who "has lived and lived on all kinds of shortages"
and "been compelled to spin gold/ thread from straw" ("Sojourn in the
Whale") can best tell us this. "The Rigorists" as a poem may not be a "good"
poem except in a moral sense, yet it helps illuminate its author's cast of mind
even if we are too sated with comforts to feel we need its advice.
    "He 'Digesteth Harde Yron'" begins:

                Although the aepyornis
                or roc that lived in Madagascar, and
            the moa are extinct,
            the camel-sparrow, linked
                with them in size—the large sparrow
            Xenophon saw walking by a stream—was and is
            a symbol of justice.

Characteristically Moore gives us not one but two names for the extinct species of Madagascar, as if naming it would bring it back, or bring it back at
least in relation to the subject of her poem, a surviving symbol of justice. The
survival of the symbol as well as of the individual bird requires vigilance.

> This bird watches his chicks with
> a maternal concentration—and he's
> been mothering the eggs
> at night six weeks—his legs
> their only weapon of defense.
> He is swifter than a horse; he has a foot hard
> as a hoof; the leopard
>
> is not more suspicious.

If animals were to put the human race on trial for deviousness and greed, the ostriches would be witnesses of consequence for the prosecution, as ostriches (the poem points out) were decoyed and killed by men pretending to be ostriches. The world of Marianne Moore's poems is a dangerous one, and the theme of danger in her poems is often connected with the need for mothering. We see it most clearly in "Bird-Witted" where the vigilant mother bird, who can hardly find enough food to feed her young, instinctively attacks the cat. The paper nautilus "scarcely eats until the eggs are hatched"; even the frigate pelican contrives a nest for his "children." There is a primal childlike fear informing these poems, and their "mothering" depends on a consciousness of evil as well as an instinctual love.

People are in moral danger because of the luxury they surround themselves with; ostriches are in mortal danger because they are part of that luxury.

> Six hundred ostrich brains served
> at one banquet, the ostrich-plume-tipped tent
> and desert spear, jewel-
> gorgeous ugly egg-shell
> goblets, eight pairs of ostriches
> in harness, dramatize a meaning
> always missed by the externalist.

Marianne Moore is no externalist. This externally ostrich-dominated banquet, dominated by the symbol of justice, is ironic; the Romans eat their own hope of salvation, but it is not the sort of internalization that lasts. The ostrich is merely decoration, dish, and transportation. What good is a symbol of justice, then, if justice is not done by it? Symbols, too, are for the externalists; the truth must go deeper in, must be invisible where "the power of the visible is the invisible," where the "hero" searches for her meaning. "Heroism is exhausting, yet/ it contradicts a greed." Justice can't survive in a world that is incapable of recognizing it. Even the ostrich, "the alert gargantuan/ little-winged, magnificently speedy running bird," will not be able to outrun greed. He is a rebel, a hero, but against what external odds? The heroic American eagle, helpless symbol that it is, nurses broken eggs. "A new pigeon cannot compensate."

CURIOUS GRACE

> *To explain grace requires*
> *a curious hand.*
>
>   ("The Pangolin")

Certain of Marianne Moore's animal poems are primarily concerned with the animal's style of being. These poems include "The Frigate Pelican," "Peter," "To a Snail," "To a Chameleon," "Tom Fool at Jamaica," "Melanchthon," "The Arctic Ox," and "The Pangolin." This group is, in a way, arbitrary, and it may be objected that some of these animals belong more to the categories of animals-as-critics or animals-as-art. Overlaps are unavoidable. These particular poems are especially related, though, in that the animals they describe are seen first and most particularly for themselves and only secondarily as models for human behavior and human art. (This is not true of all of Moore's animal poems, some of which carry a more prominent moral or aesthetic burden.) One might include the jerboa and plumet basilisk here, as the poems about them are concerned very much with the animals' own forms and beings, but they are perhaps more rewardingly considered in relation to magic, as that is where their most charming qualities seem to lie.

     "Peter," a domestic cat, does not have the brilliance of Christopher Smart's Jeffery (with which all cat poems, I suppose, must ultimately be compared), yet the poem succeeds in giving Peter an inviolable life of his own; he makes us see and appreciate catness. His human author begins by examining him in sleep, noticing eyebrow and whisker and "detached first claw." He is, like all Marianne Moore's animals, compared with a variety of forms we do

not usually associate with cats. For instance, in sleep "he lets himself be flattened out by gravity,/ as seaweed is tamed and weakened by the sun." He has
a "prune-shaped head and alligator eyes"; he may, when he is asleep, be
proxy for a snake or "dangled like an eel/ or set up on the forearm like a
mouse." He is a predator, but may be the prey of our imaginations while he
sleeps, for then he is not himself.

Still, "profound sleep is not with him a fixed illusion," nor is it with
the poet, who has certain dreamlike illusions about his inactive form.

> Springing about with froglike accuracy, with jerky cries
> when taken in hand, he is himself again;
> to sit caged by the rungs of a domestic chair
> would be unprofitable—human. What is the good of hypocrisy?

Cats do as they please, will not be tamed or misled by appearances as humans
will. A cat has no use for pretense, will change occupations at whim (as cat-
admiring poets may change images), and he will not condescend.

> He can talk but insolently says nothing. . . .
> As for the disposition invariably to affront,
> an animal with claws should have an opportunity to use them.

As, we may add, should the poet of wit who, like the hero, does not like
some things. Peter's mission is "to leap, to lengthen out, divide the air, to
purloin, to pursue." In all these activities he is not unlike the poet who names
him; curiosity may kill him and "a fight with nature or with cats" may scare
him, but he does not hide his natural responses. He expresses them. "To do
less would be nothing but dishonesty."

We are reminded again and again in Moore's poems that animals must
be preserved in their naturalness and innocence. "The Arctic Ox (or Goat)"
begins by admonishing us:

> To wear the arctic fox
> you have to kill it. Wear
>   qiviut—the underwool of the arctic ox—
> pulled off it like a sweater;
> your coat is warm; your conscience, better.

If you are attracted to these opening lines, you may like the closing ones as
well:

> If we can't be cordial
> to these creatures' fleece,
> I think that we deserve to freeze.

Despite a tone of triviality, the poem "The Arctic Ox" underlines a main concern of Moore's animal poems. She would like a suit of *qiviut* herself, so light
she wouldn't even know she had it on; in other words, she would like to possess some of their natural animal warmth without self-consciousness, without
having to kill anything, without affectation. She would like to *be* this pleasant
animal, an unpredacious poet in goat's underwear. Not that she isn't, in a
sense, just that.

There are other things Marianne Moore likes about these childlike, playful little creatures:

> While not incapable
> of courtship, they may find its
>   servitude and flutter, too much
> like Procrustes' bed;
> so some decide to stay unwed.

Just like her. And fortunately they are not known for the "egocentric scent"
of musk, although they may be called musk oxen. The anomaly is unfortunate but it cannot interfere with an actual integrity. The arctic goats use what
they have, give what they can, and get on splendidly in their "innocence and
altitude" (like the knight in "Armor's Undermining Modesty"), an innocence
that goes so far as to trivialize this poem, which must be distinguished from
her work at its evil best.

A poem that deserves special attention as an expression of style and being is "The Pangolin." The pangolin is "the night miniature artist engineer,"
"Leonardo Da Vinci's replica." The invocation of Leonardo is important in
terms of Marianne Moore's work in general. Toward the end of her career she
devoted two poems to Leonardo—one a description of his picture of St.
Jerome and the lion, which asserts the necessity of communion between beast
and saint, between protective animal and writer-artist; and the other, about
Leonardo himself, called "An Expedient—Leonardo Da Vinci's—and a Query,"
the query being Leonardo's own alleged last words, "Tell me if anything at all
has been done?" If Leonardo, as this poem tells us, "peerless, venerated/ by
all . . . succumbed to dejection," what about Marianne Moore's "night miniature artist engineer," his "replica"? What does the pangolin, and what does

the pangolin-poet, do to keep from "capsizing in disenheartenment?"

First of all, he trusts his artichoke-like armor and his explorative nature. The pangolin is Da Vinci's replica because in Marianne Moore's poem he is capable of, or representative of, both natural and supernatural wonder. He *is* a wonder. He is a master of dream "who endures exhausting solitary trips through unfamiliar ground at night,"

> returning before sunrise; stepping in the moonlight,
>   on the moonlight peculiarly, that the outside
>   edges of his hands may bear the weight and save the claws
>
>   for digging.

He is both *in* the moonlight and *on* it; he has control. The outside of his "hands" bear the weight of his progress, while the inside, the claws that are aggressive, are saved for work in depth. He has a scientist's and an artist's intuitions for the instrumentality of his own body. The artist explores within the moonlight; the scientist-engineer keeps on top of it. The pangolin may be on unfamiliar ground, but knows what he needs to find there; he has ways of dealing with both the unfamiliarity and the need.

He hisses at danger, he does not fight. His is a sound of moral disapproval; his technique is humble retreat. He is found "serpentined" about a tree, with the healthy and bodily-expressive consciousness of evil that rightly belongs to a night artist.

The pangolin's armor is partly the armor of his art, his grace. It is, like the "thin glass shell" of the paper nautilus, fragile though hard, like a "wrought-iron vine." He is covered, delicately enough, with "flattened sword-/ edged leafpoints"; compact, he is like a "furled fringed frill" on the hat-brim of an iron bust. But his grace is more than that of the wrought-iron artwork that he resembles. "To explain grace requires/ a curious hand," the poet says. "Grace" is more than a gift for precision and an appropriateness of movement. To explain grace, or as background to such an explanation, Marianne Moore asks a curious question.

> If that which is at all were not forever,
> why would those who graced the spires
>   with animals and gathered there to rest, on cold luxurious
>   low stone seats—a monk and monk and monk—between the thus
>   ingenious roof supports, have slaved to confuse

grace with a kindly manner, time in which to pay a debt,
the cure for sins, a graceful use
    of what are yet
            approved stone mullions branching out across
            the perpendiculars?

It is difficult to see exactly what Marianne Moore is trying to say here, and what its relationship to the pangolin is. The statement-question itself is highly armored in stone and complexity, yet we may try to state the meaning more clearly for ourselves, thus: If the world, or grace, is not eternal, why would artist-monks work to invent temporal meanings and applications of grace? The answer is that the world and its consequent "grace" *is* eternal, and the way to eternal grace is to be found through its temporal expressions—kindness, manners, use of art. If eternal grace could not be found through temporal grace, the monks would not have bothered to think of specific applications of it that could be adopted by ordinary men. The pangolin's kind of grace, natural animal grace as opposed to the supernatural grace that monks understand, needs to be translated into ordinary human terms in order to serve a temporal and practical purpose. The beast and saint, both needing translation from habitats of mystery into clearings of action, have a rare wisdom about the world deserving of that translation.

In the image of the artist-monks in their cold stone-decorated retreat (the "gathered to rest" suggesting death and eternity), one feels the tension between inside and outside, between death and life, between the intuition of eternity and the need for a practicality that can only be temporal and external. The same dichotomy is expressed by the pangolin's wrought-iron and stone-swallowing body, which is probably what suggested the image of the church with its retreating souls and strange gargoyles. We also find in this image the combined presence of the artist's inspiration, that eternal thing that made him choose ingeniously to express himself in stone in the first place, and the scientific construction, the architectural technique that made the artistic expression feasible. We are back to the idea of Leonardo and his own curious hand, explaining "grace" equally through artistic inspiration and practical engineering.

The pangolin has a soul, "a meaning always missed by the externalist" ("He 'Digesteth Harde Yron'"), and a body that in its graceful practicality expresses soul. He can roll himself "into a ball that has/ power to defy all effort to unroll it; strongly intailed, neat head for core, on neck not breaking off, with curled-in feet." In other words, he makes a perfect circle of himself, a defensive or a sleeping habit that is a symbol of eternity. But in motion and time he has obvious and useful appendages, unlike eternity. "The giant-pangolin-/tail, graceful tool, as prop or hand or broom or ax, tipped like/an elephant's trunk with special skin/ is not lost on this ant-and-stone-swallowing uninjurable artichoke." This is a masculine counterpart to his expression of himself as a rolled-up ball, his feminine and retreating form. In his feminine form, the pangolin's "head" is inside, "on neck not breaking off"—castration impossible. When he is feeling safe enough to venture out and is on an aggressive ant-hunt, he is vigilant; at these times "the giant-pangolin-/ tail . . . is not lost on [him]." We find in the image of monks and cathedral a combination of feminine and masculine, of inspiration and technique, "low stone seats" guarded by "ingenious roof supports." We find "a monk and monk and monk" (homunculi?) passively sitting or lying dead within a womb whose external expression is erect, actively thrusting at the sky and at eternity. These passive monks have slaved to provide external expressions of grace without themselves needing recourse to external action. They are in retreat as the pangolin curled-up is in retreat.

There may be no way of knowing how consciously Marianne Moore used this imagery of the circle and tail, monks and edifice, stone and living creature. But to my mind, a passion for armor is a passion to be both femininely withdrawn and protected and masculinely explorative and aggressive, to be equipped for all exigencies of mind and body. One wants to be directed outward, to conquer truth and time, to penetrate the mysteries of the world, but in this there is always the danger of being cut off suddenly, killed, castrated, silenced. On the other hand, one wants to be curled within oneself, safe and passive; but in this position there is no hope of penetrating, or of being penetrated either—there is only a self-sealed mystery. True grace may be seen as a balance between the two, a proper rhythm of alternation between external and internal, armor and soul, masculine and feminine, temporal and eternal. This the pangolin has, this the world at large has with its

> sun and moon and day and night and man and beast
>   each with a splendor
>   which man in all his vileness cannot
>   set aside; each with an excellence!

This sudden outburst from the soul of "The Pangolin," the poem, the artist, comes as a surprise. It has the splendor of naturalness, of natural duality and rhythm that leaves room for epiphany and that cannot be spoiled by an unspontaneous humanity. The poem is about the particular habits and individual excellence of the pangolin, but it is also about the condition of man, as the pangolin has "certain postures of a man."

Beneath sun and moon, man slaving
to make his life more sweet, leaves half the flowers worth
having,
needing to choose wisely how to use his strength.
. . .
Bedizened or stark
naked, man, the self, the being we call human, writing-
master to this world, griffons a dark
"Like does not like like that is obnoxious"; and writes error
with four
r's. Among animals, *one* has a sense of humor.
Humor saves a few steps, it saves years.

How are we to fit these things together? If, as we may suspect, grace—
the idea of it, or the curious explanation of it—is at the center of the poem, at
the eternal center between the alternations of sun and moon, day and night,
man and beast, then grace is also the concept which informs these sudden and
random observations. Given temporality ("*beneath* sun and moon") man
slaves (as the monks slaved) to choose the best way to act, and acting, as we
have seen, is the only way of externalizing the eternal-internal concept of
grace. So man writes, an activity peculiar to him; it is his own excellence and
most graceful endowment, as ant- and stone-swallowing is to the pangolin,
and thus he expresses his choice. His writing is obscurely funny, but moral;
he cannot be damned for his intentions (of not liking to be like or to like
some objectionable likeness of his). His unconscious wit, certainly a form of
grace, allows him to discover coincident humor in an erroneously written
error.
    The "he" in the last stanza of the poem may seem ambiguous, but I
believe it refers to man alone, albeit, a pangolin-modeled one. The pangolin
in his night foragings and dependence on moonlight may be seen as the night-
soul that corresponds to man's day-soul. The pangolin may be regarded as the
poet's dream—a curious one, curious enough for any bestiary—combining
beast, moon, and night, with religious and sexual imagery. This energy is
carried over into the "alternating blaze" of day, with its own wit, fear, and
strength in adversity.

Not afraid of anything is he,
    and then goes cowering forth, tread paced to meet an obstacle
at every step. Consistent with the
    formula—warm blood, no gills, two pairs of hands and a few
        hairs—that

```
                   is a mammal; there he sits in his own habitat,
                        serge-clad, strong-shod. The prey of fear, he, always
                             curtailed, extinguished, thwarted by the dusk, work
                                  partly done,
                        says to the alternating blaze,
                          "Again the sun!
                               anew each day; and new and new and new,
                             that comes into and steadies my soul."
```

This is a rare combination of humor and religious awe. We have on one hand the lowly textbook definition of "mammal"—one kind of link between pangolin and man which, purely scientific, cannot be overlooked. We have this mammal's personal attitude toward life, into which he goes "cowering forth" with considerable apprehension, "the prey of fear." Each has an armor and each has an excellence, but each has a fear of curtailment also. Each must be able to "intail" himself strongly, curl into a ball or become pure soul, enlightened alternately by the eternal spheres of moon and sun. It is not "funny" but deeply humorous, this relation of low technique with such high aspiration, lowly mammal with man.

"The Pangolin" may not be a perfectly realized poem. It does not succeed in avoiding a self-indulgent obscurity (fallacy of imitative form?), yet it is magnificent in its ambition to "explain" grace. The poem tells a story of how soul comes into the world, how it comes "cowering forth" to be born, and also how it is borne once it has arrived. The pangolin is at home in a "nest/ of rocks closed with earth from inside, which he can thus darken"; he is born from this womblike place into the moonlight where he expresses the strangest of earthly beings. He must be uncurled and brought out from his nest to express his particular style of life and his life-given grace. The monk-artists also have made a dark nest for themselves from which their ideas for the outward expressions of grace in men's lives are born. Man's soul is born from such dark, cold, and eternal places. He is a decision-maker by daylight, a technician, an artist with a sense of humor awaiting the sun, the expression of his soul. In "Sun" Marianne Moore says to the sun, "You are not male or female, but a plan/ deep-set within the heart of man"; and she asks the sun to "be wound in a device of Moorish gorgeousness." "The Pangolin" is remarkable for its attention to miniature engineering techniques, to the machine-like body, in short, to a highly specialized individuality of both poem and animal. At the same time the poem proposes to be about the soul and eternity. One grows out of the other; they grow together, as beast and man in "Leonardo Da Vinci's" where "astronomy/ or pale paint makes the golden pair in Leonardo Da Vinci's sketch seem/ sun-dyed. Blaze on, picture, saint, beast." Beast and man, male and female, light and dark, science and soul—all converge and conspire against permanent dejection. This is the answer to Leonardo's query "has anything at all been done?" The pangolin is wound in devices, not of gorgeousness exactly, but in devices that are Moorish with wit and brillance of analogy. He expresses his duality as "night miniature artist engineer"; he is a communication of self. This is what has been done, and all that can be done.

PICKING AND CHOOSING

> *Literature is a phase of life. If one is afraid of it,*
> *the situation is irremediable; if one approaches it familiarly,*
> *what one says of it is worthless.*
> ("Picking and Choosing")

Marianne Moore often employs animals as critics of art and life; their criticisms are related to their survivals and individual beings as the poet's criticisms are, in turn, related to hers. The two poems I intend to discuss in this section perhaps do not properly belong in a consideration of Moore's "animal poems," as they are not really *about* animals so much as they are about literature; and the criticism of literature and of literary criticism in them is explicit, rather than implicit as it is in, say, "To a Snail" or "Melanchthon." The animals in "The Monkeys" and "Critics and Connoisseurs" are seen with as much precision as animals in other of Moore's poems, but somehow their naturalness as animals is undercut by their author's ironically intended self-consciousness in observing them. These are two poems that have puzzled me and continue to puzzle me somewhat, and being as adamant about the wickedness of critics as they are, they rather successfully resist criticism. But even if they cannot be unraveled to satifaction, they do make a point about Marianne Moore's vision of animals as spokesmen, about the paradoxical fallenness of that vision.

"The Monkeys" is a peculiar poem. It involves a sketchy memory of a visit to a zoo in which four or five different animals are dimly recalled. This is followed by a speech on aesthetics, given surprisingly by a very clearly remembered and distinguished cat, a "Gilgamesh among/ the hairy carnivora." The poem was originally titled "My Apish Cousins"—which suggests the humanity of the relations that gather about these dim memories of animals.

I recall their magnificence, now not more magnificent
than it is dim. It is difficult to recall the ornament,
    speech, and precise manner of what one might
        call the minor acquaintances twenty
            years back; but I shall not forget him—that Gilgamesh.

The poem was first printed in Kreymbourg's *Others* in 1917. Twenty years
earlier, if Marianne Moore is being truly autobiographical, the poet was nine
or ten. Somehow—in a dream?—this hazily remembered experience merges
with a distinct memory of a cat, and an idea, clearly not that of a ten-year-
old, about art. The other zoo animals seem also to have spoken, but "it is
difficult to recall" what they said or how they said it. What is recalled is their
separateness and "magnificence, now not more magnificent than it is dim."
The elephant had "fog-colored skin," the zebra was "supreme in its abnor-
mality," the hummingbird simply "trivial and humdrum." The talking cat,
however, is recalled with more striking detail, as sometimes only one figure of
a complicated dream can be recalled. The poet insists that she will not forget
him with "the/ wedge-shaped, slate-gray marks on its forelegs and the resolute
tail." He is oracular, like the Cheshire cat of *Alice in Wonderland,* and the
reader may tend to accept what he says as wise by virtue of its mysteriousness
rather than its comprehensibility, which is neither immediate nor ever, in
fact, guaranteed. Here is what the cat "astringently" remarks:

                "They have imposed on us with their pale
    half-fledged protestations, trembling about
        in inarticulate frenzy, saying
            it is not for us to understand art; finding it
        all so difficult, examining the thing

    as if it were inconceivably arcanic, as symmet-
    rically frigid as if it had been carved out of chrysoprase
        or marble—strict with tension, malignant
            in its power over us and deeper
                than the sea when it proffers flattery in exchange for hemp,
            rye, flax, horses, platinum, timber, and fur."

"They" I take to mean obscurantist and elitist critics; and "us"—I'm not sure
—the animals in the zoo? us ordinary-talking cats? "They" say art is difficult,
arcanic, of Parnassian *l'art pour l'art* strictness; and that it has "power over
us." Given the prejudicial first part of the cat's speech, we must assume he

does not agree. He does not agree that art has power over us simply because it offers flattery (insincere words or difficulty that flatters the initiated "understanding" of the self-ordained priests of interpretation) in exchange for the raw materials of life, the commodities of world-market exchange. The artist must offer flattery, fulfillment of arcanic expectations, in exchange for the necessities of life. Whereas it should be the other way around? The cat attacks vain literary work and the suspect livelihood of a conspiracy of artist-critics. Quite rightly.

Critics are silly, "trembling about/ in inarticulate frenzy," and their silliness lets them be victimized by what they are told is "art" or what they assume to be "art" by virtue of its incomprehensibility. They are silly when they feel obliged to attribute true substance and the real commodities of thought to what any animal in the zoo could tell them is merely superficial. The critics who do not dare trust their common senses about what makes sense and what is just fooling around are obliged to produce valuable raw materials in exchange for plastic trinkets and to say that the trinkets were made of them. To revise superficiality so that it seems to read profoundly deserves the scorn of any sensibly talking animal. The naturally wise "Gilgamesh among/ the hairy carnivora" will read poetry with a suitable "perfect contempt" for it, finding in it, perhaps, a place for the genuine. Finding that place empty, he will not hesitate to say so.

"The Monkeys" tends to make monkeys of all who attempt criticism of artistic products that are not perfectly clear to them, and my reading of this poem in no way makes me feel exempt. I feel that the "place for the genuine" ("Poetry") in this poem is the cage of the animal and that the talking cat is genuinely there. Still, and to put it in the silliest way possible: this poem illustrates the fact that difficult poetry which is difficult in illustration of the fact that it hates difficulty should hang up a sign on its cage: NOLI ME TANGERE, and beneath that, PLEASE DO NOT FEED THE ANIMALS. Would gaping critics be able to decipher those warnings? Could they manage to keep their hands and their peanuts to themselves and simply look?

Probably not. Not when it is something of ourselves that we see pacing in the cage, wanting to be touched and fed.

Animals and poems do not belong in cages, but that is how we are forced to view most of them. We do not expect them to talk back, necessarily, but when they do, it is with a power that is not related to flattery or to the gross national product. And this is how Marianne Moore would have her animals and her poems differ from the uncommunicative specimens that her talking cat would scorn. The critic who finds this scorn incomprehensible may simply move on to the next cage. But she will not forget him.

"Critics and Connoisseurs" begins with that much quoted, fêted, and baited assertion, "There is a great amount of poetry in unconscious fastidious-ness." It may be applied to any number of critical arguments, but Marianne Moore seems to have something very particular in mind—namely a kind of natural determination that is not self-conscious and that expresses itself with-out any thought to what one might gain. Certain Chinese art seems to fit her criteria, but best are the

> mere childish attempt to make an imperfectly bal-
> > lasted animal stand up,
> similar determination to make a pup
> > eat his meat from the plate.

Here the child performs with respect to his animal friend the ideally uncon-scious task of the artist with respect to her art, or critic with respect to what she criticizes; she tries to make the subject behave according to her own in-stincts of propriety. This approach must demonstrate that one is not afraid of one's subject, but it must not be over-familiar either, ending by breaking the animal's bones or spirit or forcing unwanted nourishment down its throat un-til it bursts. The child in a certain way makes her subject her equal by assum-ing it is so, by practicing on it the unselfconscious and affectionate fussing that the child herself, if she has been well loved, has been subject to.

Following the opening remark about "unconscious fastidiousness" and its modest illustrations are the two animal associations which dominate the poem: the over-critical swan and that foolish connoisseur, the ant. Marianne Moore's relationship to the swan is like the child's relationship to the puppy. Her affection for the animal is demonstrated by her close observation and recreation of it.

> I remember a swan under the willows in Oxford,
> > with flamingo-colored, maple-
> > > leaflike feet. It reconnoitered like a battle-
> > ship.

So far the poet rather admires the bird, but she is put off by the swan's own attitude of "disbelief and conscious fastidiousness." What she is really indig-nant about is the fact that the swan ignores the food thrown to it. Finally the swan condescends to take what she gives, but she still does not approve. Who is the critic? The transition between swan and ant is effected through the "you" to whom the poem is critically addressed:

        I have seen this swan and
    I have seen you; I have seen ambition without
understanding in a variety of forms.

"Ambition without understanding" is a very wicked thing and awful to be accused of, yet what is the difference between it and "unconscious fastidiousness," fastidiousness to no conscious ends, the ambition to make an animal stand up without understanding that the animal is not built for standing up, the ambition to make the swan leave his guard by throwing food to him? Are those ambitions of understanding? Of critics' bafflement? They are, rather, corruptions of innocence, and of natural behavior. The poem may contain more irony than it bargained for, and the result is an ambiguity we cannot resolve or defend. That is acceptable; if all the irony were consciously fastidious, there would be too great an amount of prose in it.

        Opposed to the swan, but without any moral superiority, she has noticed an ant,

        a fastidious ant carrying a stick north, south,
            east, west, till it turned on
        itself, struck out from the flower bed into the lawn,
            and returned to the point

    from which it had started. Then abandoning the stick as
        useless and overtaxing its
            jaws with a particle of whitewash—pill-like but
        heavy—it again went through the same course of procedure.

The ant is criticized for aimless activity, for carrying something around in a circle without understanding that carrying something should have a purpose. It should transport whatever it is to a new location. The ant is unconsciously fastidious about touching all points of the compass and about having something in his mouth whether it is useful to him or not. He is an aimless connoisseur, a poet or a critic with nothing to say, his mouth being full of pills or particles of whitewash. Yet what is the difference between what the ant has done and what the poet herself does in first observing the swan, then the ant, in nearly perfectly regular stanzas (14, 8, 12, 12-14, 6, 14, 6, 12, 6—there are a few anomalous lines, but very few) and then drawing no real conclusion from her fable? What kind of understanding has prompted the poet's ambition—to make the swan leave its defense to eat crumbs from the stream, to make the purposeless activity of the ant have a poetic purpose? Unconscious fastidiousness, presumably, in which one finds poetry. Poetry and a question. The poem ends:

> What is
> there in being able
> to say that one has dominated the stream in an attitude of self-
> defense;
> in proving one has had the experience
> of carrying a stick?

The attitude with which this question is put would seem to dictate the answer: there is absolutely nothing in it. But there *is* unconscious fastidiousness in it; there is poetry and at least one highly quotable line. The critic will defend her ground no matter what; the connoisseur will carry his latest "find" around in her circle and then abandon it for something else. The artist, ideally aware of dialectics, will try not to be rigid with self-defense nor thoroughly and unconsciously aimless. The critic can be an artist, and vice versa.

"The Monkeys" and "Critics and Connoisseurs" were written at nearly the same time and help to illuminate each other. Both poems invoke childhood. "The Monkeys" begins with a dim memory of childhood, of visiting a zoo with an attitude of fresh wonder. But this wonder gives way to an adult complexity beginning with the speech of the cat—a complexity which is characteristic of the fallen adult world and which deals with it. "Critics and Connoisseurs" begins by praising a "childish" practice that is straightforward even if a bit silly, that of trying to make animals do tricks they were not by nature intended to do. One cannot force words either, although one can have the hope of a child in the matter. The grown-up world of criticism with its meaningless manipulations comes as a shock in both poems. The cat delivers a diatribe; the swan and ant affront us with affectation and pointlessness. As Moore says in a review of Wallace Stevens' *Auroras of Autumn*, "The child is sane, however many times he asks 'what is it?' whereas the adult succumbs to an 'enfantillage' of intrusiveness and asks you who you are."[6]

Whatever else these poems are about, they are certainly partly about growing up, about loss of innocence, about learning to see things critically and learning to be seen critically. When one's relationship to animals changes from the unnameable wonder of naming to critical name-calling, one is no longer in Eden. The animals themselves tell us this. They say things one does not want to hear, and they do things one does not understand. One cannot forget the impertinence, but one need not quarrel. The only retort is offering an image that rediscovers the capacity for natural delicacy leading to an imperturbable and unconsciously fastidious natural piety. The aim is to accept—at least to tolerate—the universe as one finds it. This means accepting dreams and childhood, talking animals and the dumb ambitions of swan and ant. There is in "The Monkeys" an unforgettable diatribe; there is in "Critics and Connoisseurs" a confrontation with two polarized modes of unmeaning.

The animals have no answers, but they are didactic. They preach to us and present us with bad models, but they are surviving nevertheless. They are, to this purpose, described entirely with respect to the attitudinal style each has developed to cope with the chaos of the world. They do not ask you who you are, but they may ask you who you *think* you are. Marianne Moore has been called "arcanic"; she has dominated a certain stream with self-protectiveness; and she carries a moral stick. But she walks most softly, and she does have somewhere to go. Her eyes are open. Her compass is neither broken nor closed.

MYTHOLOGY'S WISH

the basilisk portrays
mythology's wish
to be interchangeably man and fish—
("The Plumet Basilisk")

Animals are one of the oldest and most natural subjects for art. The relationship between live animals and those magically preserved in art is various and often brought to our attention by the poems of Marianne Moore. Foremost among these are "No Swan So Fine," which describes a Louis XV candelabrum; "An Egyptian Pulled Glass Bottle in the Shape of a Fish"; "Sea Unicorns and Land Unicorns," dealing with the use of these animals as emblems on maps, shields, and in literature; "Charity Overcoming Envy," an essay on the allegorical animal figures in a tapestry; and "Tippoo's Tiger," about a king's mechanical toy tiger. Throughout all Moore's poems there are passing references to animals as art: the toys of the Egyptians in "The Jerboa," the bronze fireplace dogs in "People's Surroundings," the fairy-tale mice in "Tell Me, Tell Me," and the goat, real but imagined as a statue on an antique pedestal, in "An Octopus." Marianne Moore whimsically invokes the animal-rich art of the elite, animals that are turned into the unnecessary-vital ornaments of a court, animals as magicians' middlemen, and animals as actors in fairy tales. Moore's poems invite us to explore connections among the powers of kingship, imagination, magic and animal life.

"No Swan So Fine" asserts that there is no live swan, "no swan,/ with swart blind look askance/ and gondoliering legs, so fine" as the china one among its finely sculptured and polished flowers in the Louis XV candelabrum. The last half-line of the poem reads, simply and abruptly, "The king is dead." A way of life that went along with the king's life is also dead. The swan is alive only insofar as art is, but dead in its extravagant finality of form. Insofar as kings represent unprogressive ceremony and permanent superfluity, the swan and the king share a fate. The poem is a compression of an important ambivalence toward animals petrified as art. This swan appeals to Marianne Moore with its delicacy, elegance, and perfection; it appeals more than a live swan with "gondoliering legs." Yet, attractive as it is to her, she must admit that it is dead; it represents, more than a way of life, a royal fatality. The attraction is vital and fatal.

The first part of "The Jerboa," subtitled "Too Much," lists certain arts of the Egyptians which compromise the lives of animals by making possessions of them. The poem suggests that this particular excessiveness is both emblematic of success and prophetic of demise. The Egyptians

> understood
> making colossi and
> how to use slaves, and kept crocodiles and put
>   baboons on the necks of giraffes to pick
>   fruit, and used serpent magic.
>
> they had their men tie
> hippopotami
>   and bring out dappled dog-
>   cats to course antelopes, dikdik and ibex;
>   or used small eagles. They looked on as theirs,
>   impalas and onigers,
>
> The wild ostrich herd
> with hard feet and bird
>   necks rearing back in the
>   dust like a serpent preparing to strike, cranes,
>   mongooses, storks, anoas, Nile geese;
>   and there were gardens for these.
>
>   ("The Jerboa")

There is awful but artful appropriateness in the Egyptians' keeping ground rhinoceros horn in an intact rhinoceros horn "and locust oil in stone locusts." Moore sees the same irony here as she does in the Romans' use (described in "He 'Digesteth Harde Yron'") of "an ostrich-plume-tipped tent" to shelter a feast of ostrich brains. A symbol of the live whole animal presides over the animal's destruction and consumption, charms the act of greed, makes it magically "right." Attractive and appalling, this sort of "fantasy and . . . verisimilitude . . . were/ right to those with, everywhere// power over the poor./ The bees' food is your food." Exploitation of animals is wrong, even when combined with artistic reverence. Poem-animals as well as life itself may retaliate with irony:

> [the Egyptians] made
> basalt serpents and portraits of beetles; the
>   king gave his name to them and he was named
>   for them.

The situation is similar in "No Swan So Fine," where the swan wears a "toothed gold collar" "to show whose bird it was." The candelabrum is known as a Louis XV candelabrum. The king gives his name to the art-enshrined animal and the animal is magically elevated, but the art contains a seed of the king's own mode of death, the stylized executions of his cere-monial life. The king and the animal in art are united by a sharing of names; in the petrification of naming they are both preserved and lost.

Man's first power with respect to animals is to name them. The art of taming and the art of symbolic representation are related. Animals are tamed to feed us and protect us; they are named and classified to give us the precise illusion of order in the world, specifically our naming power over it. As op-posed to and in relation to the animal community, we are defined by our definitions of animals. Their bones preserve a natural record, and we a written one—this being for us as natural as death. Marianne Moore never loses sight of the relation of natural animal precision to natural human illusion. "Such power as Adam had and we are still devoid of" is the power of seeing the ani-mal kingdom for the first time and being able to name it with an uncontrived and unfallen awe. First definitions of this sort contain discovery free from guilt. Verbal ownership is symbolic ownership, the sort every child must learn to substitute for actual realization of his wishes, the sort that wealth allows kings to forget.

"Tippoo's Tiger" relates the power of kingship and identity with ani-mals. It begins by observing of Tippoo that: "The tiger was his prototype./

The forefeet of his throne were tiger's feet." And it continues with descriptions of the splendors of Tippoo's court—silver stairs, an emerald carpet, and

> Tipu owned sixteen hunting-cats to course the antelope
> until his one great polecat ferret with exciting tail
> escaped through its unlatched hut-door along a plank
> above a ditch; paused, drank, and disappeared—
>   precursor of its master's fate.

> His weapons were engraved with tiger claws and teeth
> in spiral characters that said the conqueror is God.
> The infidel claimed Tipu's helmet and cuirasse
> and a vast toy, a curious automaton—
> a man killed by a tiger; with organ pipes inside
> from which blood-curdling cries merged with inhuman groans.
> The tiger moved its tail as the man moved his arm.

>   This ballad still awaits a tiger-hearted bard.
>   Great losses for the enemy
>   cannot make one's own loss less hard.

The tamed animal disappears and takes its owner's power with it; the mechanical and magical totem animal contains its owner's fate, as well as that of his enemy. Only a poet who is willing to identify with the "tiger" of this poem and share a violent fate can do the theme justice. The poem ends abruptly with this realization. "The king is dead."

Marianne Moore is not the "tiger-hearted bard" the story requires. Her poem is about loss, the inevitability of it, the seed of which is contained in the act of identifying one's possessions with one's self. The king is no different from the commoner in this, although he offers more elaborate illustration. The poet closes the poem like the door of a room she does not want to see or to enter. She has seen enough just walking past—seen that the greatest loss is always personal, that only "a tiger-hearted bard" can make an impersonal epic; she has seen that art, ingenuity, and magically contrived protection cannot really protect us, but can only predict our martyrdom to our illusions.

"His Shield" presents another example of kingship associated with the protection of art and animals. The poem begins with the prickly dullness of a porcupine's "shield," but the poet rejects the armor of the "spiny pig":

> Pig-fur won't do, I'll wrap
> myself in salamander skin
> like Presbyter John.

The Presbyter John referred to is Prester John, legendary ruler of Abyssinia. In twelfth-century imagination, according to Elaine Sanceau:

> There was no king on earth like Prester John. His robes were washed in fire and woven by a salamander. . . . His kingdom was the land where dreams come true. The fountain of youth flowed there and subterranean streams of gems. There might be picked up the magic stone that gives sight to the blind or makes a man invisible. No poor were in the land of Prester John, nor misers, nor thieves, nor murderers, nor even flatterers.[7]

Moore's poem persists in this medieval view of a perfect land with a perfect Christian king. Prester John was surrounded by luxury, reported in "His Shield" as consisting of gold "so common none considered it," "rubies as large as tennis/ balls conjoined in streams so/ that the mountain seemed to bleed," and "household lion cubs" who accompanied the linen-clad king on his outings. Despite all this, we are told, "his shield was his humility."

This poem, if it does nothing else, reveals a deep wish to have irreproachable irresistible power in a realm that is both material and spiritual—to have armor, animal protection, magical protection, largesse, kingship, and last but not least humility. The moral, and this poem is one of those that has an adamantly stated one, does not coincide with the obvious wish of the rest of the poem. In fact, it is contradictory: relinquish what you would keep, be dull, do not judge. The contradiction between obvious pleasure in the power, magic, and riches of humble Prester John and the warning to be dull and self-sacrificing at the same time (neither of which Prester John was, by any real historical accounts) is similar to the contradiction implied in "Tippoo's Tiger," "The Jerboa," or "No Swan So Fine." The basic and unresolvable contradiction in all these poems is between the wish to possess, through vision or magic or art, everything, and the need at the same time to give it all up. The contradiction approaches resolution only in the poetic grasp of paradox, in the simultaneous possession and sacrifice inherent in acts that are symbolic. Obscurity can be a by-product of the symbolic process, and the end of "His Shield" is an example of this; it is a recurrent obstacle in the reading of Moore's poems and one she is aware of. In the essay "Subject, Predicate, Object," she says, "As for the hobgoblin obscurity, it need never entail compromise. It should mean that one may fail and start again, never mutilate an auspicious premise."[8] We cannot condemn honesty for inconsistency; if the premise is paradox and if the poems seem to tell us two things at once about where the good life lies, we must accept them both.

In "Elephants" the role of the animal as example and magical protector is central and explicit. The poet describes a man, the elephant's keeper, asleep on a sleeping elephant:

> And the
> defenseless human thing sleeps sound as if
>
> incised with hard wrinkles, embossed with wide ears,
> invincibly tusked, made safe by magic hairs.
> As if, as if, it is all ifs; we are at
> much unease. But magic's masterpiece is theirs—
>
> Houdini's serenity quelling his fears.

Houdini managed to escape his imprisonments through "serenity," a state of mind that told him he was not really imprisoned for good. The elephant is "a life prisoner but reconciled"; he is reconciled through a serenity that transcends the reality of his situation. He may not escape as literally as Houdini, yet he escapes.

> With trunk tucked up compactly—the elephant's
> sign of defeat—he resisted, but is the child
>
> of reason now. His straight trunk seems to say: when
> what we hoped for came to nothing, we revived.
> As loss could not ever alter Socrates'
> tranquillity, equanimity's contrived
>
> by the elephant.

The elephants, who can "change roles with their trustees," share certain traits with the pangolin, another animal whose habits are seen by Moore as spiritually beneficial to itself and worthy of emulation by man. The pangolin, resisting, "rolls himself into a ball," "strongly intailed." And when he revives his tail is once more "a graceful tool," "tipped like/ an elephant's trunk with special skin." The response of both these animals to loss of dignity, to being symbolically castrated by fear of encroachment, is to retreat, but only temporarily. Both come back again to display the tail or trunk as instruments of experience and knowledge. The elephants are related to Socrates; they "expound brotherhood" to "man the encroacher" through the Sanskrit verb *bŭd*; they are "knowers." It is thus that they are like "the sea in a chasm" in the poem "What Are Years?" which "struggling to be/ free and unable to be/ in its surrendering/ finds it continuing."

To "know" these elephants as Moore has described them, and to participate in their "magical masterpiece" of equanimity, is to be protected from the experience of loss. All of the animals specifically related to art or magic in Moore's poems are concerned in some way with loss. The solution always seems to lie in an identification with an animal who replaces in us what we lack—the grace of the china swan neck "at ease and tall"; the engineering practicality of the pangolin's "graceful tool"; the escape of the "great polecat ferret with exciting tail" and the aggressiveness of the mechanical toy tiger; the salamander coat of Prester John; the "serpent magic" and taming arts of the Egyptians; the strong, quick, moon-steeled, and fish-shaped Jerboa in his dry happiness; and, of course, the elephant's trunked surety. In an early poem, "Diligence Is to Magic as Progress Is to Flight," we find the wish of a lifetime expressed with a joyful childlike faith that is, however unsubstantiated, ever renewable in Moore's poems: "With an elephant to ride upon— 'with rings on her fingers and bells on her toes,'/ she shall outdistance calamity anywhere she goes."

But loss, experience—these are just as renewable. "Melanchthon," another elephant upon which the poet's imagination rides, expresses an aspect of the poet's use for sad experience:

> The sediment of the river which
> encrusts my joints, makes me very gray but I am used
>
> to it, it may
> remain there; do away
>   with it and I am myself done away with, for the
>   patina of circumstance can but enrich what was
>
> there to begin
> with. This elephant skin . . .
>
>   . . . rut
> upon rut of unpreventable experience.

"The Fish," not properly an "animal poem," though its title suggests it, deepens our sense of this "unpreventable experience," this quality of life that despite the exuberance of living forms and immortal art, contains our death. It is an immensely powerful and bitter poem. It is full of a sense of infringement, violation, and injury; it is also resigned. "The Fish/ wade/ through black jade." It is not an easy, fishlike movement, but laborious; and the water is not liquid but stone, not translucent, but dark. One of the morosely-colored "crow-blue" mussels "keeps adjusting the ash heaps" on which it lies by opening and shutting itself; it is not a happy animal expression. The shell moves "like an injured fan." "The barnacles which encrust the side/ of the wave"—again the water is seen as an unpleasantly solid substance—do not have privacy; "the submerged shafts of the/ sun . . . move themselves . . . into the crevices—/ in and out." It is deliberate, not playful; not an expansive sea, through which anything can freely move, but a "sea of bodies." (Recall the sea of "A Grave" into which "men lower nets, unconscious of the fact that they are desecrating a grave.") The water, this evilly forceful and solid mass, "drives a wedge/ of iron through the iron edge of the cliff." This violence is followed by a chaos where starfish, jellyfish, crabs, and submarine toadstools "slide each on the other." The sea is full of internal revulsion. What stands out on the "defiant edifice" of the cliff are "all/ external/ marks of abuse . . . ac-/ cident—lack/ of cornice, dynamite grooves, burns, and/ hatchet strokes." The side of this chasm is dead. The poem ends:

> Repeated
>   evidence has proved that it can live
> on what cannot revive
>   its youth. The sea grows old in it.

The accident is lack. The chasm side is permanently mutilated and abused by some mysterious unpurposeful purposefulness of nature. This strange poem is the work of a thirty-year-old woman whose rather unnervingly cool sympathies lie with a battered and violated nature. It is a poem about injury of wholeness, resentful but resigned deprivation. It contains the prophecy of "foiled explosiveness" that is suggested by the late poem "Then the Ermine:." The sea, with all its rushings of individual lives, all its bodies injured and insulted, grows old within its "dead" walls. How does one make up for such unintentional, natural desecration?

For what it is worth, one can invent a personal myth. One can try and convince oneself that life is worth efforts of affection and loving observation, that vicarious pleasures are real, that loss and desecration are only temporary setbacks in a vision that is essentially whole and infrangible. Myths, like dreams, express wishes, wishes to do away with limitations. Marianne Moore expresses her wishes with as much directness as she does her sense of limitation. Here is one of her most famous wishes:

O TO BE A DRAGON

If I, like Solomon, . . .
could have my wish—

my wish . . . O to be a dragon,
a symbol of the power of Heaven—of silkworm
size or immense; at times invisible.
Felicitous phenomenon!

Between the writing of "The Fish" (1918) and "O to Be a Dragon" (1957), Marianne Moore wrote a poem of major importance to her work which develops and relates the contents of both. "The Plumet Basilisk" (1933) is divided into four parts; the first and last, subtitled "In Costa Rica," deal with the plumet basilisk proper and frame between them "The Malay Dragon" and "The Tuatera," suggesting that any dragon or lizard may be delimited by the specific vision of the basilisk. Geographically the poem leaps from South America to China to New Zealand to Copenhagen. "Dragons" are a universal phenomenon as well as a felicitous one.

Like many of Moore's animals, the plumet basilisk is specifically related to kingship and loss. He *is* a kind of king, and he has the power of invisibility, the power to lose himself at will:

He leaps and meets his
likeness in the stream and, king with king,
helped by his three-part plume along the back, runs on two legs,
tail dragging; faints upon the air, then with a spring
dives into the stream bed, hiding as the chieftain with gold body
hid in

Guatavita Lake.
He runs, he flies, he swims, to get to
his basilica—"the ruler of Rivers, Lakes, and Seas,
invisible or visible," with clouds to do
as bid—and can be "long or short, and also coarse or fine at pleasure."

Marianne Moore's most powerfully visioned and envisioned animals have "knowledge" of both land and water; land animals are usually suggestive of sea-creatures in shape and movement even if they are not actually amphibious. In "Like a Bulrush," which considerably predates "The Plumet Basilisk," the poet sketches the importance of being amphibious. As it has not been printed since 1921, the whole poem follows:

LIKE A BULRUSH

Or the spike
of a channel marker or the
moon, he superintended the demolition of his image in
the water by the wind; he did not strike

them at the
time as being different from
any other inhabitant of the water; it was as if he
were a seal in the combined livery

of bird plus
snake; it was as if he knew that
the penguins were not fish and as if in their bat blindness,
                                        they did not
realize that he was amphibious.

This animal "superintended" the dissolution of his image; he is in high office, an overseer, manmade or extraterrestial. His ability to extend his relations from land to sea or sea to land is as pleasurable and deliberate as the poet's. His power is also secret, suggested but belied (at least to the blind) by his "combined livery." Neither his sea-acquaintances nor his land-acquaintances suspect his "other" life. Does he know that penguins are not fish? Anyway, it is *as if* he did, and *as if* that gave him special power.

"As if, as if, it is all ifs; we are at/ much unease" ("Elephants"). It is precisely the *as if* that does confer power, power of sight and oversight together. *As if* he saw, and as if "they" didn't. As if, it makes a difference. It gives the feeling of power, of control over environments not necessarily one's own. The special relation, often amounting to interchangeability, between bird and snake is also *as if,* and it is recurrent in Moore's poems. The humblest most powerful members of Moore's bestiary partake of this mythic conjunction. Even the jerboa is compared to both bird and snake, and in "The Tuatera" it is observed, with quiet amusement, that "bird-reptile social life is

pleasing." "Like a Bulrush" derives what force it has from a vision of amphibiousness, and a notion that amphibiousness confers vision unavailable to those
whose imaginative or imagined lives are confined to one habitat. Best of all,
the amphibious creature has the widest choice of hiding places.

The hidden body of the king, the image which closes the first part of
"The Plumet Basilisk," is the central metaphor of the whole poem; this magical golden body that is ritually renewed by plunging to the depths of mystery and lost treasure, and that brings a power back with it. This mystery
dominates the second section subtitled "In Costa Rica" (the last of the poem),
but before we reach it we are introduced to other "dragons," both the land
sort and the sea sort.

To emphasize the symmetry of dragonhood, West and East, "The Malay
Dragon" opens with the line "we have ours, and they have theirs." The ensu-
ing comparison includes colors, leaping habits, appendages, and decorations.
The body of the Malay dragon is "boatlike," but he does not go near water;
he is a "harmless god" and "serpent dove." He is rather objectively perceived,
unmysterious compared to other dragons, similed to many diverse forms of
life, and lovely in his delicacy. "The Tuatera" is not about the tuatera exclusively, but includes references to "sea lizards" congregated with friendly
birds who are "innocent of whom they neighbor," the "non-serious" lizards
who are more frightened than frightening, and the "two pairs of dragons
standing on their heads" that top the Copenhagen stock exchange as a symbol
of security, "the four green tails conspiring upright." This last image seems
odd at first but is related to the thematic material of the poem in several
ways. It demonstrates the use of dragons as art and art as symbol of security
in a poem where a sense of danger is pervasive, and it goes along with a sense
of mystery. This dangerous mystery, symbolized first by the king's "gold
body," has to do with treasure and the mystery of wealth. The plumet basilisk is America's dragon, guardian of its most secret treasure, which is not to
be found in the cold bourses of the North, where one might think the treasure is, but in the mysterious South, among "the yet unfound jade ax-heads,/
silver jaguars and bats, and amethysts and/ polished iron, gold in a ten-ton
chain."

Neither the Malay dragon nor the assortment of dragons culminating
with those in Copenhagen can lead us to the supreme treasure of the Ameri-
cas. This treasure consists not only of the unfound material wealth mentioned
so specifically, but of the wealth of imagination that is inspired by a hidden
and mythic past. It is a past that is contained not least in the aspiring dreams
of the individual in search of the treasure of self.

Marianne Moore's imaginative vision of the "basilisk," the little amphibious animal-king with the interesting little body, is in many ways a childlike vision, suited to a more wishfully innocent American way of thinking than the visions of greed that inform some of her other poems. Her genius lies partly in her ability to recapture with more success than most that unbusy child's state of mind that allows one to stop and count the whiskers on a cat or the spots on a leopard's portrait, to ask what a thing eats and what a tail is for, to ask for the name of everything in a picture, every plant and flower. Thus we learn that the basilisk "feeds on leaves and berries and has/ shade from palm vines, ferns, and peperonias." We see that "eight green/ bands are painted on the tail—as piano keys are barred by five black stripes across the white." Yet the adult is here, too, calling this configuration on the tail an "octave of faulty/ decorum" (how so?) and realizing the element of primitive fear in both lizard and man with more than childlike circumspection. She speaks of the lizard's hiding until nightfall, "which is for man the basilisk whose look will kill; but is// for lizards men can/ kill, the welcome dark." She describes the frightening sounds of the tropical jungle, reminiscent of the dark sounds in "The Hero" that the "hero" in cowardly fashion does not like. There are drums, bagpipes, monkey whistlings, weird tappings, the scream of a frog.

Then, retreating once more to idea rather than sensual imagining, we are told that

> the basilisk portrays
> mythology's wish
> to be interchangeably man and fish.

These lines come directly from a poem published in 1909 in the Bryn Mawr magazine *Tipyn O'Bob*. The poem, "Ennui," expresses its wish as clearly as "O to Be a Dragon," but it conveys more adolescent depression than "felicitous phenomenon." Here is this brief thought in its entirety:

> He often expressed
> A curious wish,
> To be interchangeably
> Man and fish;
> To nibble the bait
> Off the hook,
> Said he,
> And then slip away
> Like a ghost
> In the sea.

Twenty-four years have not dulled the force of "his" wish in the life of the poet. To "slip away," to become invisible at will: this is the other side of the wish to see, and see, and see; the other side of the wish to be in visible control of everything. On one hand the poet is greedy for as much experience as can be wrung from minute observation, to include as much of the world as possible in a single, momentary, animal-animated form, to see the world in a grain of sand; on the other hand she wishes to slip away, to disappear—the same thing in a way as wanting the world itself to disappear. "The Plumet Basilisk" is an all-or-nothing affair. In the end the little king is made to disappear as the wish of "Ennui" disappears by losing itself in the sea. Like the lizard who is "Like a Bulrush," the basilisk "superintend[s] the demolition of his image in/ the water."

Before this happens, though, the poet must wring every last bit of experience from the image. The following three stanzas need no comment, as we watch the basilisk and the poem together

>   traveling rapidly upward, as
>   spider-clawed fingers can twang the
>   bass strings of the harp, and with steps
>   as articulate, make their way
>   back to retirement on strings that
>   vibrate till the claws are spread flat.
>
>   Among tightened wires,
>   minute noises swell
>   and change, as in the woods' acoustic shell
>   they will, with trees as avenues of steel to veil
>
>   black opal emerald opal
>   emerald—the prompt-delayed loud-
>   low chromatic listened-for down-
>   scale which Swinburne called in prose, the
>   noiseless music that hangs about
>   the serpent when it stirs or springs.

The basilisk is "no anonymous nightingale," he is a complex of most mysterious things, a king not of decorous civilization but of the deep American "swamp, fed on/ sound from porcupine-quilled palm trees/ that rattle like the rain." He is our American consciousness, "our Tower of London/ jewel that the Spaniards failed to see." We may fail to see him, too, if we discard faith and imagination; he is the strange baby American Excalibur, "gold/ defending dragon that as you look begins to be a/ nervous naked sword on little feet." He has the "courage" spoken of in "Walking Sticks . . ." that "achieves/ despaired of ends inversely,—// mute with power and strong with fear." He is "nested" within his own body, more a spirit than a thing, and like the pangolin, the basilisk will recoil from what scares him and hide. Yet "he is alive there/ in his basilisk cocoon beneath the one of living green." And he is the poem.

A hidden aliveness, a hidden power, a hidden treasure: why are these always and in best form concealed, armored, pent, waiting, secretly watching? Myth (whatever it is, besides a fashionable literary term) may be motivated by quandary; it may be an answer or a kind or restitution for a limitation in the world that is felt as loss, an accident of lack, or want of the proper equipment for freedom—freedom found through affect, force, and clarity. Myth may be the "feminine" answer to "masculine" fact, the muse's contribution to the thrust of inquiry, the unborn baby of uncertain sex.

In "Radical" "the world is but a circumstance" for the growing carrot; it is, in fact, just a mass of uncompliant, crushing earth. The fictional force by which the carrot is seen by the poet to fulfill its destiny, which is "to be thick," is self-creative and determined. This force by and large links all Moore's imagery to her central myth. In the poem "Nevertheless" "frost that kills/ the little rubber-plant leaves . . . can't// harm the roots; they still grow in frozen ground." Often the ground of feeling, and of life itself, in Moore's poems seems threatened by freezing. But, like the carrot in "Radical,"

> with ambition,
> imagination, outgrowth,
>
> nutriment,
> with everything crammed belligerent-
> ly inside itself, its fibres breed mon-
> opoly—
>
> a tail-like, wedge-shaped engine with the
> secret of expansion, fused with intensive heat
> to the color of the set-
>
> ting sun and
> stiff.

It denies its impotence like a man; it wills to be stiff and to penetrate the earth. This radical carrot grows by volition, the bare *will to be* a thing, an instrument of completion, the will to complete the predestined self. The wish is only the beginning of the will, and here is where the great "myth" of Moore's poetry lies—in wishing to be that which is self-creative; to be a dragon, visible or invisible at will, or a plumet basilisk, "long or short, and also coarse or fine at pleasure," able to disappear and to reappear like a king with the mysterious knowledge of wealth and power that a king has.

The wish is the dream-half of the poem; the will is expressed in craft. Moore's wishes are often a child's wishes, and all of us share them. In childhood the myths that claim we can know and be mysterious and powerful creatures at will make important restitution for our weaknesses. In all poets, this childhood myth of the power of volition and of verbal insistence as a means to power lives on, but it seems to have a special and almost obsessive poignance in the alternating assertiveness and withdrawals of self in Marianne Moore's poetry.

She has described "creativeness" as the closest thing to "soul."9 Creativity is the *will* to create, yet this will is partly fate; perhaps the word *determination* is more exact, as it is something one acts upon as well as something which, like a wish, seems to be laid upon one from without. The myth, substantially, is that you can be what you are determined to be—alive, creative, powerful, and mysterious—and you can be what you look at, or look for, despite a very flawed existence. "Might verse not best confuse itself with fate?" ("Saint Valentine"). Verse for Marianne Moore is a determined and creative thrust toward being truly alive and truly what one was meant to be in the end, silent. The conception is imaginative because the thrust is not felt to be there anonymously, to be given or taken without thought proper to the naming of the act. *Fate* is the chosen word. It is placed, nominally and stylistically placed, with one's own conception, conviction, and silence in mind.

We have postulated certain relations among kingship, imagination, magic, and animal life. "The Plumet Basilisk" makes the myth that joins them most clear, as the basilisk, the thing whose look can kill yet who hides in the night and leaf-shadows, combines the powers of all. The basilisk's armor is no more than its mystery, as the poet's in the end is no more than an obscurity which pretends to breed clarity and sometimes mysteriously succeeds in this. But clarity, the "rock crystal thing," is just another mystery: that there should be any answer at all. The myth at the core of all this is that by looking you will be filled with the light you see; you will be powerful, invisible, a king, a magician, a knight-in-armor, a bird—anything, in fact or in fiction, which will make up for the opposing fact that in reality you are naked, fearful, "pent . . . hard pressed . . . abased" ("Like a Bulwark"). The basilisk is alive there in his cocoon, like the meaning of an obscure poem, the meaning of the jungle, or of the earth. He is alive there in his own primal scene. You had better not peek at him because (the eye not always being innocent, as Moore reminds us in "To a Giraffe") you will be frightened if not killed. But he is *alive* there, he is *alive*. You can't see him when he is at the bottom of the lake or inside you working his magic, and you can't have him appended to your body as you might like, or even hold him in your hand. But you can feel his presence *as if*.

"He is alive there." This assertion is the climax of the poem called "The Plumet Basilisk." From there on he disappears, but not really for good; we are asked to imagine

> his quicksilver ferocity
> quenched in the rustle of his fall into the sheath
> which is the shattering sudden splash that marks his temporary loss.

His "quicksilver ferocity" links him to Mercury, the messenger; the basilisk is the messenger between land and sea, the poet and her wish, life and death, male and female, one mystery and another. He is "a nervous naked sword" and his "sheath" and protection comes from his impact upon the water, the splash that reveals his whereabouts at the same time as it conceals his body. "The shattering sudden splash" is a metaphor for the impact of the poem itself. And after, there is a kind of loss; but peace comes with it, for the basilisk, representing the power of sight in darkness, the king, and the dragon's art, will return. "'The ultimate poem,'" Moore says, quoting Stevens (in a review of his *Auroras of Autumn*), "Truly is 'far beyond the rhetorician's touch'; is as reliable as the bird, the waterfall, 'these locusts by day, these crickets by night.'"[10] Such a poem creates an illusion of peace. Peace—

> This is that figure stationed at our end,
> Always, in brilliance, fatal, final, formed
> Out of our lives to keep us in our death,
>
> . . . a king as candle by our beds
> In a robe that is our glory as he guards.

Marianne Moore quotes these lines from Stevens because they offer shelter to someone who herself needs to be protected and to offer protection through a precision of words, an illusion of peace and safety in life, an illusion of illusion, if you will.

FIGHTING AFFECTIONS

MARRIAGE

Unhelpful Hymen

Truly as the sun
can rot or mend, love can make one
bestial or make a beast a man.
*   Thus wholeness—*

wholesomeness? best say efforts of affection—
attain integration too tough for infraction.
    ("Efforts of Affection")

MARIANNE MOORE'S "MARRIAGE" begins with superb lack of passion,
on the far abstract end of the continuum of meaning that reaches between it
and dream. It is a purely verbal consideration:

> This institution,
> perhaps one should say enterprise
> out of respect for which
> one says one need not change one's mind
> about a thing one has believed in,
> requiring public promises
> of one's intention
> to fulfill a private obligation.

Enter Adam and Eve, not as immediate protagonists, but as absent mentors
who, having been the first to propose conjugal bliss, so the myth has it, might
have some useful observation to make. Their answer is of course entirely a
matter of our own imaginations. It is really we who are asked to reflect on

the glint of a wedding ring and some cynical words drawn from Francis Bacon. Not love, but an "enterprise," is the center of attention as the poet wonders

> what Adam and Eve
> think of it by this time,
> this fire-gilt steel
> alive with goldenness;
> how bright it shows—
> "of circular traditions and impostures,
> committing many spoils,"
> requiring all one's criminal ingenuity
> to avoid!

Moore's quotation of Bacon, so aptly placed for rendering the symbol of love into an image of social greed, and the eternal circle into an image of unprogressive self-interest, applies as much to a style of writing and speaking as it does to the life style of prospective husbands and wives. Social mores, ingenious in the enshrinement of the original *felix culpa,* must be fought with like ingenuity. What Adam and Eve might think of it is certainly no consolation.

The "hand" that is offered the reader in "Marriage" is, like the hand offered in marriage described by the poem, "impatient to assure you" that its groping is free of obligation. Whatever they say, though, both poet and lover know that this is not true. The poet beginning an ambitious poem is not unlike the applicant for marriage in that there is an obligation to fulfill at least one's own definition of a plausible poem, and at most to make a lasting and public union of words and sense. The applicant for marriage is squeezed between the danger of uncontrollable affection, something alive with goldenness which requires criminal ingenuity to obtain as well as to avoid, and a certain abstract bondage to universal meaning. To maintain a balance between the inner irrationality and the outer reasonableness of any such "enterprise" leads almost inevitably to a moral strain; it is perhaps this strain, more than any other, that holds the fragments of a life, a marriage, or a poem together.

Late in the poem "Marriage" someone is quoted as saying:

> "Married people often look that way—
> seldom and cold, up and down,
> mixed and malarial
> with a good day and a bad."

Marriage is a strain. A poem of more or less loosely "married" images also looks a bit "mixed and malarial," with a good line and a bad, according to its various mental predispositions, chance associations, and a certain amount of unconscious fastidiousness. Part of the strain of "Marriage" is due to the intended comprehensiveness of it despite the knowledge, or intuition at least, that such an enterprise is to be necessarily incomprehensible in the end. What Allen Tate has said about Hart Crane's poem *The Bridge* is splendidly true of Marianne Moore's "Marriage." He is speaking of the image or central idea of "bridge"; we can easily substitute "marriage."

> Because the idea is variously metaphor, symbol, and analogy, it tends to make the poem static. The poet takes it up, only to be forced to put it down again *when the poetic image of the moment is exhausted.* The idea does not, in short, fill the poet's mind; it is the starting point for a series of short flights, or inventions connected only in analogy—which explains the merely personal passages, which are obscure, and the lapses into sentimentality. . . . Crane's difficulty is that of modern poets generally: they play the game with half of the men, the men of sensibility, and because sensibility can make any move, the significance of all moves is obscure.[1]

"Marriage" is obscure for these reasons, for the brevity of its insights and the lack of smooth transitions between them. The poem is true to the "conscientious inconsistency" of the mind described by Moore in "The Mind Is an Enchanting Thing"; it is a poem that describes the poet's mind with as much faithfulness as it describes what is in the poet's mind. "Marriage" is constantly changing tones, seemingly in response to itself, its own inner need to leave an unsatisfactory phrase or unexplainable or unenlargeable image. Clearly Moore thinks of "marriage" not so much as an event as a set of attitudes toward a hypothesis. It is centrally concerned with mental, not physical actions, and it leads eventually to a marriage within one mind of its various attitudes toward marriage rather than to a marriage of different minds.

Moore's initial picture of Eve, for instance, marries the old mythy attractiveness with a very peculiar mental ability:

> Eve: beautiful woman—
> I have seen her
> when she was so handsome
> she gave me a start,
> able to write simultaneously

> in three languages—
> English, German, and French—
> and talk in the meantime;

This Eve gives us a start, too, but not because of her alleged handsomeness. Moore's note on this passage refers us to an article in the *Scientific American* entitled "Multiple Consciousness or Reflex Action of Unaccustomed Range." We are done with Eden. Babel is behind us. *Finnegans Wake* is before us, unwritten as yet, a threatening potential of multiple consciousness turned literary. Eve is modern and it is her mind, the incomprehensible comprehendability of it, that attracts us. But if amazing Eve is busy scribbling and talking at the same time, relying on unconscious fastidiousness, we suspect, as she could not possibly be *thinking* of everything "equally positive in demanding a commotion/ and stipulating quiet," where is there room for dense old Adam? He enters the room of the poem and of the scribbling Eve when we are not looking; he is an unwelcome "visitor." "*I* should like to be alone," says preoccupied Eve,

> to which the visitor replies
> "I should like to be alone;
> why not be alone together?"

A modest proposition, surely. On the surface it is good natured enough, or pleasantly devious. Any second thought about it, though, is sure to be made uncomfortable with its glibness, vulgarity, and sad presumption with regard to what could be a sacred human relation. There is an insidious remoteness and literally embarrassing sentiment in the proposal of being alone together. It is all mildly funny, too, but the poem, resisting its own impulses with a vengeance, glances suddenly back to Eden and seriousness, as it was seen to glance for just a moment near the beginning, at a live goldenness. Here, despite a warning given earlier that "psychology . . . explains nothing," we are offered a psychological reason:

> Below the incandescent stars
> below the incandescent fruit,
> the strange experience of beauty;
> its existence is too much;
> it tears one to pieces
> and each fresh wave of consciousness
> is poison.

We welcome the new inspiration and relief from the offhand proposition that immediately precedes it, but are we to welcome the news that each such fresh wave is poison? Although sudden beauty saves us from the poetic sterility of "alone together," it transports us to the only slightly more poetically fertile ground of being alone *alone,* savoring a disjunction of senses that we know is poison.

From affectation to affection, in poem after poem, Marianne Moore writes, or seems to write, in self-defense against this poison. At the same time she cannot help seeking it out. She may remind one of the small animal, observed observing, in her poem "An Octopus,"

> the victim on some slight observatory,
> of "a struggle between curiosity and caution,"
> inquiring what has scared it.

This is a "victim" not only of some hidden predatory thing in man or in nature, but of its own sturggle between the instinctive desire to *know* and the fear that by venturing out to know, it will *be known.* In the poem "Marriage," no matter how much the mind wants to be alone, there is the very existence of "Adam" to contend with. Adam is tantamount to a world; he is the general "other" as well as the particular "other" who is dangerous to the self precisely because he is equipped by beauty to invade it, because he may not remain quite "other" enough.

> And he has beauty also,
> it's distressing . . .
> a crouching mythological monster.

The "beauty" in "Marriage" seems always to be crouching and waiting for a chance to break in and overwhelm the careful cerebrations, the witty satire, the pure descriptions, in short, all the defensive maneuvers, the silences, the necessary restraints.

In *The Philosophy of Literary Form,* Kenneth Burke assures us that

> when you begin to consider the situations behind the tactics of
> expression, you will find tactics that organize a work technically
> *because* they organize it emotionally. . . . Hence, if you look for a
> man's *burden,* you will find the principle that reveals the struc-

ture of his unburdening, or in attenuated form, if you look for his problem, you will find the lead that explains the structure of his solution.[2]

The burden of the poem "Marriage" is one with the witty confusions (read con-*fusions*) of style in the poem. The poet, in presenting her broad subject in a way that is so willfully confusing, is also stipulating a kind of solitude. The woman of "multiple consciousness" defies "psychology" to explain her abilities.

> Psychology which explains everything
> explains nothing
> and we are still in doubt.

She should like to be alone. It is possible that in solitude the poet finds the complexity of consciousness, and its ability to change energy states like an excited electron, less frightening. "In the Days of Prismatic Color" is a poem that considers the fine clarity of the world "when Adam was alone." Alone he is able to perceive things clearly and with no obscurity, as a green thought in a green shade perhaps. The entrance of Eve is not an explicit event in this poem, but we are made to know that when Adam's solitude was lost, so was his uncomplicated vision. Admit the presence of an "other," explain or try to explain yourself and exactly how you see things, and all becomes complex, obscure.

The obscurity in Marianne Moore's vision of marriage lies in attempted explanations that are highly personal and shared only through "efforts of affection" not quite *equal to* affection. The obscurity, the single self confronting another with marriage in mind, says to the reader in each unprepared-for leap of sensibility, "*I* should like to be alone." But here *we* are, and the poem, pulled in the direction of silence by its desire for solitude and unapproachability, is acknowledging us in every image restrainfully given over to language. It is also daring us to make at least equal efforts of affection on its behalf. It is an effort of communication, an uncomfortable one. Nevertheless, in that discomfort is a real truth about the human predicament. We can never have the occasional comfort of affection, of the beautiful image that strikes love in us, without the pain of reaching out, offering something too personal for words, in words, in other words, and in yet other words.

"Marriage" begins with Adam and Eve. The poem is "about" a mythical situation. Without telling us the whole story, it makes jerky guesses pertaining to the meaning of it. This reflects the critical modern quandary of a literature that is over-conscious of itself. The question we are expected to ask of literature is not an absorbed "what happens next?" but a beard-stroking "what does it mean?" Each fragment has its burden. Each must *signify*. Divorce—between absorption in a mythic story and detached analysis of its parts—is written into the engagement.

"Mythological statements lead to questions," observes Elizabeth Sewell.[3] Whether the statements really *do* precede the questions as Sewell's phrasing would have it, or vice versa, it is true that in Moore's poem "Marriage" both are present and are connected causally, however casually. We do not want to see the same old Adam and Eve go through their old routine, we want to know what they *think* about our own blundering imitation of it. We want to see them respond to *our* myth. We imagine their responses in our own fears and hesitations, desires and aggressions, and last but not least, rhetorical persuasions.

The poem "Marriage" may be seen as a rhetorical response to the idea of marriage, to the myth of confrontation between man and woman, a man and woman who may be asked to stand for opposed forces in general. The "Eve" and "Adam" of the poem are each imagined in the separate rhetorics of each, their separate self-persuasions and persuasiveness. Underlying all the rhetoric, however, we are always aware that there is a question as motivation. And the one affirmative answer, "I do," is never given.

"Unhelpful Hymen!" the poet exclaims near the center of the work, after giving us images of the beauty and monstrousness and triviality of marriage. "Hymen," that purely mythical tissue, that rhetorical ploy, cannot solve the insoluble elements of "Marriage." "Hymen" is described as

> a kind of overgrown cupid
> reduced to insignificance
> by the mechanical advertising
> parading as involuntary comment,
> by that experiment of Adam's
> with ways out but no way in—
> the ritual of marriage,
> augmenting all its lavishness.

The "criminal ingenuity" of "mechanical advertising" replaces childlike dreams with those of adult-infantile cupidity. Simple self-expression learns calculation and the art of seeming to be what it has lost by calculation, the artlessness of being itself. The poet has no choice but to fight fire with fire.

The poem "Marriage" parades as "statements that took my fancy which I tried to arrange plausibly" (Moore's first note on the poem). Actually, it is forced to partake of the same evilly conscious rhetorical techniques that it damns. It courts us, woos us with the propaganda of poetry, wants to bond our senses to it for life. It is greedy for our affections. There the difference begins. Moore wants our affections not for a material greed which goes beyond them, and not for a social-commercial commitment, but for a spiritual and moral commitment. We cannot escape the original greed of Adam's experiment, but we can recognize that it was a greed for life and love and not twist those things to mean aimless possessiveness and a willingness to be possessed.

If Moore's cynicism throughout the poem seems excessive, we might note that cynicism, although not always so witty, is a part of every mythic quest and every quest for meaning. Adam and Eve mistrust their creator and accept the cynical rhetoric of the serpent; Psyche turns her light on what should be dark, and loses what is central to her life; the Red Cross Knight abandons Una and tends to believe the rhetoric of Despair. All these stories illustrate the moral strain of life itself. There is something right and realistic about what all of them do, even when they are broken, having broken their words. Words are made to be broken, and some of the tentative answers to mythical questions *have* to be informed by the consciousness of evil in order to make new words, new promises, new lives, and new poems for ourselves.

Moore's allusion to "mechanical advertising" follows kind and lovely images of affect—dazzlement of apple and nightingale and fire. Her crafty alternations are analogous to the reversals and surprises that must be a part of any narrative quest. Here the "victim" of reversals, the "hero" of the "story," is the reader insofar as she lets herself be involved. If we are not involved by the very technique of the poem, in other words, then we are doomed to read a story without character and without point. "Marriage" is boring for those with no "way in" to the myth. Life can be boring for the same reason.

> Life, friends, is boring. We must not say so.
>
>   . . .
>
> and moreover my mother told me as a boy
> (repeatedly) 'Ever to confess you're bored
> means you have no
>
> Inner Resources.'
>
>   (John Berryman, *Dream Song* #14)

Berryman confesses, for the moment of this song, that he is bored, and that this is the reason. It is a warning (among other things) to the reader of modern poetry, whose "inner resources" are constantly in demand in the reading of poems that come close to the confusions of life, confusions which, when we cannot meet them with "inner resources" or find a "way in" to the myth, we are quite ready to ignore or to dismiss as "boring." If we believe that "the mind is an enchanting thing," we must admit that its inconsistencies and confusions, inseparable from most of its most interesting functions, are by no means the least of its enchantments. Nevertheless, in the interests of integrity, the poet presenting such confusions must not herself be confused, as the poet presenting us with his boredom must not, in the writing itself, be bored or boring. "Unconfusion submits/ its confusion to proof," says Moore in "The Mind Is an Enchanting Thing," and the burden of the "proof" lies with the reader, the observer of the mind and the life of the mind.

"Good art never bores one," says Ezra Pound in the preface to *The Spirit of Romance.* "By that I mean that it is the business of the artist to prevent ennui; in the literary art, to relieve, refresh, revive the mind of the reader —at reasonable intervals—with some form of ecstasy, by some splendor of thought, some presentation of sheer beauty, some lightning turn of phrase— laughter is no mean ecstasy. Good art begins with an escape from dullness." Marianne Moore accepts this responsibility and proves it in the technical brilliance of the poem "Marriage," a technical brilliance that illuminates confusion, controls it, and presents it as central to life and the decisions one must make about it. She pays her readers the compliment of trust in their inner resources. She does this by never explaining or visibly pontificating; by sharing carefully selected and suggestive facts, quotations, and images without enslaving them to a single vision; by never staying too long with one of these, and by never forcing an issue. She assumes that we have an interest in the way our minds leap between mundanity, ecstasy, and humor and that we can bear the tension of never quite coming to a conclusion. She assumes that we do not find life boring.

If in all the reversals and surprises of the poem, the accumulations of words around a single magical image, or in suddenly changed pace the reader feels she is approaching a climactic statement of some kind, something that will suddenly make all the pieces fit into the puzzle, she will be disappointed. "Marriage," like life, presents anticlimax after anticlimax with only slight build-up and, significantly, no climax at all. There is no "I do" in the poem, no consummation, and by the time we do catch a glimpse of an actually married couple they are already seen to be preparing for divorce. In the essay "Feeling and Precision," Moore comments on the madness behind this method:

Intentional anticlimax as a department of surprise is a subject by
itself; indeed, an art, "bearing," as Longinus says, "the stamp of
vehement emotion like a ship before a veering wind," both as
content and as sound; but especially as sound, in the use of which
the poet becomes a kind of hypnotist—recalling Kenneth Burke's
statement that "the hypnotist has a way out and a way in."4

The poet's technique is not superadded to an enchanting story. It is an enchantment in itself in its provision, not of continuity, but of a continuous
and (if we can allow ourselves to submit to it as we would to the continuity
of dream) hypnotic tension.

According to Marianne Moore's intentionally anticlimactic summaries
of marriage up to the point of the Hymen passage quoted earlier, Adam's experiment has "ways out but no way in—/ the ritual of marriage,/ augmenting
all its lavishness." That is, the ritual aspects of marriage, in providing and
perpetuating a kind of false and lavish substitute for the largesse of the re-
linquished garden, only make the original sin more contemptible, not necessarily more bearable. Hymen—the myth of Hymen—is unhelpful unless we are
capable of reevaluation. The poem "Marriage," with its ability to withdraw
from the mythical situation and to disdain the "way out," mythical escape
from real consequences, makes a new myth in the process of examining itself.
It has a "way in" to an interior reality and the devious workings of the mind
that make myth attractive and necessary in the first place.

Manipulation by sound is used as a "way in" with the same "criminal
ingenuity" in poetry as it is used in advertising, but with quite a different
moral intent. The rough sound of "insignificance," "mechanical advertising,"
and "involuntary comment" wakes us from the trance of "unnerved by the
nightingale/ and dazzled by the apple"; it spoils the illusion with a purpose. A
matter mainly of the arrangement of long and short syllables, of consonance
and assonance, it is a "way out" of the illusion of Eden or a childhood paradise or whatever fine nostalgic fantasy one would dream oneself into. Technical manipulation is a "way out" as Adam's tasting the fruit of consciousness
was a "way out." Paradoxically, it is also a "way in," as only through this
kind of withdrawal from illusion can one retrieve a precise understanding of
it. Only the Adam who does not willingly give up Paradise in favor of the enchantments of mortal and moral confusions, the Adam who once he is forced
out tries to imitate a lost lavishness and convince himself it is the real thing,
has no "way in" to the meaning of the myth. It may sound melodramatic,
but it is true: the meaning of the myth contains, like the flower its seed, the
meaning of Adam's existence.

Treading Chasms

Marianne Moore's style and structuring of poems is what provides for her the balance between the fight to be affectionate and the fight not to be. It is for this that the paper nautilus "constructs her thin glass shell." She guards her "eggs," scarcely eating until they are hatched:

> Buried eightfold in her eight
> arms, for she is in
> a sense a devil-
> fish, her glass ram's-horn-cradled freight
> is hid but not crushed.

The poet's "freight" is the substance of her poems; they will hatch as the tentative communications that come from efforts of affection. Feelings, in Marianne Moore's scheme of things, must be hidden but maintained whole in hiding. Their existence, more than any other force, dictates the form and beauty of the shell that holds them. Perhaps this is why the typical man and the typical woman who seek each other and each other's feelings in marriage must use, at least in Moore's poem "Marriage," the careful rhetoric they use, and why the poet must arrange her poem so as neither to express too early an unformed and unprotected feeling nor to deny the loving motives that underly and oversee the finished form.

The poet may have the appearance, in jumping from image to image, of a ship veering in the wind, like the cruising frigate pelican "allowing the wind to reverse [his] direction," "quiver[ing] about/ as charred paper behaves—full/ of feints," but the apparent aimlessness is important; it reflects the true character of wind, wings, and words—an end that is not at all aimless. The poem "Marriage" veers in the wind, so to speak, on both rhetorical and psychological levels; this is one of the things that makes the poem "work." The poet no more makes her cynical comments on the lavishness of the false rituals of marriage, than she must be off again, with extraordinary lavishness of her own, describing it with images of eccentric beauty:

> its fiddlehead ferns,
> lotus flowers, opuntias, white dromedaries,
> its hippopotamus—
> nose and mouth combined
> in one magnificent hopper—

[its crested streamer—
that huge bird almost a lizard,] *
its snake and the potent apple.

*(bracketed lines in 1923 Manikin edition only)

Henry James, speaking of "men of largest responding imagination before the human scene," notes that they provide generous mixtures of the two tones or attitudes toward experiencing the world that James calls the romantic and the real. "His current," says James, "remains therefore extraordinarily rich and mixed, washing us successively with the warm wave of the near and familiar and the tonic shock, as may be, of the far and strange."[5] Certainly the poem "Marriage" is evidence of this sort of "largest responding imagination before the human scene." In it we are given the most realistic, not to say prosaic, view of marriage at the outset ("an enterprise . . . requiring public promises/ of one's intention/ to fulfill a private obligation") and we are given as well the "tonic shock" of strange beauty below incandescent stars and incandescent fruit where "each fresh wave of consciousness is poison." The "real" says James, is composed of "things we cannot possibly *not* know," and the romantic or strange, of "things that can reach us only through the beautiful circuit and subterfuge of our thought and our desire." The word "subterfuge," associated here with desire, seems particularly apt with respect to the work of Marianne Moore, for many of her most beautiful images seem to come, not through the conscious fastidiousness that informs her observations of the "real," but through that unconscious fastidiousness which lets certain "efforts of affection" bloom into real longing. The lavishness of exotic detail in the Persian miniature that she describes at one point in "Marriage," for instance, is a desired extravagance. In the very remoteness of its fantastic animal-figures and jewels from "real" life is hidden the remotest (to common sense) and the nearest (to sensibility) object of the imagination—the "crouching mythological monster" that is seen to be Adam himself. Or Love, or Evil. In "An Octopus" Moore describes the mysterious bear's den "composed of calcium gems and alabaster pillars/ topaz, tourmaline crystals and amethyst quartz" where the bear, unseen for all this extravagance, is known to lurk. The danger is not dangerous when it is hibernating in such dreamed beauty. The mythological monster is never fully revealed; what is revealed in Moore's poetry inspired by him is the primal desire for excess and love that escapes her everyday ascetic attitudes toward marriage and life. The greediness that she despises is a greediness that she knows, as we all must know it, from self-inspection.

One finds in Moore's calculated alternations between lavishness and stoicism, "rigid fidelity and the most fanciful extravagance" (to use Hazlitt's words concerning Burke's style), a coincidence of moral and psychological responses to the possible richness of experience. Whether it is called, with moral prejudice, "the garden of earthly delights," or, with psychoanalytic prejudice, the "nurturing other," the reader must have an affection for it, as Marianne Moore herself does. One must have both moral and psychological defenses against the hunger and the affection, however, as well as ways of expressing both. The questions and the statements Moore presents us with by first indulging and then damning material and verbal extravagance embody her method, make up the "story" that almost, but never quite, answers the mythical quest for meaning. When the artistic defenses become too rigid, one begins again "the fight to be affectionate" as in "Marriage." One must begin the fight over and over, as one loses it.

Thus Eve must be introduced, and introduced again, as she loses her original brilliance and, chameleon-like, takes on a new but still transitory brilliance.

> "See her, see her in this common world,"
> the central flaw
> in that first crystal-fine experiment,
> this amalgamation which can never be more
> than an interesting impossibility
> describing it
> as "that strange paradise
> unlike flesh, stones,
> gold or stately buildings,
> the choicest piece of my life:
> [I am not grown up now;
> I am as little as a leaf,]*
> the heart rising
> in its estate of peace
> as a boat rises
> with the rising of the water."
>
> *(bracketed lines in 1923 version only)

In this rather long description of Eve describing paradise in Richard Baxter's words, there are actually two descriptions of paradise—the one the poet sees surrounding Eve, surrounding "the central flaw," and the paradise within her. Outside of her it is disaffected, or disinfected, by intellect and abstraction; it is an "experiment," an "amalgamation," and "interesting impossibility" (a good description, incidentally, of the poem "Marriage" itself). Within Eve,

Paradise or "marriage" is associated with nostalgia for childhood, "the choicest piece of my life." But there are problems beyond inner and outer paradise in this passage; there is a central flaw deeper than simple Eve.

Eve is "in this common world" describing marriage as a strange "paradise" (an idea she picked up from "mechanical advertising" most probably) or quality of soul that is unlike material wealth. She describes it as "the choicest piece of my life." We have assumed she refers to a real childhood on the basis of the lines later removed, but there is another possible reading, also based on the excised lines but more closely connected with the rest of the poem. Later on the woman, the "she" of the lovers' debate, is described in rather unfavorable circumstances and in a nasty tone by the "he" of the debate as "uniquely disappointing,/ revengefully wrought in the attitude/ of an adoring child." In the earlier passage we hear only Eve's thoughts on the matter, in which the idea of marriage seems to remind her of being a child. This makes her heart rise exactly as Richard Baxter describes the hearts of ambitious and covetous men rising in the passage from which Moore quotes to supply her Eve with words. Could it be that her "innocent" heart rises with the expectations of what she will get by marriage, by returning to weak dependency? One suspects that Moore certainly thought so. Seen in this cynical light, the loveliness of the passage partakes of the "circular traditions and impostures/ committing many spoils" that were part of Moore's initial definition of marriage. If the lines specifying childhood are removed from the passage, the connection is lost. For better or for worse?

In Marianne Moore's own retreat from beauty that "tears one to pieces" (a retreat which is at least partially distinct from Eve's), we note that she first pulls back to the safety of abstraction, in the description of Eve's outward circumstances, then allows a measure of release in giving us her inner perceptions of "paradise." We are, in this reflection of Eve's, still safely removed from the place where consciousness itself is poison. The Eve of this common world needs this safety, for she is

> constrained in speaking of the serpent—
> shed snakeskin in the history of politeness
> not to be returned to again.

Because Eve cannot speak of the serpent, she reminds herself of childhood, when one is "as little as a leaf," free from consciousness that can kill, and ignorant of the potency of the apple. Marianne Moore, however, often speaks of the serpent, which in one poem she describes as

This animal which from the earliest times, importance has attached,
fine as its worshippers have said—for what was it invented?
To show that when intelligence in its pure form
has embarked on a train of thought which is unproductive, it will
    come back?

                ("Snakes, Mongooses, Snake Charmers, and the Like")

"There is something attractive about a mind that moves in a straight line," as Moore observes in "People's Surroundings," but there is a remedy for, as well as something attractive in, one which does not. The snake was "invented" so that we can, when thinking scatters itself (as it so consistently does in Moore's poems and in the reading of them) come back to snakedom as to a basic premise, a hidden principle of consciousness, of life and evil. For instance, when one sets one's "intelligence in its pure form" a task, such as defining so broad a thing as "marriage," and when one finds oneself talking instead about somebody or other's ability to write in three languages simultaneously and the unproductive paradise of childhood in which you are a vegetable and there is no serpent to speak of, one finds oneself returning to intelligence in a less pure form, a kind of ur-intelligence of images. The dazzling image throughout Moore's work more often than not comes back to a simple and dangerous consciousness of the identity of beauty and evil in the snake or some related animal—the chameleon in "People's Surroundings" for example. Possibly more central than Adam to the various hypotheses of the poem "Marriage" is the serpent that constrains us.

The encounter between Eve and the evil beauty of serpentine intelligence is referred to in the poem as "that invaluable accident/ exonerating Adam." This allusion to Eve's seduction is a little resentful, but mostly witty, as is the "shed snakeskin in the history of politeness." The humor relieves the tension underlying Eve's attraction to "the strange experience of beauty" that will tear her to pieces. It begins with Adam:

And he has beauty also;
it's distressing—the O thou
to whom from whom,
without whom nothing—Adam;
"something feline,
something colubrine"—how true!
a crouching mythological monster
in that Persian miniature of emerald mines,
raw silk—ivory white, snow white

oyster white, and six others—
that paddock full of leopards and giraffes—
long lemon-yellow bodies
sown with trapezoids of blue.

Adam is so distressingly beautiful, and Eve's dependence on him so utter, that he must, like a god, be seen in the mystery of creation that surrounds him to be seen at all. We cannot look at him directly. Adam's being swallowed up by this particular Persian miniature characterizes one aspect of all of Marianne Moore's poems; in her the experience of intense beauty inspires both fear (of her own seduction by it) and praiseful wonder, and she summons all creatures here below to help her, to help her conceal and control her feelings through their own artful armorings and their lending of them to her. Animals and the art of others help her praise the origin of an individuality that cannot be explained, but that must be proved. Art provides a necessary retreat from the feline and serpentine beauty of Adam, specifically from his sexual attractiveness. Sublimation is the fate of this poet, whose fate is con-fused with verse:

> Alive with words,
> vibrating like a cymbal
> touched before it has been struck.

The crash never comes, but the instrument lightly agitated keeps trembling out a message of possibility. It is a possibility that could not help but call attention to itself among the rest of Moore's orchestration, her "tuned reticence with rigor" that belongs to her "Propriety."

The image of vibration in the touched cymbal is attributed to the words of someone who "has prophesied correctly," but the reader is left in doubt about the prophecy itself and the person who made it, and the passage in quotation marks is not acknowledged in the notes.

> Alive with words,
> vibrating . . .
> he has prophesied correctly—
> the industrious waterfall
> "the speedy stream
> which violently bears all before it,
> at one time silent as the air
> and now as powerful as the wind."

The stream, related to the Pierian spring perhaps, is, in all its violence, the same stream that at another time was quiet. The latent power of the stream is analogous to the latent power of still air, which as wind can be felt. This power is analogous to the latent power of sound in a vibrating cymbal, or the latent power of words that, as prophecy, can become truly enacted. It encompasses possibilities within realities. Verse *can* become fate. "The power of the visible is the invisible" ("He 'Digesteth Harde Yron'"). The associations that these ideas of latent power have with marriage are made clearer by the statements that caught Moore's fancy in presenting the second proposal scene in the poem:

> "Treading chasms
> on the uncertain footing of a spear,"
> forgetting that there is in woman
> a quality of mind
> which as an instinctive manifestation
> is unsafe,
> he goes on speaking
> in a formal customary strain,
> of "past states, the present state,
> seals, promises
> the evil one suffered,
> the good one enjoys,
> hell, heaven,
> everything convenient
> to promote one's joy."

The first proposal was a simple "Why not be alone together?" This, its "formal customary strain" more apparently calculated and seriously thought about, nevertheless has similar dramatic and ironic elements. We as readers have information about Eve's mental qualities—in the first such scene they were the freak ones of "multiple consciousness" that allowed her to write in three languages with both hands and talk at the same time, and here they are informed by sinister instincts connected with the garden of Eden and a childish greed. Into such hostile or unsafe atmosphere comes the man with his inept proposals. He is persistent here, though his proposal may seem to go off in many different directions at once—heaven, hell, past, present, and everything convenient, coming together. Moore, by quoting Hazlitt on Burke's style in this passage, is commenting on the style of the proposal and on the style of the poem as a whole. Because it contains such an important double commentary, here is the quoted passage and environs from Hazlitt:

Burke's style is airy, flighty, adventurous, but it never loses sight of the subject; nay, is always in contact with and derives its increased or varying impulse from it. It may be said to pass yawning gulfs "on the unsteadfast footing of a spear": still it has an actual resting place and tangible support under it—it is not suspended on nothing. . . . The principle which guides his pen is truth, not beauty—not pleasure, but power. He has no choice, no selection of subject to flatter the reader's idle taste or assist his own fancy: he must take what comes and make the most of it. . . . It is all the same to him, so that he loses no particle of the exact, characteristic, extreme impression of the thing he writes about, and that he communicates this to the reader, after exhausting every possible mode of illustration, plain or abstracted, figurative or literal. . . . The most rigid fidelity and the most fanciful extravagance meet and are reconciled in his pages.[6]

One can easily see how this praise of Burke can be turned into a rationale for the poem "Marriage," which does proceed by fancy and by "exhausting every possible mode of illustration, plain or abstracted" in offering us its hand. And we have seen how it does not cater to the reader's natural idleness. The man proposing marriage within "Marriage" does not flatter the idle tastes of the woman to whom he speaks, either. He is like the writer who assumes his readers must admire him because of the integrity he knows is inside himself. Marianne Moore makes fun of this, but it is also something which the writer or suitor or reader must believe in order to go on.

In the situation at hand, then, the suitor continues his little lecture without seeming to be aware of the woman's mental state, which is, like his, one of lonely calculation. So he goes on talking to himself, unaware that he is on dangerous ground with respect to her and that there are chasms between them which his rhetoric barely crosses, "speaking/ in a formal customary strain" which has to do with customs that are a strain for both of them. We feel it is the woman in the poem—the mental Eve—who appreciates the wit of "everything convenient" in his talk of good and evil, heaven and hell. For her, joy is different than for him. It is from her point of view that his joy is mocked in the following passage:

> In him a state of mind
> perceives what it was not
> intended that he should;
> "he experiences a solemn joy
> in seeing that he has become an idol."

Is this really what he sees or what he is made to think he sees by the "masked ball attitude" ("Nothing Will Cure . . .") in her, an attitude that is instinctive and self-destructive.

Marianne Moore abandons this particular irony for a different level of consciousness in this "Adam" in which his mental state is taken much more seriously; and it is, as are all the most emotionally charged insights of the poem, conveyed by image rather than by verbal wit or abstract rhetoric.

> Plagued by the nightingale
> in the new leaves,
> with its silence—
> not its silence but its silences,
> he says of it:
> "It clothes me with a shirt of fire."
> "He dares not clap his hands
> to make it go on
> lest it should fly off;
> if he does nothing, it will sleep;
> if he cries out, it will not understand."

Efforts of affection are efforts of communication and this Everyman has chosen to appeal to a creature who, although she may be able to understand many languages simultaneously, cannot seem to understand or respond to *his* language. The situation is similar to one Moore presents in "Half-Diety," where a butterfly, conscious that a "nymph" is pursuing it, proves to be inaccessible to her efforts of affection toward it; the butterfly is "indifferent to her. Deaf to ap-/ proval." The nightingale is, like the butterfly, or the unicorn, a creature of "miraculous elusiveness" ("Sea Unicorns . . ."); it is hidden and silent where visible and affirmative responsibleness is most fervently desired of it. The pursuer of this elusive creature knows that it will be frightened by too obvious a gesture, yet will ignore him if he makes no gesture at all.

Later in "Marriage" the man is described as an "orator," master of rhetoric, skillful but of questionable sincerity; there is no real or personal communication between him and the lady he importunes. Whims and studied effects cannot compose themselves into a whole; perhaps "Marriage" is partly about the divorce of poetry and prose. Both bad poetry and bad prose, or whimsical arbitrariness and sterile rhetoric, are meant to appeal to the psychology of the auditor, as advertisement and cliché do. But calling the prospective or actual husband "orator" looks not just to the ironic scene of private argument or imprecation, but beyond that to the culminating figure of the poem, Daniel Webster, an orator who failed to make a "marriage" work between civil warriors. "Marriage" becomes more and more a poem about political America at the same time as it is a critique of the personal lives of Americans.

The man, despite his being on stage, an "orator," has deep feelings that lessen our possible contempt for him. The following presentation of "Adam" balances Eve's meditation on paradise quoted earlier.

> Unnerved by the nightingale
> and dazzled by the apple,
> impelled by "the illusion of fire
> effectual to extinguish fire,"
> compared with which
> the shining of the earth
> is but a deformity—a fire
> "as high as deep
> as bright as broad
> as long as life itself,"
> he stumbles over marriage,
> "a very trivial object indeed"
> to have destroyed the attitude
> in which he stood—
> the ease of a philosopher
> unfathered by a woman.
> Unhelpful Hymen!

The vision of the nightingale—a creature of myth in its own right—and the apple, which in this context is the apple of dazzling and poisonous consciousness identified with Eve's accident, creates in the aspiring suitor the illusion of an eternal love, "compared with which/ the shining of the earth/ is but a deformity." It is the highest illusion possible; it defies the precision of a certain woman's freak multiple abilities, of the definitions of paradise as "crystalfine experiment" and "interesting impossibility," and of the particularization of shades of white in the Persian miniature. It may be the highest possible illusion, but it is still only illusion. It is the shocking irrelevance, or perhaps it is relevance (the issues are so mixed on this level), of this image of desire, of "fire effectual to extinguish fire" that jolts the poem back to the relative clumsiness of wit and verbal precision. The suitor "stumbles" over the reality of marriage, over the realization that it is not a legalization of his affection for his own images of desire but legalization on an earthly plane, "a very trivial object indeed"; and somehow—he cannot understand how—this trivial object is able to destroy the ease of his imaginings and his narcissistic philosophy of eternals. His extravagant desire was "unfathered by a woman." She obviously can "father" nothing. He has fathered his vision himself, plagued by her uncanny silences.

Just as the "O thou/ to whom from whom,/ without whom nothing— Adam" was at the center of the "emerald mines/ raw silk—ivory white, snow white/ oyster white, and six others—/ that paddock full of leopards and giraffes," Adam is at the center of the ritual of marriage with its ferns, flowers, prickly pears, dromedaries, hippopotamus, crested bird-lizard, snake, and apple. The hippopotamus is described specifically as a huge mouth, a "magnificent hopper," and this is, perhaps, one of the most germane images in "Marriage"—the mouth that needs to be filled—with vows, with irony, but most important, with beauty and love. We have seen how Moore extends and retracts, extends and again retracts the feelings of her poem. She will envision a scene, be filled with it, and make us passive in looking at it (i.e., we do not act upon it intellectually, ask is this true, are giraffes "sown with trapezoids of blue"?); she will then turn against this instinct for beauty and mock it with words that require from us, as well as from her, an active intellectual evaluation.

In the following passage from "Marriage" the Manikin edition is used because it contains lines, indicated by brackets, that the other editions do not possess and that in my reading of the poem are significant. (One might speculate that they were taken out because their private significance was greater than their artistic contribution to the poem; but one can contend, too, that they are poetically justified.)

["When do we feed?"]
We Occidentals are so unemotional,
[we quarrel as we feed;
one's] self [love's labor] lost
the irony preserved
in "the Ahasuerus *tête-à-tête* banquet"
with its small orchids like snakes' tongues,
with its "good monster, lead the way,"
with little laughter
and munificence of humor
in which "four o'clock does not exist,

> but at five o'clock
> the ladies in their imperious humility
> are ready to receive you'';
> in which experience attests
> that men have power
> and sometimes one is made to feel it.

"When do we feed?" is a slyly vulgar question at this point in the poem. It is a barbarian talking, surely, or a husband demanding service. The animal-monster and the prospective husband are not always separable, and the gratification of food is not always far from that of the marriage bed. It is a more jocular than affectionate communication, and it leads to the observations which follow, on the prearranged meetings of men and women over food. Dining, which could be an intimate and serious mutual occupation between husbands and wives, is called "feeding," is denied grace and communion. The "quarrel as we feed" is perhaps the only communication, and is engaged in for its own sake. The "quarrel as we feed" may also be a witty but not complicated slur against those whose tastelessness in love is brought to table; or it may be a quarrel with the food itself, fighting against what one knows one needs, as a poet may fight her own images.

The line "one's self love's labor lost," which is shortened in subsequent printings to "self lost," has, in its original willful ambiguity the tone of preoccupation with one's own language that Moore makes fun of in the language of the lovers throughout the poem. One's self is one's greatest labor of love, of course, and it is a labor in vain. There is no real love left, or no self, but there is irony, the irony of having unwittingly made one's efforts of affection in the wrong direction.

The "Ahasuerus *tête-à-tête* banquet" is a reference to the story of Esther (chaps. 5-7) and the two banquets she prepares to give Haman his just desserts. Ironically, Haman feels himself to be specially favored by the royal attentions the first night, only to be hanged upon the second. The small orchids with snakes' tongues are Moore's own sinister decoration of the banquet table; we know *her* attitude toward feasting together and betrayal. Esther's story emphasizes the power a wife may have over her husband while he still retains the illusion of freedom. The quotation from *The Tempest*, "Good monster, lead the way," is associated with Esther's banquet by virtue of the scene in which it occurs. In this scene (Act II, scene ii), it will be remembered, Stephano and Trinculo discover Caliban, get him good and drunk, and enlist his services in their scheme. Caliban, poor monster, under the influence of their spirits, thinks mistakenly that he has found new freedom whereas he has merely found new bondage. "O brave monster, lead the way," ends the act, and the next act opens with a love scene between Ferdinand and Miranda wherein she offers to be his wife, or servant, however he is willing to take her —another example of bondage exchanged for a new bondage. The "monster" has led the way; feasting, drinking, loving, one must beware.

The feast is set "with little laughter/ and munificence of humor," much as the gems of warning are set into the poem "Marriage." We do not laugh at the ironies, but they have a "quixotic atmosphere of frankness" that makes us smile to ourselves as we imagine the civilized gentlemen and ladies at their tea. The ladies who serve it have "imperious humility" because they know the men have the real power and because they have learned in their own way how to manipulate it. Only sometimes is it felt. The whole passage beginning with the uncivilized "When do we feed?" and progressing through time and literature—from the Bible to Shakespeare to a dissertation on *La Thé* (by the Comtesse de Noailles)—attests to the fact that the obligation to satisfy one's own body and to serve another's are inseparable in life and ritualized by art.

In this passage, as in most of Moore's poems, the conscious fastidiousness of the rhetoric of the sequence and the unconscious fastidiousness of the motives behind it are equally thorough. The close association of the *tête-à-tête* banquet, the drunk monster, and the affectatious tea, is not unlike the "condensation" of dreamwork. Kenneth Burke, in "Freud and the Analysis of Poetry," argues that poetry uses such phenomena as "condensation" and "displacement" as dreams do, and that poetry is therefore susceptible to the kind of analysis that is applied to dreams. "In so far as art contains a surrealist ingredient (and all art contains some of this ingredient), psychoanalytic coordinates are required to explain the logic of its structure."[7] The "psychoanalytic coordinates" of the passage just discussed, and perhaps of the whole poem "Marriage," would seem to be on one hand the desire to be satisfied, to be "fed" and treated royally, as if one had power; on the other hand, we have the coordinate of fear of betrayal, enslavement, and physical injury to which any intimacy with another human being makes one vulnerable. It is summed up in "the spiked hand/ that has an affection for one/ and proves it to the bone." The "displacement" of this desire and this fear is, as is characteristic in Moore's poetry, raised to the level of art—the Old Testament, the Elizabethan play, and the western tea ceremony—and to the level of occasions where people get especially dressed up and speak in carefully calculated phrases which invariably mean something other than they seem to mean. Sublime sublimation.

Next we overhear a debate between a "he" and a "she" which shows superlative lack of mutual understanding.

> He says, "What monarch would not blush
> to have a wife
> with hair like a shaving brush?"
> The fact of woman
> is "not the sound of the flute
> but very poison."

In other words, if she must be at all, she must be beautiful; but it would be even better if she were invisible and inaudible. This little speech shows Moore characteristically using negatives to introduce associations as extraordinary as possibilities. If she is not getting ready to symbolically castrate him with her shaving-brush hair, she will poison him with her decidedly unflute-like assaults on silence. What he would like is something sublime and artistic, not physically embarrassing and humanly noisy.

She answers his rebuke with one of her own:

> "Men are monopolists
> of 'stars, garters, buttons
> and other shining baubles'—
> unfit to be the guardians
> of another person's happiness."

This observation, Moore's notes tell us, is taken from a Mount Holyoke Founder's Day address (1921) in which Miss M. Carey Thomas goes on to say that these "baubles" are "so valueless in themselves and yet so infinitely desirable because they are symbols of recognition by their fellow-craftsmen of difficult work well done." This does not seem to convey the insult intended by Moore's woman's statement. The Holyoke address, furthermore, reads, "men practically reserve for themselves," not "men are monopolists of," the latter being much more definitely denunciatory. Moore is outdoing her sister feminist as well as paying tribute to her.

"He" is allowed to rally, though, with a stranger insult than he has received:

> He says, "These mummies
> must be handled carefully—
> 'the crumbs from a lion's meal,
> a couple of shins and the bit of an ear';

> turn to the letter M
> and you will find
> that 'a wife is a coffin,'
> that severe object
> with the pleasing geometry
> stipulating space not people,
> refusing to be buried
> and uniquely disappointing,
> revengefully wrought in the attitude
> of an adoring child
> to a distinguished parent."

The physicality, and it is not a sheer but a dense one, of his perceptions of woman is meant to be appalling. These "mummies" are delicate, for they exist only as the leftovers of a lion's meal. The quotation is from the book of Amos (III, 12): "Thus saith the Lord; As the shepherd taketh out of the mouth of the lion two legs, or a piece of an ear; so shall the children of Israel be taken out that dwell in Samaria in the corner of a bed, and in Damascus in a couch." Now what makes Moore think of this particular verse of Amos in connection with marriage? The passage in Amos has nothing in it about marriage, but it is about punishment for transgression, the punishment being to be all but eaten by the metaphorical lion of Assyria. The remains from the lion's meal are moral remains, and they must be retrieved from the beds and couches of the Samarians. One commentator on the Bible suggests that the morally despoiled people are found in the corners of beds because they have grown to love the evil luxury of soft cushions; another suggests that they are there out of cowardice, hiding with only legs and perhaps an ear showing. In the context of Moore's poem we think of the marriage bed, of course, but this is not the sort of bed anybody thinks Amos had in mind—except her.

What is the speaker's interest in "mummies?" Is he simply talking to himself about some archeological interest apart from women, or is he suggesting that these "mummies"—mothers?—are like the horribly evil remains of women after the "lion" has satisfied himself? Can we see in the lion a continuance of the animal and monster imagery in the rest of the poem? This would be to see him as the pursuing lover. Can we connect the "meal" with the other references in the poem to feeding? "But questioning is the mark// of a pest!" ("For February 14th"), and these may be too monstrously leading.

If the lion's meal is not enough to convince us that we are on dangerous ground when debating marriage, we can "turn to the letter M"—for Marriage, Murderousness, Moore?—and find Ezra Pound's claim that "a wife is a coffin." She is, in fact, less than two shins and an ear; she is an "object," a "geometry," a "space" unaccommodating of living people. You would like to bury her like a coffin, but unfortunately she is only *like* one, and in reality is a dependent object "wrought in the attitude/ of an adoring child." The remains of passionate wickedness, the helplessness of a child—what compliment can the "she" of the debate return?

> She says, "This butterfly,
> this waterfly, this nomad
> that has 'proposed
> to settle on my hand for life'—
> What can one do with it?
> There must have been more time
> in Shakespeare's day
> to sit and watch a play.
> You know so many artists who are fools."

There is "munificence of humor" in this transition, and considerable irony. He speaks of lion's hunger, and death, and ponderous object-worship, with allusion to punishment by an angry God, and she comes back at him with butterflies and waterflies, nomadic and undependable creatures.[8]

The lady is obviously flustered. She is almost muttering to herself when she says "What can one do with it?" "It," not "him"; he is an object to her as she is an object—no more—to him. She goes on to speculate on what two people can do together. Go to a play? One can only guess why she thinks there was more time in Shakespeare's day. Perhaps she believes that if one did have time one would find out enough about the trials of love not to want to try it out oneself. Or that one would find out enough about writing plays to be more than just a *foolish* artist. It does not matter much; she may be stalling for time, filling her part of the conversation with whatever occurs to her, as if she were free-associating. It is practically her last freedom.

When the lady criticizes the proposing or imposing gentleman for having so many foolish artist friends, he immediately retorts that she has foolish friends who are not even artists. I suspect this is one of the "statements which took Moore's fancy" that is inserted into the poem merely for the delight of it. We may think of it as an overheard and remembered conversation. Here ends the "debate,"

> The fact forgot
> that "some have merely rights
> while some have obligations,"

> he loves himself so much,
> he can permit himself
> no rival in that love.

He cannot let anyone love him more than he himself does, but it doesn't matter, because she feels the same way about herself: "she loves herself so much,/ she cannot see herself enough—." "She" sees herself as an object in a household of objects,

> a statuette of ivory on ivory,
> the logical last touch
> to an expansive splendor
> earned as wages for work done.

She believes she deserves this fate, and she does. Moore caps this little aside on the utter barrenness of narcissistic enchantment with a moral: "one is not rich but poor/ when one can seem so right." One that does not question one's position has no way into the meaning of the myth. These people are poor in their self-satisfied segregation from each other. The "vermin-proof and pilfer-proof integration/ in which unself-righteousness humbles inspection" that Moore indicates would be welcome in "Efforts of Affection" would be welcome here.

A Striking Grasp of Opposites

> *What can one do for them—*
> *these savages*
> *condemned to disaffect*
> *all those who are not visionaries*
> *alert to undertake the silly task*
> *of making people noble?*

Lovers are "savages" in Marianne Moore's book because of their primitive self-interest. The "savage" asks, "When do we feed?" and, as we see in the poem "Marriage," this savage sentiment is only thinly disguised by such civilized ceremonies as tea at five o'clock precisely. We recall that Moore has said first of all in the poem "New York" that it is "the savage's romance." The city is the center of the fur trade, commerce, excessive materialism, and has a "dime-novel exterior" which she imagines as portraying "Niagara Falls, the calico horses and the war canoe"—in other words, honeymoon sentimentality, animal-wildness, and battle. Not that she objects to these things unequivocally, but she does make fun of all of them as they are related to "Marriage." In the end, "New York" is seen as important *not* for all these qualities but for "accessibility to experience." This is also one importance of courtship and marriage and all thought about these, but does not make them any less a "savage's romance."

The "savages" must inevitably alienate all those who see the world plainly and unenchantedly, "all those who are not visionaries." "Visionaries" is an extravagant word here and, I think, meant to strike us as funny and impossible—like "Marriage"—impossible that a "visionary" *would* want to undertake the task of making ordinary and narcissistic people into noble and true lovers, to go so far as to see them as Adam and Eve. The only "visionaries" who would undertake it are the politicians, like the Daniel Webster of dubious morals with whom "Marriage" will end, or those visionaries who make up the "mechanical advertising" that sells *Bride* magazine and home insurance, and we know what *their* visions are. But Moore's "Marriage" is an American poem about American-style marriages, and we have been blessed with many visions of low nobility. There is another breed of visionaries however—visionaries in the sense that Moore might be said to be one—those who see the "rock crystal thing", or at least know that it is there to see. These will not be alert to the "silly task." They will produce instead the witty commentary called "Marriage" and save vision for the pangolin or plumet basilisk.

Up to this point the poem "Marriage" has been about the uncomfortable preliminaries, the initial attractions, self-interested courtship, and mutual abominations. We skip the marriage ceremony itself and come next upon a glimpse of the couple after they have been married a while:

> This model of petrine fidelity
> who "leaves her peaceful husband
> only because she has seen enough of him"—
> that orator reminding you
> "I am yours to command."

The words which describe this "model" wife are, Moore's notes tell us, taken from an advertisement in the *English Review* of June, 1914 (actually the *English Review Advertising Supplement*), for new Paris fashions. The adver-

tisement is mostly descriptive of new tissues and colors and shapes of bodices
and other "elegancies," except for Madame Puget's one indulgent condescen-
sion to women of bad taste, and it is revealing of Marianne Moore that she
was enough struck to enshrine this piece of prose in a poem fashioned eight
or nine years after.

> Now everything has changed, without any other reason
> than "for change." Thus proceed pretty dolls when they leave
> their old home to "renovate their frame," and dear others who
> may abandon their peaceful husband only because they saw
> enough of him.
> The worst is that the alteration is far to be a success. The
> elegant of 1914 are actually hoisting a few horrid imaginations
> that one must declare, and try to ruin under the weight of their
> own ridicule.
> It is first the coiffure in the shape of a pumpkin which un-
> covers foreheads and lengthens occiputs.
> The "Simple Simon" collar with its absurd long points.
> The flounces and different engines which play an anker's
> effect round the middle of the body.
> And then the awful evident little drawers.

Clearly Marianne Moore fancied this sort of "advertisement" with as much
enthusiasm as she felt for the need to ridicule such things. This double feeling
—curiosity and fantasy about the richness of a fallen world and simultaneous
disdain—corresponds with her feelings toward marriage itself and toward her
own poem about it. On one level, she regards courtship as no better than a
"mechanical advertising" of the self. In "Armor's Undermining Modesty"
she quotes an advertisement put out by a publishing firm which seems ambivalent in its intent to mock. In "The Arctic Ox" she says, in a lighter vein,
"If you fear that you are/ reading an advertisement,/ you are." Neither wom-
en nor strong native attitudes of any sort can make true and workable marriages of different styles—that of freedom and bondage, New York and Paris,
evident underpants and modesty—with mere rhetorical rufflings. Poems,
which are also a kind of advertising of the self, cannot do it either. The point
is that advertisement, the often deceptive rhetoric of change, is central to
affectation as well as to affection, meaning to stir and invent no more than
the illusion of affection.

Moore is both in and out of sympathy with Noras who slam the door. If
they had not let themselves be so easily carried over the threshold in the first
place such scenes might be avoided altogether. Fashion and marriage along

with most social attitudes are centrally pretense; they are awful-ly attractive. Awe-fully. "Certain white crapes embroidered with coloured cotton wool," remarks Madame Puget in the same article from which Moore quotes, "are fascinating when they are new, but the effect is deceitful after washing." Moore is constantly aware of this danger of "style" and may not always be able to avoid it herself, despite the "criminal ingenuity" that at the beginning of the poem "Marriage" she attributes to both social impostures and means of avoiding them (poetry being one of the latter).

> One sees that it is rare—
> that striking grasp of opposites
> opposed each to the other, not to unity,
> which in cycloid inclusiveness
> has dwarfed the demonstration
> of Columbus with the egg—
> a triumph of simplicity—.

"That striking grasp of opposites" is a concisely humorous way to describe the relationship of Moore's model marriageables—her Adam and Eve, her poetry and prosy rhetoric, her ideas of freedom and bondage, her own feelings and the things she "quotes." All are striking out at each other in the poem "Marriage" as well as striking us. "Striking" is associable with aggressiveness and attractiveness both, as is the "spiked hand/ that has an affection for one" that occurs earlier in the poem. And the "grasp" may be one of affection, or bondage, or abstract understanding. And the "opposites"—well, they are, both abstractly and particularly, "opposed each to the other, not to unity," which is to say they are, and they aren't. They tend most strongly, though, to the protection of abstraction, the first abstract view of "Marriage" as "this institution/ perhaps one should say enterprise."

This unity in its "cycloid inclusiveness" makes other explorations, other "sciences," look insignificant. Columbus, when challenged to make an egg stand on end, realized he had to break the shell, and sacrifice wholeness to do so. To Moore's way of thinking, making a marriage stand solidly also requires sacrifice, and to a much more complicated degree. The poem itself stands on broken ends, for to pretend that any one perception about her subject could be perfectly conceived as an egg would be less than honest. Columbus is also invoked because of his discovery of America, and if we see this as a poem that comes to be about America as well (the "integration" of North and South), we see that Moore is comparing Columbus' discovery in its relative insignificance to the discovery of a first love, each leading in its own way

to the quarrels of compromise, and of settling in. "Marriage" shows us the
New World with all its paradisal illusions unveiled, its unnoble savages having
tea at five o'clock and calculating spoils, its bickering Adams and Eves submitting to each other's serpentine logic.

In Moore's anti-epic, Columbus' important discovery was not of the
roundness of the world, but discovery of a joke with cynical implications, the
discovery of gravity, and of "uniting strength with levity" ("The Frigate
Pelican"). Moore breaks the myth of "Marriage" to make it stand up; it is
done with style and an air of innocence, acquisitiveness and wit, a willingness
to sacrifice meaning without sacrificing moments of accuracy.

She sees

                              that charitive Euroclydon
                              of frightening disinterestedness
                              .which the world hates,

admitting:

                              "I am such a cow,
                              if I had a sorrow
                              I should feel it a long time;
                              I am not one of those
                              who have a great sorrow
                              in the morning
                              and a great joy at noon."

"That charitive Euroclydon" is identified syntactically with "that striking
grasp of opposites"; it is another metaphor for love that is rare, that has both
destructive and constructive qualities. Euroclydon is the name given to a
tempestuous wind, which in Acts 27 threatens the lives of Paul and other
prisoners as they sail near Crete. An angel of God comes to Paul and explains
that the men will be saved but the ship will be wrecked, the connection with
"Marriage" being, one must suppose, that the tempestuous wind, like love
and wars fought for love, is both charitive and dangerous. The wind, like a
tempestuous emotion, has a "frightening disinterestedness" or may seem to
by virtue of its blindness; the world hates this wind because it is a force which
cannot be controlled with human reason. The allusion to storm and ship-
wreck is not surprising in connection with what Moore feels to be dangerous
and attractive—we may see the image invoked by her to represent uncon-

scious emotion in many different poems. Again, if this poem is "the vestibule to experience" of an American "epic" and we are approaching civil war, the "charitive Euroclydon" is the wind that will wreck the ship of state.

This rare thing, this love of unified opposites and storm of simultaneous charitiveness and disinterestedness must be hated by a world that cannot accept paradox. It must see marriage, or any other enterprise, as either bountifully good or bountifully bad. This world, which cannot accept the simultaneity of joy and sorrow, of freedom and slavery, admits, "I am not one of those/ who have a great sorrow/ in the morning/ and a great joy at noon";

> which says: "I have encountered it
> among those unpretentious
> protégés of wisdom,
> where seeming to parade
> as the debater and the Roman,
> the statesmanship
> of an archaic Daniel Webster
> persists to their simplicity of temper
> as the essence of the matter:

> 'Liberty and union
> now and forever';

> the Book on the writing table;
> the hand in the breast pocket."

The war is over, but the rhetoric and the sorrow persist. The "statesmanship" of a Daniel Webster, as far as the simple masses of Americans are concerned, is the essence of the wise democracy that spawned and protects them. He is part of our tradition. The essence of Webster's statesmanship was, however, less than a moral success. Moore uses the word *parade* at one other point in the poem, also placing it strikingly, where "mechanical advertising" is seen "parading as involuntary comment." Devious rhetoric is an American tradition. Daniel Webster had complete mastery of the rhetoric of resistance and secession; he had celebrity; he had plenty of money and plenty of power. He said, as if it came as naturally as leaves to the trees, "Liberty and union, now and forever," and died. His statue remains, and the sorrow of disunion remains, in this peace of art.

The cowlike world admits its unrelieved state of unhappiness, admitting it is not in its nature to change from sorrow to joy. Neither divorce nor civil war will bring instant cure to a family or country whose union was brought about in the first place through selfish verbal manipulation. Is there, somewhere behind this confession of the "world," the sentiment that worldly things and a heavy, cowlike existence are inextricably bound to long sorrow and that joy is to be reserved for some unearthly place, not the noon of everyday, but the Noon that Emily Dickinson sees as Heaven? The poem "Marriage" is permeated with the wickedness of mundane aspirations, the most thoroughly pessimistic work Marianne Moore ever produced for public consumption. It admits the attractiveness of earthly affection, of the idea of love, of the possibility of a new world, a paradise that "works," but love is damned in every instance by false affection, by affectation and insincere speeches, by the "savage's romance." Marianne Moore does not say that there is another kind of love in this poem, unless it is love of art; but the earthliness, the "faulty excellence" of this love too is undercut, here as in other poems of hers.

"Marriage" appeared in 1923, one year after T. S. Eliot had shown the literary world what could be done with a fragmented experience in *The Waste Land*. An extraordinarily long poem for Marianne Moore to have written, running to ten pages in the *Complete Poems*, it was first brought out by the Manikin Press in London (was it thought to be unacceptable in America?) as a book in itself. "Marriage" is seldom, if ever, mentioned in connection with what have come to be known as the standard long poems or neo-epics of the present century, including *The Waste Land*, the *Cantos*, certain long poems of Stevens, Crane's *The Bridge*, and Williams' *Paterson*. Though Marianne Moore's "Marriage" is not as flamboyant as some of them, not perhaps as painstakingly conceived (though one may have doubts about this), or as successful, it shares with these poems certain origins in late nineteenth-century (French) and twentieth-century poetic speculations, and certain "originalities"—disjunctiveness, obscurity, implied criticisms and cynicism about modern society, a free combination of poetic styles. The relations these poems bear to each other and to literary and social traditions are expressed not by logical or continuous argument, but by glancing allusions and sly parataxis. It is helpful to think of Moore's "Marriage" in relation to these poems, as an experiment partly influenced by other experiments in poetry and partly by the social and literary *Zeitgeist* that influenced them all. She refers both to marriage and to Adam's mishap as "experiments," and almost certainly she considered her poem as a similar consciousness-expanding experiment. Experimenting is, after all, something one does when one is not satisfied with the way things are and wants to find something better; an experiment is also often a bid for power, whether it occurs in Eden or in a fallen world.

"Marriage" may be seen as a woman's bid for power in a man's world, or a poet's bid for power in a prosaic world. Yet "Marriage" was never acclaimed as the men's experiments were. It was perhaps felt too strongly that a woman could not propose it. When she did, there was an embarrassing silence. Somebody blushed to imagine "a wife/ with hair like a shaving brush." Years later T. S. Eliot chose to admire "The Jerboa." Marianne Moore is best known for her elegant and eccentric descriptions of harmless animals. Her passion was for baseball. No one until lately has thought of her in connection with marriage. But enough of that.

All the long poems produced in and about America in the modern period, in addition to what they were trying to "say" about the state of the external world, say something also about highly personal states of being. Their very "original" confusions and inturnings of sense seem somehow purposeful and necessary to the poets' own lives as well as to the poets' observations upon the disorder of the human community. The institution of marriage, certainly, is as flexible an image for the joining of disparate elements, in self or society or both, as is the bridge, the growth of a city-man, a general quest in a wasted land, the journey of a comic Crispin or blue guitarist. The concept of "marriage" is as abstract as the basic concepts of any of these. The poem "Marriage," proposes, as the other long poems do, to investigate rather abstractly, through all its imagistic and rhetorical particulars, the possibility of joining, of making sense of bits and scraps of experience—a past there, a present here, and so forth. These go forth to some implied future and have no small pretensions to a kind of prophecy. Whether it is the clairvoyance of a Madame Sosostris, the babble of the falls in *Paterson* that contains history and prefigures the future, or the statue of the failed statesman at the end of "Marriage," all look to some difficult future, some further fall of man which, like past falls, may not be without its rewards (mainly for sensibility, one suspects), but which is somehow without epic, or even true or traditional poetic dignity.

So, after the long-range ineffectiveness of everything, what is left? "The statesmanship/ of an archaic Daniel Webster" seems to be all. The victim of lingering sorrow in Moore's poem says, "I have encountered it." Love? The grasp of opposites? The birth of a nation? The God-exploited storm? The sorrowful world has encountered a language of "cycloid inclusiveness," as the sorrowful poet has, which can transform hopeless complexity into simple statements, a language that can arrange marriages between entities that are as fundamentally opposed as North and South. The summary: "Liberty and union/ now and forever." Liberty is not union and now is not forever, but one can say it; it sounds nice and people want to believe it, and they do. They

even say "I do." Marianne Moore, a Secretary of State in her own right, as
Daniel Webster was in his, finds this remarkable, and the poem "Marriage"
may be regarded as her series of remarks on this very peculiarity of language,
its ability to persuade.

I find the last two lines of "Marriage" devastating in their anticlimactic
oddness and complacency: "the Book on the writing table:/ the hand in the
breast pocket." After all that! After a poem of such strange complexity, after
all the wit and the rich allusiveness and elusiveness of style, we are left with
a cold statue, paralyzed. The Book on the writing table is naturally the Bible.
That must be all that is left if the world has failed one utterly: hypocrisy and
self-satisfaction punished, heaven promised. The hand in the breast pocket is
not the hand given in "Marriage," or, if it is, it has been retracted to the self
in a stiff pose, for the sake of an image really. And what is in the breast
pocket that the hand should go after it? Is it love, or money? If "Marriage" is
to be seen ultimately as an act of statesmanship, a record of articulate language and worldly calculation, which is worth its while whether it works or
not, this, I suppose, is a good way to end.

THREE CONFUSING POEMS

Sainted Obsession

While not incapable
of courtship, they may find its
*   servitude and flutter, too much*
like Procrustes' bed;
so some decide to stay unwed.

("The Arctic Ox (or Goat)")

In 1948, 1950, and 1952, Marianne Moore published "Efforts of Affection," "Armor's Undermining Modesty," and "Then the Ermine," three
poems which her critics since have often related to "Marriage" (1923), if only
for the fact that they are similarly obscure. Previous efforts at elucidating
these very elliptical poems have not been satisfactory, although critics have
been honest about the difficulties. With respect to "Efforts of Affection" and
"Armor's Undermining Modesty" the explicators agree that the poems are:
(1) obscure and (2) generally about the paradox of love (the most suggestive

comment coming from Donald Hall, who says, "The obscurity seems to lie entirely in the suppression of the copula"[9]). With respect to "Then the Ermine": we are agreed that (1) it is a puzzle and (2) it uses color symbolism and therefore may be about truth. My own approach to these poems depends on certain complexes of imagery that link all three together with "Marriage."

These images, which occur together strangely and which indicate a similar emotional content in the poems are the following: (1) a "striking grasp of opposites," i.e., opposition between forces (always able to be reduced to male and female) that can never be unified except by a labored illusion; (2) the presence of a saint, knight, or hero; (3) the presence of a butterfly, moth, or flying "pest" of some kind; (4) deep attraction that must be resisted; (5) advertisement or flattery or use of words (as in a motto) of which one should be wary; and (6) an assertion of the wish for purity (untarnished armor, wholesomeness, spotless ermine). It seems that the first two of these late poems also bear, as "Marriage" does, political meanings; the failure of politics to unite the world may be seen as a metaphor for the failure of affect in uniting the poet with any other single being. In both themes—failure of politics and failure of human affect—we are reminded of the impossibility of accurate judgment and a subsequent fear or mistrust.

Armor seems the only answer. All these poems may be seen as revolving around certain rationalizations for avoiding marriage and sexual love. It is odd that poems combining the particular images mentioned above in an elliptical style so clearly reminiscent of "Marriage" should occur from twenty-five to twenty-nine years after "Marriage." Possibly the death of Moore's mother in 1947, which left her more alone than she had ever been, made her rethink the solitude in her life. Or possibly these poems are completions or revisions of poems begun some two decades earlier.

"Efforts of Affection" begins at the beginning, with the book of Genesis, and moves through Shakespeare and La Fontaine to a statement of Moore's own conception of "integration."

> Genesis tells us of Jubal and Jabal.
> One handled the harp and one herded the cattle.
>
> Unhackneyed Shakespeare's
> "Hay, sweet hay, which hath no fellow,"
> Love's extraordinary-ordinary stubbornness
> like La Fontaine's done
> by each as if by each alone,
> smiling and stemming distraction;
>   How welcome:

Vermin-proof and pilfer-proof integration
in which unself-righteousness humbles inspection.

The biblical twins have opposite tasks in life, one to provide spiritual nourishment, the other physical. It does not matter whether they are explicitly of
opposite sex, as all oppositions in the poem quickly gather implications of
sexual as well as social opposition. We have the same situation in "Marriage,"
where there are two voices with opposite concerns, also beginning with Genesis and widening in reference to include the romances of Shakespeare and
La Fontaine's wisdom concerning love. In "Marriage" the banquet prepared
by Esther leads by association to the drunken, good monster of *The Tempest.*
In "Efforts of Affection" the allusion to the twins—opposed as naturally as
they are one—of spiritual and material nourishment in Genesis leads straight
to a scene from *Midsummer Night's Dream,* where Bottom with his ass's head
on ("cattle") and Titania (poetry, a spiritual, harp-handling fairy queen)
make love. The "hay, sweet hay"—something to eat—also links the passages.
To make hay and to lie in it are not irrelevant to this rustic sophistication
either. This leads to the proverbalizing La Fontaine, another reminder that
the business of animals and poetry, though opposed, may well coincide. Love
between different and opposed species of animals does not usually work out
well in La Fontaine, as it does not between the fairy-queen and artisan-ass in
Shakespeare, or between woman and man, South and North, in "Marriage."
Yet at the beginning there is always the illusion, maintained "by each as if by
each alone,/ smiling and stemming distraction." (Recall the private jokes and
persuasive distractions of "Marriage.")

The "How welcome!" is slightly incredulous and wishful, saying, more
or less, "Wouldn't it be nice if this all worked out, ostracizing rats and thieves
for good." As for unself-righteousness humbling inspection, it may be connected with a remark Marianne Moore made in a review of an art exhibit for
The Dial: "One hesitates to appraise work—even to praise it—the inspiration
of which is spiritual."[10] The alliances referred to in the first verses of "Efforts
of Affection" may be irrational and doomed to failure, but in so far as they
are inspired we might as well not appraise their success. It is too highly a personal matter.

In "Combat Cultural" Moore is inspired by the same problem of "integration." The poem begins with images of things acting contrary to their
base natures—horses "turned aerial" and "a drooping handkerchief snapped
like the crack of a whip." Its guiding image is that of a Russian dance where
one person pretends to be two:

> These battlers, dressed identically—
> just one person—may, by seeming twins,
> point a moral, should I confess;
> we must cement the parts of any
> objective symbolic of *sagesse*.

The "integration" of this cultural combat is not just that between the fighters who are "'sacked' and ready for bed apparently" but between objects at rest and those in motion, between mind and body through the "mist/ of swords that seemed to sever/ heads from bodies." The ultimate integration is between "cold Russia" (the Russia of the cold war) and "old Russia"; beyond that, between Russia and America.

Another example of Marianne Moore's obsession with the "grasp of opposites" is found in the beginning of "Elephants" where two elephants in combat appear to share one trunk:

> The opposing opposed
> mouse-gray twined proboscises' trunk formed by two
> trunks, fights itself into a spiraled internosed
> deadlock of dyke-enforced massiveness.

Combat and unity do seem always to be an "objective symbolic of *sagesse*" in Moore's work, whether it is one appearing to be two in combat or two appearing to be one. The objective is always cemented by illusion, torn apart by precision. Both illusion and precision are necessary for the objective *sagesse*.

The second half of "Efforts of Affection" takes the poem away from its domestically warring literary illustrations and amplifies the personal meaning of affection and integration.

> "You know I'm not a saint!" Sainted obsession.
> The bleeding-heart's—that strange rubber fern's attraction
>
> Puts perfume to shame.
> Unsheared sprays of elephant-ears
> Do not make a selfish end look like a noble one.
> Truly as the sun
> can rot or mend, love can make one
> bestial or make a beast a man.
>   Thus wholeness—

wholesomeness? best say efforts of affection—
attain integration too tough for infraction.

"You know I'm not a saint!"—it would seem to be a lover's protesta-
tion, a denial of the illusion, or stated illusion, of the opposing lover. One
would make saintliness a quality of a person loved in order to displace an interest in the physical aspects of love. It is a "sainted obsession" on both sides.
On one hand, to deny sainthood is a necessity of saintly humility. On the
other, to protest that the loved one is a saint is to assure a spiritual motive
for the love, to make it wholesome.

The bleeding-heart is a kind of fern, more attractive (to this poet, anyway) than perfume. It is a metaphor for the lover's frustration, but also, one
might conjecture, a peculiar allusion to "bleeding-heart" liberals. "Unsheared
sprays of elephant-ears" are not attractive, but they present no flamboyant
illusions about the nature of the world, the plainness or even ugliness of some
things in it. If we read Republican conservatism into the "elephant-ear" we
have the opposition, bordering on joke, between the liberal politicians who
dress their selfishness in the language of humanitarian love and concern, and
the conservative politicians who accept the ugly nature of things, advise
people to pull themselves up by their bootstraps, and let ignoble selfishness at
least appear to be what it in fact is: selfish. The poem appeared in an election
year in *The Nation,* and we know from various sources that Marianne Moore's
political preferences were with the elephant-ears. It is not inconsistent with
her love of scientific accuracy, astringency, self-reliance, and the Edsel.

The little moral about the paradoxical force of the sun and of love has
been leapt upon quite naturally by all critics as the "message" of the poem. It
is a little too glib, though, to bear the weight of the whole. It avoids the main
issue, which asks how far we can let "efforts of affection" take us into the
dangerous world of love and illusion. Love has two faces, as does the politics
of love, but neither is fully turned to us in the conclusion of the poem. "Efforts of Affection" will not take us all the way to effortless love. These efforts
remain a means of maintaining a balanced, or rationalized, solitude, as the
efforts in "Marriage" do.

None of the examples of "integration" in the first half of the poem are
too tough for infraction. There are wars, disenchantments, eventual inspections (such as La Fontaine's) which break them despite the spiritual base of
the original illusion. In the second half of the poem integration that has no
illusive and spiritual base is sought on realistic and physical bases. The
elephant-ear is realistic, the rotting and mending of the sun is physical. The
only wholeness, or integration, that is too tough for infraction is the integra-

tion within a single illusionless self, an unbreakable "wholesomeness." In her essay on T. S. Eliot in *Predilections*, Moore refers to "wholeness" as "the condition of ecstasy." It is "to be 'accepted and accepting'" and its opposite is unbelief. Thus any wholeness, whether of style or subject, is a matter of faith, the reader's faith as well as the writer's. We would like to be persuaded.

A Pest

> *One may be a blameless*
> *bachelor, and it is but a step*
>   *to Congreve. A Rosalindless*
> *redbird comes where people are, knowing they*
>   *have not made a point of*
>   *being where he is—this bird*
> *which says, not sings, "Without*
>   *loneliness I should be more*
>   *lonely, so I keep it."*
>   ("Smooth Gnarled Crape Myrtle")

The poem "Marriage" presents a woman's attempts to protect herself from the awful persuasions of the man and the marital estate. She has no such strong rhetoric as the poet who speaks of "efforts of affection." "She says," rather despairingly:

> "This butterfly,
> this waterfly, this nomad
> that has 'proposed
> to settle on my hand for life'—
> What can one do with it?

The Arctic Ox does not like the "servitude and flutter" of courtship, and the butterfly, or fluttering (flattering?) creature is associated with failed or failing courtship in at least three other poems—"Half-Deity," "Armor's Undermining Modesty" (at least in my opinion), and "Then the Ermine." We must look at "Half-Deity," a poem inexplicably dropped from Moore's canon, to understand the associations the fluttery, flying thing brings to the two late poems we are about to consider.

"Half-Deity" is a poem about courtship, the imprecations of a "nymph" chasing a butterfly who is "half-deity,/ half worm." This flying creature is attractive as a work of art, "on whose half-transparent wings, crescents en-grave// the silken edge with dragon's blood," and it is desired by a "nymph . . . in Wedgewood blue." This nymph has discovered the butterfly in a kind of Eden. As she follows it from crabapple to pear to pomegranate tree, she is "forced by the summer sun to pant." It is hinted that she, perhaps because of her innocence, is looking at, and looking for, something forbidden, as "some are not/ permitted to gaze informally/ on majesty in such a manner as she/ is gazing here." The butterfly, although it is "afraid of the slight finger" knows that something is up; it begins to act like a restless horse, "pawing" the flower it has lighted upon. The butterfly is furred, like the moth's wings in "Armor's Undermining Modesty"; "unaware that curiosity has/ been pursuing it." It is nervous,

> for she with controlled agitated glance
> explores the insect's face
> and all's a-quiver with significance.

This is no ordinary butterfly as the moth in the later poem is no ordinary moth. The confrontation of nymph and insect, moreover, is no ordinary con-frontation: "It is Goya's scene of the tame magpie faced/ by crouching cats."

In the poem "Marriage" Adam is associated with a "crouching mytho-logical monster" surrounded by intricate art. In "Charity Overcoming Envy," Envy, on a dog, faces Charity on her elephant, "crouching uneasily/ in the flowered filigree, among wide weeds/ indented by scallops that swirl, little flattened out sunflowers,/ thin arched coral stems, and—ribbed horizontally—/ slivers of green." In both cases the monster to be feared and avoided—misled affection, covetousness—is overcome by displacing interest to a surrounding context, letting the sense become confused and distracted from the "mon-ster" by the monster's chosen camouflage. The "acacia-like lady" in "People's Surroundings," like a butterfly in her delicacy and elusiveness, "shiver[s] at the touch of a hand,/ lost in a small collision of the orchids—/ dyed quick-silver let fall/ to disappear like an obedient chameleon in fifty shades of mauve and amethyst." What disappears?—the dangerous hand? the lady? the orchids? It is all one. The monster and victim both merge with what surrounds the incident of their coming together, or their possible coming together. Dis-tractability is a saving grace.

The tone in "Half-Deity" changes abruptly, as it does in "Marriage" when any near-crisis is reached, and for similar reasons. The following passage provides no transition between epithetical anger and detached observation:

> Equine irascible
> unwormlike unteachable butterfly-
> zebra! Sometimes one is grateful to
> a stranger for looking very nice; to the
> friendly outspread hand. But
> it flies.

The hand is "an ambiguous signature" ("Those Various Scalpels") in all of Moore's poems. In "Half-Deity" the "hand" of the west wind, enters a few lines after the nonexistence of a "friendly outspread hand" is regretted. The west wind's hand would be quite acceptable to the butterfly, however, because it hides "no decoy in half-shut/ palm since his is not a/ covetous hand." In an early poem, "Roses Only," the thorns "are not proof against a worm, the elements, or mildew/ but what about the predatory hand?" And in "The Plumet Basilisk" we find a "look of whetted fierceness,// in what is merely/ breathing and recoiling from the hand."

It makes no difference who is pursuing and who is pursued (as they are always in some sense to be confused with each other); the point is that there is an antagonism between monstrousness and beauty which can be preserved in irresolution and made harmless by some art that makes them one. Moore chooses to give us a detail in "Sea Unicorns and Land Unicorns" reminiscent of the "equine" butterfly and nymph in Wedgewood blue. She sees the land unicorn "etched like an equine monster of an old celestial map,/ beside a cloud or dress of Virgin-Mary blue." Here, as in "Half-Deity," the virgin is the pursuer-with-intent-to-tame, and to the extent that she is dangerous to what might be dangerous to her, her dress is magical, "improved 'all over slightly with snakes of Venice gold/ and silver, and some O's'." The unicorn is "engrossed by what appears of this strange enemy" and ends up in her lap, unlike the more successful butterfly who gets away; yet the "courtship" is similarly dangerous and ambiguous; it has all the qualities of the fight between affection and disaffection that we find in the various scenes of "Marriage."

The moth is the opening inspiration of "Armor's Undermining Modesty":

>   At first I thought a pest
>   must have alighted on my wrist.
>   It was a moth almost an owl,
>   its wings were furred so well,
> with backgammon-board wedges interlacing
> on the wing—
>
>   like cloth of gold in a pattern
>   of scales with a hair-seal Persian
>   sheen. Once self-determination
>   made an ax of a stone
> and hacked things out with hairy paws. The consequence—our mis-set
> alphabet.

The abundantly attractive moth in "Armor's Undermining Modesty" leads to a statement that seems far from delicate mothdom, namely, that man's primate predecessors rudely and roughly prepared the way for our "mis-set alphabet" and the "faulty etymology" referred to later in the poem. Somehow, these verbal transgressions are associated in Moore's mind with the aggressiveness that prompted primitive creatures with "hairy paws" (an unfair description even of a monkey's delicate fingers and hairless palms) to invent axes "to hack things out with." This primitive "hack" will come back to haunt the derivation of "unhackneyed solitude" at the end of the poem.

   The moth is associated with a kind of aggressiveness in Moore's poem "Wood-Weasel," where the animal "is his own protection from the moth// noble little warrior." Again, we may ask, exactly who is the warrior? And in "Blue Bug" the poet claims there is "nothing more punitive than the pest/ who says, 'I'm trespassing,' and does it just the same." The moth at the beginning of "Armor's Undermining Modesty" is trespassing by alighting on the author's wrist. The nomad-butterfly-waterfly-suitor is seen as a trespasser in "Marriage." "Forgive us our trespasses as we forgive those who trespass against us": Moore forgives and forbears; she integrates the pests in her art, extending her hand to them, making an effort.

   Persian art, "contrarities," and a moth are all integrated in an early poem, "Diogenes." It was printed in *Contemporary Verse*, January, 1916, and is not in any of Moore's collections; here it is in full:

>   Day's calumnies,
>   Midnight's translucencies.
>   Pride's open book
>   Of closed humilities—
>   With its inflated look;

Shall contrarities
As feasible as these
        Confound my wit?

Is Persian cloth
One thread with Persian sloth?
        Is gold dust bran?
Though spotted Ashtaroth
        Is not a Puritan,
Must every gorgeous moth
Be calico, and Thoth
        Be thanked for it?

The question of whether "contrarities" shall confound the poet's wit is one of the overriding questions of Moore's life's work. It is a question we cannot ignore, especially where her "contrarities" confound our own wits, as indeed she means them to. Again and again she asks this question, always involved with the moral and cultural combat between excess (in love, art, anything) and asceticism. The difference between day and night *should* be plain as day; yet "day" in which everything should be clearly seen and which should represent itself with no mystery, contains misrepresentations. Midnight, the magical time of deepest obscurities, is unnervingly translucent. Even the evaluation of pride and humility does not present itself as an open and shut case. The moth that pesters the poet in the opening lines of "Armor's Undermining Modesty" is related to Persian art, the art in which "Adam" is hidden in one scene of "Marriage." Persian art is an art of religious sensuality toward which the Presbyterian Moore feels ambivalent attraction, for is it not wrong to absorb oneself in such obvious luxury when creatures of the spirit should be spare?

Ashtaroth is the Hebrew equivalent of Astarte, goddess of fertility and reproduction. She is "spotted." "Then the Ermine" opens with the words "Rather dead than spotted." It is this decoration, apparently, that marks the annoying romance with the butterfly or moth. We may recall that in describing the "Carriage from Sweden" Moore praises its "unannoying romance" as opposed directly to the city in which it is found, New York, the "city of freckled integrity." "Must *every* gorgeous moth/ be calico?" she complains. Calico is a poor substitute for Persian cloth, yet it, too, in its own common way is spotted. It is to be avoided as the beauty of the "Half-Deity" is to be avoided, despite, or because of, the beautiful dragon's blood that spots its wings. And the feminine sexuality that it arouses? Half of it is deity, the other half is worm.

Why thank Thoth? He is the Egyptian god of wisdom, learning, letters, numbers—all those ambivalences of precisions, persuasions, and distractions. As scribe of the gods, he resides at the center of the ability to name and enumerate contrarities that perplex and attract us. In "Armor's Undermining Modesty" this ambivalence of language is traced to that predecessor who "hacked things out with hairy paws." (Is it merely coincidence that Thoth is often portrayed with a baboon's head?) The source of our evil and our revenge, our highest good and our praise of it, is identical with the source of language. We cannot help it if sometimes it immodestly obtrudes (as the moth-pest does); it becomes both armor and enemy of our sense and sensibility.

"Armor's Undermining Modesty," despite unresolved questions of "day's calumnies," goes on to advise us:

> Arise, for it is day.
> Even gifted scholars lose their way
> through faulty etymology.
> No wonder we hate poetry
> and stars and harps and the new moon. If tributes cannot
> be implicit,
>
> give me diatribes and the fragrance of iodine,
> the cork oak acorn grown in Spain;
> the pale-ale-eyed impersonal look
> which the sales-placard gives the bock beer buck.
> What is more precise than precision? Illusion.

"Arise, for it is day," the advertising motto for the John Day Company, contains in itself a complex of allusions having to do with the love-language nexus in Marianne Moore's work. First, the fact that the motto is a typically ingenious American advertisement links it with the "mechanical advertising" and self-advertisement that is scorned in "Marriage." Second, the John Day Company was a publishing firm, and there is a sense in which all publishing is self-advertisement. Moore may have been reminded of something Ezra Pound wrote in his "Paris Letter" to *The Dial* (November 1922, p. 549) where he connects American literature with advertising and greed (and this passage may very well have influenced the poem "Marriage," which appeared in 1923):

> If people like to eat an advertising medium, it is their own
> affair; no advertising medium has yet proved to be nutritive. . . .

literature is regarded in America as an advertising medium. . . .
   The producers of 'advertising medium' apparently make no
effort to protect themselves. They arrive as live beef at the doors
of their respective armours, they leave canned, and die in a few
years anonymous, after having 'reached millions.'

It is remarkable how closely Pound's image of "armours" coincides with
Moore's image of armor in "Armor's Undermining Modesty." This connection
may seem silly at first, even a parody of close critical reading, yet it persuades
us to reconsider the title of the poem in light of the allusions to writing and
advertising that dominate it, and in light of Marianne Moore's apparently ambivalent attitude toward the armor she regards as a personal and literary necessity. "Armor's Undermining Modesty" may be understood as the following:
(1) armor is something that belies and subtly destroys modesty; (2) armor is a
sign of modesty that thwarts or reduces the effectiveness of something unnamed—one's own plans or desires, perhaps, or those of another, or armor itself, suggesting (3) that armor is being undermined by modesty. Or, instead of
reading "Armor's" as "Armor is . . . ," we may read it as a possessive form,
yielding the thought that (4) living or hiding or fighting from within armor
is a knight whose modesty is undermining, of and in itself or of an enemy.
Either armor is *opposed* to modesty, a form of advertising oneself as a person
specially equipped to put up a good fight in the ways of the world; or it is
identified with modesty, a retreat from exposure and a sign of submission to
one's convictions. Armor is either *surrounded* by something undermining or
contains something undermining. Armor is alternately the victim and the per-
petrator of this ambiguity. The tenor and the vehicle are one.
   For "armor" read "a poem in its published form," or "any formal use
of language that advertises illusions," or "public self-advertisement." "The
producers of 'advertising medium' apparently make no effort to protect
themselves," laments Pound. "They arrive as live beef . . . ." Marianne Moore
is not one of these. Her psychic economy demands home canning and her
modesty stipulates a small distribution among friends. This does not mean
that she is not tempted by the advertising medium that Pound talks about.
She goes so far as to regard it as literature, to add "canned" products to her
own concoctions, risking the undermining of both integrity and modesty by
doing so. The confusions of her ambivalence and the unconfusion that submits them to proof (see "The Mind Is an Enchanting Thing") may be nutritive or not, depending on the reader's willingness to cooperate with an undermining wit.
   Advertising is the result of hunger for illusions; it is indispensable to

politics, to corporations whose business is to feed us whatever they can convince us we need, and to art. The "day" associated with the John Day publishing firm's advertisement may very well be associated in Moore's mind with the playwright of the early seventeenth century whose name was John Day. His *Ile of Gulls* (1606) is a play that would surely have appealed to Moore's sense of the world as reflected in "Armor's Undermining Modesty." It refers to contemporary political scandals and parodies puritan sermons and, in short, contains every sort of "advertising medium" that would be gleefully eaten up by the court, including one of those ridiculous Elizabethan love-story mixups involving mistaken identities. Moore may have this John Day in mind, or she may be remembering T. S. Eliot's parody of Day in *The Waste Land* where the honking horns of taxis bring Sweeney to Mrs. Porter, a modern perversion of Day's "A noise of horns and hunting, which shall bring/ Actaeon to Diana." Immodest assignation, misuse of words and literature in advertising, daylight full of puns and obscurities—no wonder gifted scholars lose their way.

Etymology (close, as a sound, to entomology and hence moth-infringements) is one of the precisionists' methods of understanding language, but although we are all precisionists in a way, as Moore says in "Bowls," this method leads to difficulties as often as to elucidations. "Contrarities" such as the ones that perplex the poet in "Diogenes" and "Marriage" and "Efforts of Affection" cannot be set straight by looking up "day" and "night," or "beast" and "man" in a dictionary. In "Bowls" Moore puts her tongue in her cheek and says,

> I shall purchase an etymological dictionary of modern English
> that I may understand what is written,
> and shall answer the question
> "Why do I like winter better than I like summer?"
> and acknowledge that it does not make me sick
> to look playwrights and poets and novelists straight in the face—
> that I feel just the same.

There is a big difference between experience and the words used to describe it, but writers and advertisers must pretend that there is not and believe above all in the precision of illusion. Why one happens to like summer better than winter or one product better than another or one poet better than another is a matter of preference, not evidence. It is a matter of illusion that is more precise than precision because it involves one's personal feelings. When language pretends to be something else, we hate it. It sometimes makes us sick to meet the propagators, even when we are one of them. "Bowls" also contains a reference to the pushy sales of magazines. "No wonder we hate poetry. . . ." "I, too, dislike it. . . ."

Poetry can too easily fall into the trap of greedy and aggressive rhetoric, and this is why we may hate it with all its insincere romantic trappings. Moore prefers honest "diatribes and the fragrance of iodine," astringency that does not claim to be other than it is, like the unsheared elephant-ear plant. And this is what we are shown also in the lovers' debate in "Marriage." Moore herself refuses to make poetry that is no more than an extension of the most primitive weapons, or that is self-important and devious. Give her the kind of advertising that is pale and impersonal, like the stare of the buck on a sales-placard. Moore's poems are openly didactic. Live not by easy or false illusions, but by the most precise illusions that feelings can honestly create. Let us *not* live by commodity or flattery.

Undermining illusion is the object of "knights we've known":

> like those familiar
> now unfamiliar knights who sought the Grail, they were
> *ducs* in old Roman fashion
> without the addition
> of wreaths and silver rods, and armor gilded
> or inlaid.

> They did not let self bar
> Their usefulness to others who were
> different. Though Mars is excessive
> [in] being preventive,[11]
> heroes need not write an ordinall of attributes to enumerate
> what they hate.

Ideal knights like ideal suitors or ideal words, are not dressed up with an arty irrelevance. They have extrapersonal convictions, like the knights who sought the Grail. The Grail is associated with a primitive nature cult, and the task of the hero with bringing health to a sick land. Moore's hero's task would seem to be the purification of American tastes, letters, and illusions through accurate perceptions of nature. The hero sets aside personal wishes in favor of the task. Renunciations are a necessity and they are natural; they needn't be in writing. In fact, they may be dangerously compromised be being in writing when to renounce writing itself is one of the requirements of an armored modesty.

"Mars is excessive/ in being preventive" insofar as a knight advertises a willingness to do battle by wearing armor. Aggressive or excessively self-protective rhetoric invites a like response. Moore's obscurities are excessively preventive of understanding, preserving the solitary crusade at the cost of straightforwardness. Allison Heisch, in an essay on Queen Elizabeth I's parliamentary rhetoric, shows that there was a direct correlation between her political insecurity of the moment and the obscurity of her language.[12] Obscurity can help in the exercise of power, as any political speech-writer knows. Obscurity is an armor of undermining modesty, defying its adversaries to say clearly what is wrong with it.

An understood thing about being a "hero" is that a hero hates some things and knows instinctively what these things are. She lets the world know of her ability to discriminate through actions, not words. In the poem "The Hero" Moore begins by telling us that "where there is personal liking we go. . . . We do not like some things and the hero doesn't." No chivalrous and insincere trappings, please; speak your mind, be stringent; meet foes directly, don't write around the bush in inky flutterings. Yet, as we have repeatedly noticed, Marianne Moore has a penchant for flouting her own admonitions.

The following passage might prompt one to ask whether Marianne Moore is more interested in giving or receiving advice on the subject of knighthood and its armoring:

> I should, I confess,
> like to have a talk with one of them about excess
> and armor's undermining modesty
> instead of innocent depravity.
> A mirror-of-steel uninsistence should countenance
> continence.

There is another question here which we can see no way of resolving. Does the poet want to talk about armor's undermining modesty as a subject in itself, as opposed to the subject of innocent depravity; or does she want to talk about the fact that armor undermines modesty whereas it should undermine innocent depravity? The unbelievers that knights are supposed to fight are depraved, certainly, but unenlightened and thus innocent of their depravity. Does armor undermine the knight's own modesty (and/or innocence) in her attempt to enlighten others? "Undermining modesty" and "innocent depravity" are both oxymorons, both threatening, both inseparable from the business of the hero who must compromise himself in his uncompromising conviction that to lose is to find, to destroy a life is to save it, to surrender is to conquer, and so on. Whatever Marianne Moore decides to talk about, with the knight or with herself, it will be a contrarity. Her garden grows according to her confusions, a forbidden and forbidding unity of good and evil at the center. She offers us the potent fruit of it as she offers her hand in "Marriage," ambiguously.

What one intends, by donning armor, is to protect one's honor, express one's modesty, defend against all kinds of depravity, and in some way or another bring home the Grail. Spenser's Red Cross Knight puts on armor not only to protect himself from external dragons, but also to strengthen his own image of himself as a righteous and incorruptible person, safe from internal "dragons." He insists too much on his modesty and armor, abandoning the real Una and becoming immodestly aggressive. Whereas, if he'd had a talk with Marianne Moore about it, she could have told him that "a mirror-of-steel uninsistence should countenance/ continence." She could have told him not to insist so much on the power of his defenses, that it would have been enough for him to go around in his armor, simply reflecting the world in his polished surface; this alone would have been enough to give a plausible appearance to his knightly self-restraint. She would have said to him:

> What is our innocence,
> what is our guilt? All are
> naked, none is safe.
>
> ("What Are Years?")

This is, after all, what Moore seems to be telling herself in "Armor's Undermining Modesty"—one of the things, anyway—that "armor" may belie one's deference by insisting too much on the illusion of pilfer-proof integration and wholesomeness that resists infraction, the illusion that one is safe. Safe from what? Self-doubt, prying eyes, attractive monsters, "wooden spears" that can pierce an elephant's soul, wishes, deceptive rhetoric, pride, despair, any such "pest" of the imagination that one can imagine.

"Armor's Undermining Modesty" seems to me to be not so much about knighthood as about Marianne Moore's own attitudes toward affect, "the fight to be affectionate," language, and self-protective art. The poem began with a moth, a "pest" landing softly on the wrist of the writer. What may have been the writer's first impulse? To smash it, probably, but that is no way to treat a muse. The moth is not just a pest; when looked at as a "hero" looks, with rock-crystal-seeking attention, it becomes irresistibly beautiful, with wings "like cloth of gold in a pattern/ of scales with a hair-seal Persian/ sheen." The tension that underlies the whole poem is that between the desire to own and appreciate the beauty of the "pest" and the desire to kill it for its presumption, its trespassing upon one's hand. Attractions alternate with repulsions. The hero's response to this tension is to invent a defense, to protect her own interests, to preserve her wholeness, or at least the illusion of it, in a hopeless waste land of self-interested advertising and aggressions. The tension is also between *wanting* to like something (poetry, for instance) and *needing* to hate it.

"Integration," a thoroughly countenanced continence of both the instincts of excess and the instincts of restraint in love, in writing, and in moral or political or sexual conflict of any kind, the integration suited to heroes, should be

> objectified and not by chance
> there in its frame of circumstance
> of innocence and altitude
> in an unhackneyed solitude.

These lines invite us to recall the frigate pelican, the steeple-jack in his "innocence and altitude" gilding the star on the steeple, the sad Leonardo of "An Expedient," the mountain glacier of "An Octopus," the unpsychological and unconversational giraffe who lives on top leaves, and more. These situations are "framed by circumstance"; there is a kind of perverse (per-verse) fate about them. The solitude is "unhackneyed." "Unhackneyed," it will be remembered, is a word applied also to the situation of Bottom and Titania alluded to in "Efforts of Affection." It means pure. It means original. It means free. To be "hackneyed" may mean to be kept for hire (as a writer or a horse), made commonplace (as the "advertising medium" Pound and Moore refuse to swallow); and, in the seventeenth century, when the namesake of the twentieth-century-publishing-company John Day was writing, "hackney" often meant prostitute. Marianne Moore flaunts her freedom from all accusations, as do her heroes who seek the modern Grail.

Yet there is something seriously lacking in her sort of solitude, unhackneyed as it may be. "There is the tarnish; and there the imperishable wish" ends the poem about armor. The imperishable wish is the eternity to be gained by wholeness, wholesomeness, "integration." The "efforts of affection" are doomed to be impersonal and lonely. There is the tarnish. Much as we polish our heroic efforts at communication, it is difficult to say no, *and* yes. Marianne Moore comes as close as she possibly can.

"Rather Dead than Spotted"

> *"Everything to do with love is mystery;*
> *it is more than a day's work*
> *to investigate this science."*
>   ("Marriage")

"Then the Ermine" is the most personal and puzzling of the three late poems most often seen in relation to "Marriage"; read in conjunction with these other poems, however, we find that "more is discernible/ than the intensity of the mood" ("When I Buy Pictures"). The poem begins abruptly, as if in the middle of a conversation, with the title:

THEN THE ERMINE:

> "rather dead than spotted"; and believe it
>   despite reason to think not,
> I saw a bat by daylight;
> hard to credit
>
> but I knew that I was right. It charmed me—
>   wavering like a jack-in-
> the-green, weaving about me
> insecurely.

"Rather dead than spotted" is a motto introduced in Sidney's *Arcadia* in the middle of a courtly battle. Several knights, each defending his own loved lady, have been defeated before Clitophon's turn comes. He enters;

> his device he had put in the picture of Helen which hee defended. It was the *Ermion,* with a speach that signified, *Rather dead than spotted.* But in that armour since he had parted fro Helen (who would no longer his companie, finding him to enter into terms of affection) . . . Basilius in the ende gave sentence against Clitophon . . . who yielded the field to the next commer.
>   (Book I, chap. 17, para. 4)

The Lady Helen, "rather dead than spotted," withdraws from the knight's endangering affections. The same phenomenon is stressed in "Marriage," where the poet herself withdraws from image after image of affection. Here too she withdraws suddenly and strangely from her allusion to failing court-ship and asks us to believe that she really *has* seen a bat by daylight. This is presumably one of "day's calumnies" referred to in "Diogenes," and its ob-trusion throws dark on the poem's opening motto. The bat "charmed" her, offering magic protection and enchantment, perhaps, by virtue of its incon-gruity. The bat is elusive like the butterfly. It may be seen as the butterfly's night counterpart or may be related to the moth—also a night creature, also furred—of "Armor's Undermining Modesty." In any case, the anomaly "wa-vers" in striking contrast to the unwavering voice of the motto "rather dead than spotted."

The jack-in-the-green is a man who hides in newly green branches as part of ancient May Day celebrations (in England). This ritual figure is in-voked as part of the traditional game of courtship. The annual May Day cele-bration involved all the maidens and all the young men of a village, who went to the woods to "gather in the May," one of the significant consequences being that very few maidens came back maidens. A related notion fancies May an unlucky month for marriage. The impertinent jack-in-the-green, remi-niscent of Adam hiding in the seductive Persian miniature or the "monster grown to immaturity" who appears in "See in the Midst of Fair Leaves," is altogether pertinent to questions of affection and honor. He is everyone's hidden wish for defilement—to be gathered in like the May, to be taken in by a wavering phenomenon, not felicitous.

The next stanzas of "Then the Ermine" as they appear in the *Complete Poems* differ from the version that originally appeared in *Poetry,* and the im-portance of the difference is partly in the triviality of it. The stanzas are as follows:

Instead of hammer-handed bravado	Instead of hammerhanded bravado
strategy could have chosen	adopting force for fashion,
momentum with a motto:	momentum with a motto:
Mutare sperno	*non timeo*
vel timere—I don't change, am not	*vel mutare*—I don't change or
craven;	frighten;
on what ground could one	though all it means is really,
say that I am hard to frighten?	*am* I craven?
Nothing's certain.	Nothing's certain.
(Complete Poems)	*(Poetry)*

The "hammer-handed bravado" recalls Sidney's *Arcadia* again, where knights are prone to hammer each other's heads with their swords. In the first version of "Then the Ermine" this is described as "adopting force for fashion"—not a particularly good excuse for violence—and the revision offers no elaboration but emphasizes the element of choice involved. The knight *could* have chosen a symbolic rather than a physical force. This is clearly the poet's choice. "Strategy could have chosen," and *should* have. Strategy, here an allegorical figure, should persuade through words and not blows. "Hammer-handed" recalls the suspicious and ambiguous activities of those hands from which Moore's animals recoil and which, even when (or especially when) they have an affection for one, should be avoided. The motto provides its own undangerous momentum. It expresses a wish, and nothing more, although a wish may have plenty of spiritual momentum. (One might even say that motto is a form of prayer.) Both versions of the Latin may be translated to mean roughly the same thing. It seems the change was made to have the order of the Latin correspond with the order of English: first spurning change, then fear. *Mutare*, "to change," can also mean "to stain"—usually to improve, not soil—and may thus be related to the fear of "spotting" expressed in the opening motto. Working against the motto in both versions is the word *craven*, in both occupying a conspicuous place. The word is not related except in sound to *craving*, yet craving is covertly involved in all the preceeding images and allusions. Faulty etymology notwithstanding, there is some cravin' in it.

In both versions of the poem the motto affirms constancy and bravery by denying their opposites, change and fear; and here affirmation by denial is not unsuspect (as Freud would be happy to substantiate). The first version of the poem wastes a line in announcing a meta-translation of the motto, which is the question of itself: *am* I what my motto says I'm not? As this is a little confusing, the second version asks rather "on what ground" has bravery been proved, or what proves the motto true? The first version has an apologetic tone; the second, as if in answer to an incredulous question, is reiterating the question. In both instances the question modestly undermines the firmness of the motto. The answer to the undermining question is, in both versions, no answer. A motto is words only, wishing-words that do not change or penetrate fate any more than the described self does.

The difference in meaning between the two versions is small indeed, yet every word from the motto on is rearranged except the words "I don't change," and their contradiction, "nothing's certain." It is as if the first version could foresee the changeless changes in the second. One might extrapolate: the poet can write the same poem over and over in different words without compromising the purity of the one important underlying motive. If there *is* an important difference, it may be the *form* of the question: in the first instance, *"am* I craven?" as if hoping to be contradicted; in the second, "what on earth makes you think I'm brave?" asking to be contradicted and not expecting to be. The second is revised toward more modesty. Slight as the difference is, in terms of syllable-count, rhyme, and placement, this revision could not have been simple to effect. The additional modesty and pessimism must have seemed worth it. Still, only one thing is certain, and that is that "nothing's certain."

A motto, like wit, is a condensation of the world's complexity and often a defense against threatening forces one does not understand very well. Mottoes enter poems with singular verbal assurance, like knights entering a ring with shields held firmly. The meaning is usually explicit; but then, as Moore tells us with motto-like brevity, not needing to be revised, "Nothing's certain." "Tippoo's Tiger" points out the fact that a mechanical device, a toy, cannot save its master from his ill fate. Likewise the motto, a toy of poetry, cannot save the poet from her fated subject, herself. In all of Moore's poems in which a fight is felt, especially "the fight to be affectionate," and in which a knight-in-armor is presented, the most general enemy seems to be fate in one shape or another. The motto cannot contain or deny fate. It has momentary power only. A motto, like a joke, is a loser's last resort and a winner's escape from guilt.

Denial is a strong source of emotion, strong enough to pen other emotions so that they may be forced into the pent forms of imploding mottoes, elliptical hints, revisions toward obscurity, and contemptuous wit. Self-denial is praised as well as practiced in Marianne Moore's poems. Good examples of this are found in "The Jerboa," "Sojourn in the Whale," and "Nevertheless." What excess is she afraid of? The bat by daylight? Possibly, because it is a "pest" and wavers about the ambiguously pestilent May festival. The "hammer-handed bravado"? Active clash and swagger are certainly not among her predilections. The most subtle kind of self-denial is epitomized, if not clearly recognized, in "Then the Ermine," in that the connections between its parts are tenuous and the poet here is denying herself the relief of direct expression. Her only "improvement" in revising is to lessen her appearance of assertiveness.

The revision of the fifth stanza of "Then the Ermine" is toward a restricting of possibility; the skill that flowers obscurely in the earlier version gives way to a skill that is simply rare. Awe is reduced to sigh:

Fail, and Lavater's physiography	Fail, and Lavater's physiography
has another admirer	has another admirer
of skill in obscurity—	of skill that axiomatically
now a novelty.	flowers obscurely.
(Complete Poems)	*(Poetry)*

Johann Kaspar Lavater, known as "a promoter of tolerance" as well as a magician, conducted correspondence with kings, and was generally respected for his study of "man's features as the signs and characters formed by nature to reveal the inner man."[13] A poet's failure to judge men by appearances accurately, or to predict an inner quality from external form, will make her turn to the magician in admiration. The unexpected appearance of a bat in daylight must be trusted as a sign of nature's uncertain nature, as the motto of a knight claiming purity must be trusted. But these signs and the judgments that ensue still involve a certain amount of risk, and a great deal of "skill in obscurity."

Poetry, like judgment of character, is a "skill that axiomatically/ flowers obscurely," as the first version of "Then the Ermine" puts it. Axiom is related to motto, as a clear and to-be-acted-upon proposition. The difference between them is that a motto is personal and has more to do with possibility or ideal than with fact. Marianne Moore is, in "Then the Ermine," talking to herself about the need to decide once and for all about the feasibility of any kind of judgment. On a personal level, she would like to have a motto with momentum enough to defend a chaste way of life. On a more general level she would like a system like Lavater's that explains the reasons why the hero "do[es] not like some things." Lavater's kind of "skill in obscurity"—predicting a man's fate by the lines in his forehead, his nose, his ear lobes—is now a novelty. But we still need *some* way of precisely predicting character, especially when it may involve our own future.

If we could only read between and behind the lines of a poem as easily as Lavater could read between and behind the lines of a forehead, verse might best "confuse itself with fate." The condition of failure in the poem may well be directed to the reader: fail to read the external features that make up the world of this poem and the poet's character, and henceforth admire the rare skill of a Lavater. Or the poet may be saying to herself: fail to read between these overriding images of your life—the knight, the mysterious animal, the preoccupation with words and morals and the rest—and then admire the professional magician-prophet who, with your same interests (morphology, anthropology, anatomy, histrionics, and graphics) succeeded in putting everything together so well that even the king would listen to him.

One stanza of the earlier version of "Then the Ermine" was completely excised. It is about the sea, and adds to our impression that Moore may have purposely gathered an array of images here that were pervasive in her work up until the time she wrote this poem.

> Both paler and purpler than azure, note marine
> uncompliance—bewarer
> of the weak analogy—between
> waves in motion.

We have seen the sea related to unconscious force in other poems ("A Grave," "Novices") and azure is a color associated with art, via Mallarmé, and with the sky. The sea does not comply in reflecting the azure's exact color, but the two are close. Uncompliance is found secondarily between waves in motion; to continue an analogy between the sea and poetry, although waves (images, illusions) seem to move forward, the water itself (meaning) does not. Or the poet may be thinking of the way the sea draws back between waves near shore, the momentary touch followed by (what else?) withdrawal. Emily Dickinson, racing with the sea's seduction in "I started Early," has noted such uncompliance.

The poet herself is the "bewarer of the weak analogy." The uncompliance of the sea is analogous to the uncompliance of the poet and of forces within the poet, the reluctance of her "mirror-of-steel uninsistence" to reflect accurately the inner meanings of her world. Each stanza of the poem, each image of the poet's life, is a wave of consciousness that seems to progress. But *between* these waves, what? Silence, uncompliance, perhaps anger. The uncompliance is also related to the theme of marriage. The poet is saying *no: no* to the knight, *no* to the batty jack-in-the-green, *no* to the motto, *no* to all decisiveness of motion. Later she says *no* to this whole stanza, to the partiality of its explanation, and throws it out.

So let the palisandre settee ex-
        press it,
    "ebony violet,"
Master Corbo in full dress,
and shepherdess,

an exhilarating hoarse crow-note
    or dignity with intimacy.
Foiled explosiveness is yet
a kind of prophet

a perfecter, and so a concealer—
    with the power of implosion;
like violets by Dürer;
even darker.

Change? Of course if the palisandre
        settee can express
    for us, "ebony violet"—
Master Corbo in full dress
and shepherdess

at once—exhilarating hoarse crownote
    and dignity with intimacy.
Our foiled explosiveness is yet
a kind of prophet

a perfecter, and so a concealer—
    with the power of implosion;
like violets by Dürer;
even darker.

The first version of the poem is clearer. "Change?" at least links the
passage to earlier ones, and indicates that the poet has been asked or is asking
herself something involving a change in life or vision which the settee might,
in all its unlikelihood, answer. Of course she will change only if the palisandre
settee can accommodate her. The question of whether it can or not remains
open. The "change" may be seen to involve several of the poem's themes.
First of all, there is the change that is asked for near the beginning of the
poem that inspires the poet to insist on the motto: "I don't change, am not
craven." A change is something to be feared. One real fear expressed in the
poem is contained in the opening "rather dead than spotted." It is a fear, on
the knight's part, that he will be defeated and dishonored in defending a lady
(one in Sidney's book, moreover, who has already left him for fear of her
own honor). The ermine must retain pure whiteness or be given up.

White is a color of magical safety throughout Moore's work. In "Marriage" the Persian miniature in which the mythological monster crouches is
found to contain nine kinds of white helping to conceal the monster himself.
In "Sea Unicorns and Land Unicorns" the dogs derive "agreeable terror"
from the unicorn's "'moonbeam throat'/ on fire like its white coat." In "The
Sycamore" the "albino giraffe" to which the tree is compared will "stir the
envy" of the "all-white butterfly." In "Elephants" the poet obviously sym-
pathizes with the white elephant:

Though white is
the color of worship and of mourning, he

is not here to worship and he is too wise
to mourn—a life prisoner but reconciled.

Being all white puts a burden on one at the same time that it distinguishes
one. Is it possible to change? Can something that is dark express one better?
In "People's Surroundings" furniture expresses inner life. Well, then, the
palisandre settee (palisandre is purple wood or rose wood), being a place
where two people might comfortably sit, might do to express a lonely wish,
the wish to unite "Master Corbo," the gentleman in black, and a "shepherdess," in a purple dress perhaps, wearing the color of the sea and of violets.
Collier's Cyclopedia (1882), elucidating "The Language of Flowers" lists
different kinds of violets expressing the qualities of Faithfulness (blue violet),
Watchfulness (dane violet), and Modesty (sweet violet). If a settee could contain those virtues of violets along with the unsentimental screech of the crow,
Marianne Moore might be willing to settle on it.

    But "dignity with intimacy" is probably, after all, only wishful thinking.
Except for one situation, and that is the situation of the poem itself. Here the
poet can tell, or suggest, the most intimate things about her "unhackneyed
solitude," and about her imagination, precious and unconsciously fastidious
in some ways, commonplace as axiom in others. Verse, identifiable with the
countenanced continence "objectified and not by chance" in the hero's
armor, is "foiled explosiveness." Each concise image, strong analogy, or motto might be metaphorically exploded into a million prosaic particles, but it is
not. This may be because Moore feels that it is

in fact fatal
to be personal and undesirable

to be literal—detrimental as well
if the eye is not innocent—
                . . .
When plagued by the psychological,
a creature can be unbearable

that could have been irresistible;
or to be exact, exceptional

since less conversational
than some emotionally-tied-in-knots animal

                    . . . In Homer, existence
        is flawed.
                ("To a Giraffe")

"Then the Ermine" is about an existence that is flawed and "framed by circumstance," by particular circumstances and personal laws that are mysterious. All lives are subject to similar flaw and frame, and just as "foiled explosiveness" may mark one's forehead with lines that may be read as fate, it may mark the perplexed and perplexing lines of a poem. (The only drawback is that it may take a magician to read the poem.) "Foiled explosiveness" is thus a kind of clue to fate; it is in the nature of perfection, or of perfect containment, to conceal its inner working, and this is also in the nature of fate. *Ars est celare artem.* The images of Marianne Moore's poems, to a greater or lesser extent depending on the emotional or psychological load the poem is asked to bear, tend to implode, to burst inward, into themselves and into images related to them in other poems.

The lines of "Then the Ermine," fated by the isolation of the images and the isolated inner experience of their creator, are in their horrifying reticence "like violets by Dürer;/ even darker." These are far indeed from the exuberance of May flowers associated with the "jack-in-the-green." They are even far from the purples of the comparatively light-hearted palisandre settee. They are careful, particularized, and, coming as they do at the end of this poem, more than a little sad. In "Saint Valentine" where the poet offers to help the saint decide on appropriate valentine gifts, she suggests a violet, "said to mean the/ love of truth or truth of love." But these are darker, as if representing rather the love of mystery and mystery of love, deeper than any truth we could possibly hope to know. They are meant to be *impenetrably* dark, as dreams and the concisions of dreams. Albrecht Dürer has said, "He who wants to create dreamwork must make a mixture of all things." We may regard "Then the Ermine" along with "Marriage," "Efforts of Affection," and "Armor's Undermining Modesty," as well as a great many other of Moore's poems, as created dreamwork. They are not dream-reportage by any means, but conscious art informed by the unconscious fastidiousness of a dreamer who knows she dreams and that she must add strict controls to the explosive-implosive material of her inner life.

APPREHENDING HEROES

THE HERO

Unconfusion submits
its confusion to proof.

("The Mind Is an Enchanting Thing")

T<small>HE HERO</small>" describes the qualities that to Marianne Moore's mind inform an heroic style and vision. The hero is cautious; she needs to be so to survive her human frailty. The hero needs to understand social orders and manners; she has to be able to converse with them. The hero needs to discover things; she looks intently for the "rock-crystal thing." The hero needs to know about her self, origin, and end. The poem begins by asserting childlike and instinctive predilections rather than those of intellect. This approach, as we see in poems such as "Picking and Choosing," "Critics and Connoisseurs," or "When I Buy Pictures," is for Marianne Moore essential to the most genuine criticism of art and life. The poem goes on to consider the inherent unfairness of the world and the tolerance one must learn in order to have an heroic integrity. The hero must have "reverence for mystery" along with an inclination to seek and share profoundest visions—of the "inner light" of things, of invisible power. This poem shows that the energies needed for creation and criticism of creation are the same, instinctual or intuitional, and integral. We are asking for trouble when we ask the adult question, "What does it mean, literally?" There are intensities of mood, flashes of being. That is all. We should not ask if this is enough for a poem or not. It is obviously enough for "The Hero," poem and person both having retained or gained a healthy disrespect for artificial congruity.

The first thing "The Hero" claims is that "where there is personal liking we go," and then the poem proceeds to tell where we shall *not* go: "where the ground is sour;/ where there are weeds of beanstalk height,/ snakes' hypodermic teeth, or/ the wind brings the 'scarebabe voice.'" Here, we are told, "love won't grow"; and it is typical of Marianne Moore to suggest that fear of a very primitive sort inhibits love. The problem, for her, is to find an environment where love *will* grow; the hero and the hero's love can never flourish in the dark.

A catalogue of things naturally avoided by Marianne Moore's sort of "hero" follows:

> deviating headstones
> and uncertainty;
> going where one does not wish
> to go; suffering and not
> saying so; standing and listening where something
> is hiding. The hero shrinks
> as what it is flies out on muffled wings, with twin yellow
> eyes—to and fro—
>
> with quavering water-whistle note, low,
> high, in basso-falsetto chirps
> until the skin creeps.

Marianne Moore's hero cannot be accused of foolhardiness, "hammer-handed bravado," or adventuresomeness, but she is honest. Much later in her career Marianne Moore will say that "heroes need not write an ordinall of attributes to enumerate/ what they hate" ("Armor's Undermining Modesty"); but she does enumerate them here and her list is made up not of ethical transgressions but of uncertain things which are personally threatening. Uncertain meanings, uncertain words, uncertain sounds—all are stipulated by the human predicament, all equally plagues and blessings for the poet-hero. The uncertain sounds the beginning hero hears are similar to the sounds apprehended in the night in the poem "The Plumet Basilisk," where night is "the basilisk whose look will kill" and "hollow whistled monkey notes disrupt/ the castanets." The confusions of sound increase. "Taps from the back of the bow sound odd on last year's gourd,// or when they touch the/ kettledrums—at which (for there's no light),/ a scared frog, screaming like a bird, leaps out from weeds." And the skin creeps.

The hero, as a person of heightened sensibility, is more susceptible to these loveless warning-sounds (or are they love-making?) of nature than an ordinary person. "Melanchthon" says:

My ears are sensitized to more than the sound of

the wind. I see
and I hear, unlike the
        unwandlike body of which one hears so much, which was made
        to see and not to see; to hear and not to hear.

These lines follow a query about where the center of "spiritual poise" is to be found. The "unwandlike body"—the elephantine body whose physical mass is so remarkable—is not the spiritual center, is not the really important feature of this elephant. The elephant is endowed with spiritual acuity as well as external poise, and a thick spiritual armor—a metapachyderm—as well as the well-known thick physical skin. She is thus endowed because she is unusually sensitive to perceptions of spiritual danger—the wooden spear that can pierce the soul and integrity of even so massive a creature. Spiritual poise derives a center from spiritual apprehensions; the supernatural grace of the pangolin does also. Faith follows, and it is faith in one's own decisions about what is to be *avoided* in the world as much as it is an investment in positive abstractions. Poetry should have "hands that can grasp/ eyes that can dilate" ("Poetry," first version). Its source is in childhood's ready equipment, spontaneous needs and fears, likes and dislikes, not in adult inhibition. If the child-hero hears things in the night she cannot trust, she will not go willingly . . . and she is right.

The creeping skin of the frightened "hero" leads directly to a vignette illustrating injustice (also in some ways from a child's point of view):

Jacob when a-dying, asked
Joseph: Who are these? and blessed
both sons, the younger most, vexing Joseph. And
Joseph was vexing to some.

The blindness of adults, sometimes real, sometimes metaphorical, sometimes both, is just as vexing as the diurnal blindness imposed by the turning earth. Here it is implicated with injustice, the sense of which is more than a simple personal response to nature. The child feels the injustice that results from the blindness of one who has power over him; he is "vexed," but this will not prevent him from being "vexing" in turn. Later "The Hero" will turn to the problem of seeing and being seen, also a problem that begins with childhood curiosity and insecurity. In an essay on William Carlos Williams, Marianne Moore remarks:

A child is a 'portent'; a poet is a portent. As has been said of certain theological architecture, it is the peculiarity of certain poetic architecture that the foundations are ingeniously supported by the superstructure. The child [quoting from Williams]

> Sleeps fast till his might
> Shall be piled
> Sinew on sinew.

This notion illustrates both the subject and procedure proper to "The Hero," which goes on to tell us that Cincinatus, Regulus, and Pilgrim are also vexed *and* vexing. Hope, which is not hope "until all ground for hope has vanished," is praised, and the tolerance for human error that is necessary in the meantime. These are problems or solutions related to a later stage of fear than the most primitive childhood fears—the spooks and misplaced parental blessings of the first stanzas. They are fears related to one's desire for, and apprehensions about, what is *appropriate* to human behavior and what is not.

What sort of fight are you willing to put up for the spirit? Is a pilgrimage necessary? To what extent can you plague your friends by talking about it? Moore raises questions of socialization, of manner, of choosing when and how to assert one's self and when to be silent. One must learn about possibilities of failure and intolerance in oneself and in others, and how to deal with them as a "hero" would, "having to go slow . . . tired but hopeful."

The poem jumps suddenly to the present, and to the questions and entanglements of a particular-general discovery:

> The decorous frock-coated Negro
> by the grotto [who]

> answers the fearless sightseeing hobo
>   who asks the man she's with, what's this,
>   what's that, where's Martha
>   buried, "Gen-ral Washington
>   there; his lady, here"; speaking
>   as if in a play—not seeing her; with a
>   sense of human dignity
> and reverence for mystery, standing like the shadow
> of the willow.

The crux of the poem is contained in this grotesque stanza, in the very discrepancy between the innocent omens on its surface and a profound need underlying them, the need to discover true even if uninnocent origins. The "hobo" is a wanderer like Pilgrim, mentioned earlier, but a wanderer importantly with no destination in mind. She (and her gender is somewhat of a surprise, adding disgrace if anything to the description of her) is "fearless." She has a lot to learn about history and herself. The "hero" is, on the other hand, full of fears and rightly so. The casualness of the female "hobo" is in direct contrast to the decorousness of the "frock-coated Negro." Although he is obviously the costumed and "official" guide to the place of sightseeing, the hobo ignores him and asks her also-ignorant companion to explain the historic grave. She wants to know where Martha is buried. She is, although perhaps touchingly ignorant of the fact, looking for her mother, the mother of her confusing country. The guide points out the positions of both Washingtons. The irony is implicit and dramatic. The Negro plays the role of guide at the site of America's buried parentage, its primal scene, its conception of "freedom." This is the very conception by which he has, like an unequally blessed son, been made to suffer inhumanly. He is not blind, but he doesn't look at the hobo. *He* knows the undeviating headstones; *he* knows where the spirit of freedom and equality is buried, lost. And he has too much dignity to stare at the undignified curiosity of the staring woman. His personal dislike for her, for her irreverence for mystery, for the superficiality of her wanting to peek at the position of the parents in their last bed, is an heroic dislike. The hero must realize loss and mystery. He stands like the shadow of the willow because the willow is a traditional symbol of loss and mourning. He is a knower who *is* what he knows.

Here, strangely and without power, are all the themes of loss, mystery, kingship, magic, marriage, and vision that Moore explores separately and together in all the major poems of her life. They are deeply buried, but they are there as surely as the plumet basilisk is alive there in his cocoon of living green, and it is the business of the hero to discover them for herself. Not only must she bear the knowledge of the burial place herself, but the ignorance of other people, which can be just as painful. The mysterious noises and metaphysical terror of the hero's introduction to the world make up her primal scene. She may be curious but she knows that according to the rules of a civilized society she may not look at some things. The hobo would see literally where the parents lie in relation to each other, but hers is not the truest curiosity or the truest discovery. Yet she is on her way, making the only sort of pilgrimage she can think of to make. She may be on her way to becoming a hero, and her travels in this direction are part of the mystery. Perhaps all heroes start as hoboes. The accomplished hero will allow all the mystery, and discover reverence.

"Moses would not be grandson to Pharaoh" announces the last stanza of "The Hero." A pattern of life emerges. We move back and forth, but generally along a route that takes us from an individual history of conceptions and preconceptions through familial, social, secular, and political consciousness of origins and ends, to a preoccupation with religious origins and ends. Moses presents the biblical precedent for discerning one's own proper heritage—not always apparent—and for leading one's people to freedom. What is chosen and what is fated are inseparable. Moses, too, was a pilgrim and a guide to sacred places. He had power as the adopted grandson of the Pharaoh but he rejected the superficial flamboyance and the slavery of Egypt, attractive as it might have been (see "The Jerboa"), in order to be able to lead his people to a land that was to be their own, his own, free and holy, a land of selfhood for god's "chosen" people.

A hero is chosen for her ability to choose rightly, to know what she does and doesn't like and to act firmly in uncertain circumstances. The hero must have what Keats defines as "negative capability," "that is when man is capable of being in uncertainities, Mysteries, doubts, without any irritable reaching after fact & reason" (letter to George and Thomas Keats, 21, 27 (?) December 1817). This is what the visionary hero must do, or try to do, on whatever level she can. Moses was not sightseeing in Egypt or traveling for pleasure; he had a vision relating to his people's very survival, a real and moral, socially and religiously binding mission. The hero is

> not out
> seeing a sight but the rock
> crystal thing to see—the startling El Greco
> brimming with inner light—that
> covets nothing that it has let go. This then you may know
> as the hero.

The hero is both seer and a sight to be seen. She looks at that which has inner light and brims with it herself. One is always to some extent identified with what one looks at with greatest attention. In "When I Buy Pictures," Marianne Moore makes this point very beautifully by qualifying the title. She is not *really* looking to buy them, she tells us, but, "what is closer to the truth/ when I look at that of which I may regard myself as the imaginary possessor." Looking hard equals imaginary ownership. In the poem about buying pictures Moore tells us that, whatever the thing looked at happens to be,

it must be "lit with piercing glances into the life of things";
it must acknowledge the spiritual forces which have made it.

Marianne Moore's poems do this, as they critically evaluate what they see.
Rock crystal is the epitome; it may stand for the object of all vision, as the
formation of the faces of a crystal are governed by a "spiritual" or invisible
force made visible, and transparently so. Its piercing glances must penetrate
the hero as her glances penetrate it. It is spiritual exchange with the world
that the hero, retaining her heritage of childhood instinct, her curiosity, and
her freedom of choice, must seek. She must find, in order to survive and converse with her vision, her personal style. When the hobo renounces her aimless and unholy freedoms in favor of predilected and reverent ones, the hero
in her is home free.

Marianne Moore's conception of this hero is not unlike that of Wallace
Stevens' hero in "Examination of the Hero in Time of War." His vision complements hers:

> The hero is a feeling, a man seen
> As if in seeing we saw our feeling
> In the object seen. . . .
>
> (XII)

> A thousand crystals' chiming voices,
> Like the shiddow-shaddow of lights revolving,
> To momentary ones, are blended,
> In hymns, through iridescent changes,
> Of the apprehending of the hero.
>
> (XIV)

THE POET'S APPREHENSION:

Rock Crystal

> *Contagious gem of virtuosity*
> *make visible, mentality.*
> *Your jewels of mobility*

> *reveal*
> *and veil*
> *a peacock tail.*
> ("Arthur Mitchell")

The rock crystal is the thing to see, but seeing it, in any of its possible forms, does not necessarily solve the essential mystery; there will always be new questions about the spiritual force that made it. Gems and gem-clarity, or glass and ice related to gems, have an important place in Marianne Moore's hierarchy of imagery because they are the physical relatives of the elusive "rock crystal thing." Their presence in a poem indicates something hidden as cunningly as something revealed. The "gem of virtuosity" displayed by the dancer Arthur Mitchell reveals *and* veils the mystery, the "peacock tail" with all its seen unseeing eyes. In "An Octopus" the poet speaks of the bears' den

> composed of calcium gems and alabaster pillars,
> topaz, tourmaline crystals and amethyst and quartz,
> their den is somewhere else, concealed in the confusion
> of blue forests thrown together with marble and jasper and agate
> as if whole quarries had been dynamited.

We see, with brilliant imaginative clarity, at the same time as we do not see, the secret place of the bears. Marguerite Young, describing Marianne Moore's conversational brilliance, remarks on the same sort of teasing confusion of vision:[1]

> She speaks in quick, enigmatic sentences which strip away the flesh of thought and leave the bones bare and shining, so that suddenly you feel that you are seeing into the secret heart of things. You are mistaken, however, for soon you realize a further complexity—there is no secret heart, no simple solution, but another problem, fastidious and strange.

The sea appears in Moore's poems to join in this sort of conversation. It is clear, formal, and gemlike in some contexts and inherently mysterious and uncontrollable in others. Her sea, like her language in general, is one in which "jade and the rock crystal course about in solution" ("The Novices").

The park of "An Octopus" that contains all animal life and qualities of mind, including the ponies with "glass eyes," is "a glassy octopus symmetrically pointed" as rock crystal or diamond. In "An Egyptian Pulled Glass Bottle in the Shape of a Fish" the sea itself is imagined as glass, "not brittle but/ intense . . . held up for us to see" and the glass scales of the fish protect its mystery by deflecting the sun's "sword." Melanchthon is protected also by glass, "this piece of black glass through which no light/ can filter," which is at the same time an embodiment of the elephant's hard integrity. The "Four Quartz Crystal Clocks" are like "clear ice"; they are a vehicle of truth and accuracy, yet the origin of such truth and accuracy is still a deep mystery. In "England" we are asked to admire "the East with its . . . rock crystal and its imperturbability," both mysteries to us despite the clarity of their existences. The chameleon, magical and truthful to its surroundings, adapter to the sensible world, is seen as gemlike: "Fire laid upon/ an emerald as long as/ the Dark King's massy/ one." And the jellyfish is admired for its gem-likeness:

> Visible, invisible
>   a fluctuating charm
> an amber-tinctured amethyst
>   inhabits it.

The poet says to Molière, "of chiseled setting and black-opalescent dye,/ you were the jewelry of sense." And to William Yeats:

> that it pays,
> to cut gems even in these conscience-less days;

> but the jewel that always
> outshines ordinary jewels, is your praise.
>   ("To William Butler Yeats on Tagore")

One cannot easily generalize about the meaning of jewels and the crystal-like substance in Moore's poems, but these images do all share an important quality, and that is that they both represent and preserve a moral integrity in the thing looked at or in the eyes that are doing the looking. Praise, good sense, punctuality, tough individuality, all partake of a rock-crystal nature. This is why the "sparkling chips of rock/ . . . crushed down" by the steamroller ("To a Steam Roller") are so pitiable, the steamroller so invidious. One must *make* crystals, not break them, participate in or at least acknowledge the invisible power that makes them; and, with heroic vision, one must see them whole, as infrangible revelations.

T. S. Eliot, in *The Use of Poetry and the Use of Criticism*, remarks that "[poetry] may make us from time to time a little more aware of the deeper, unnamed feelings which form the substratum of our being, to which we rarely penetrate; for our lives are mostly a constant evasion of ourselves, and an evasion of the visible and sensible world."[2] Of course, it may be pointed out also that a poem, by seeing and hearing one thing very intensely may defend against the seeing and hearing of something else, and thus become only another evasion. The rock crystal and all its luminous relatives in the poetry of Marianne Moore, including all the fastidiously brilliant pictures, animals, and words she would possess and share, perform both tasks—that of heightening our perceptions of a thing and that of perceiving itself—though she may be at the same time deflecting our interest from the deepest and most secret responses of her self. She deflects our literal understanding so well in some cases that nothing remains beyond "the satire upon curiosity in which no more is discernible/ than the intensity of the mood" ("When I Buy Pictures"). In practice, she sees nothing wrong in this; in fact, she seems to enjoy it.

The strangeness of Marianne Moore's vision is translated into strange combinations of images. The light she absorbs from things and throws back on them is deflected through a highly personal verbal medium and sometimes emerges "like violets by Dürer/ only darker" ("Then the Ermine"). Yet, in studying the consistencies and inconsistencies of such reflections and deflections throughout a poet's work, it is possible to come upon some of the invisible laws, the spiritual forces, the principles that are hid in style, and to acknowledge their acknowledgments. Marianne Moore quotes Howard Nemerov (in answer to one of the questions posed by him in a written interview[3]) on the subject of vision and strangeness:

> Strangeness is a quality belonging inseparably to language and vision. . . . language is a special extension of the power of seeing, inasmuch as it can make visible not only the already visible world but through it the invisible world of relations and affinities.

Moore goes on to say that perhaps "creativeness" is the closest we can come to a definition of "soul." "Creativeness" is at the heart of the hero or the piece of art brimming with inner light that "covets nothing that it has let go." Both speech and light go gladly out of the hero's body to join what is most real and significant to her in the world. Presbyter John, celebrated in "His Shield," is this kind of hero. Surrounded by and partaking of wealth, both spiritual and material, "his shield/ was his humility. . . . he revealed/ a formula

safer than/ an armorer's: the power of relinquishing/ what one would keep;
that is freedom."

An early poem, "Is Your Town Nineveh?" is related to "The Hero" in
its progression from fears and dislikes to a vision of the light of art and the
world outside oneself:

> Why so desolate?
>   in phantasmogoria about fishes
>   what disgusts you? Could
>   not all personal upheaval in
>   the name of freedom, be tabooed?
>
> Is it Nineveh
>   and are you Jonah
>   in the sweltering east wind of your wishes?
>   I myself have stood
>   there by the aquarium, looking
>   at the Statue of Liberty.

In the poem "Light Is Speech" Moore illustrates the title with "free frank impartial sunlight" and other sorts of verbal light, concluding:

> The word France means
> enfranchisement; means one who can
> 'animate whoever thinks of her.'

The Statue of Liberty, holding up a light which implies a freedom of speech,
is for Moore a symbol of freedom not only from external oppression but
from internal and personal oppression as well. The depression that motivates
the poem "Is Your Town Nineveh?" resents "personal upheaval" by the
aquarium. It is a whale of a depression, and it is not clear that looking at the
Statue of Liberty brings any relief.

Speaking of "phantasmagoria about fishes," we are reminded of the
awful injuries and losses and the hardening against them which underlie
Moore's poem "The Fish." There is felt loss and fear of loss in the first and
next-to-last stanzas of "The Hero" also. Light of art, of words and spirit, is
the only antidote to enslavement by personal as well as impersonal forces.
Oppressive wishes must give way to the fulfilled wishes of dreams, with a
dream's faith in its own reality. Poems can express faith in such fulfillment,
and should. We must get out of ourselves, out of the confining aquarium, give

ourselves away, in order to be ourselves, the possessors of rock crystal integrity "too tough for infraction" ("Efforts of Affection").

Marianne Moore is not an original thinker. Her "message" of freedom through sacrifice could not be more commonplace, as she herself would agree. Yet she may make it strike us with an original force because it is arrived at in the poems themselves only through difficulty. It is hard for her to sacrifice silence. Then again, it is hard for her to sacrifice speech. Sacrifice alternates with sacrifice, and the freedom with which we are able to put them together, reclaiming both speech and silence "in/ the name of freedom" and as a taboo against psychical oppression, is the freedom of Moore's verse. We may take freedoms with her verses because she has given them to us. She covets nothing that she has let go.

What is commonplace as idea is not necessarily commonplace as a personally held and acted-upon conviction; in fact, commonplace, as Marianne Moore embraces it, is rare. It is for the intensely personal valuation that Moore has performed upon the common places as well as the exotic places of the world that we feel gratitude and enlightenment, if we are able to feel them. "In Distrust of Merits" shows us commonplace abhorrence of war and the Self who participates by not participating, yet it has a felt intensity, a "mountainous wave" of unconscious fastidiousness "that makes us who look, know depth." "He/ sees deep and is glad, who/ accedes to mortality" ("What Are Years?"). It is an easy thing to *say,* but difficult to *see.*

Moore's essay "Humility, Concentration, and Gusto" ends with a motto of importance to anyone interested in those three famous qualities of hers: "The thing is to see the vision and not deny it; to care and admit that we do." To admit to the self, to admit to the core of the self and others—everything— is perhaps the hardest thing. To admit that the hardest thing—the devalued commonplace—is true, is to see the hardest thing, the rock crystal thing, invisible in its prevalence, powerful with the "power of the invisible."

THE CRITIC'S APPREHENSION:

Rock Crystal

The critic should know what he likes.
("Picking and Choosing")

The poem "The Hero" originally appeared with "The Steeple-Jack" and "The Student," a trilogy designated "Part of a Novel, Part of a Play, Part of a

Poem." The student, we are told, is "a variety of hero" because of his pa-
tience, his willingness to learn when there is no reward, "too reclusive for/
some things to touch/ him, not because he/ has no feeling but because he has
so much." Whether this is an accurate description of students in general is
irrelevant, for it is an accurate description of Marianne Moore and of her
idea of one variety of "hero." In "The Steeple-Jack" there is a college student
named Ambrose whose vocation is to sit on the hillside of the town

> with his not-native books and hat
> and [see] boats
>
> at sea progress white and rigid as if in
> a groove. Liking an elegance of which
> the source is not bravado, he knows by heart the antique
> sugar-bowl shaped summerhouse of
> interlacing slats, and the pitch
> of the church
>
> spire, not true, from which a man in scarlet lets
> down a rope.

The student-hero is a quiet connoisseur of order. He does not see boats as an
opportunity for adventure, but as small white rigid specks moving in the
"groove" of an also rigid sea. He has no pretenses to loud and swaggering false
heroism, bravado, but is content to sit and memorize the details of an antique
summerhouse. His heroism is in his receptivity, his unboastful rejection of
chaos.

The student who sees everything notices that the church steeple's star
has been tilted by a storm, but it is the business of a different variety of hero
to fix it. The steeple-jack climbs beside a danger sign to straighten and gild
the town's symbol of hope and security. The steeple-jack's work is physical,
its meaning metaphysical. The student's cast of mind is metaphysical, yet he
studies only the physical surface of the landscape. The poet, the hero-hero,
moves between these other two, active steeple-jack and passive student. Her
business is to correct all extremes of vision of blindness, to see directly to the
heart of rock-crystal and to communicate it directly. She is not "out seeing a
sight" like the student, nor is she identified with the structure of order as the
steeple-jack is. She is free to comment on both, her language one with the
"free frank impartial sunlight" ("Light Is Speech") that falls on both. She is
qualified by her instinct for danger and by an instinct for truth. She stands

somewhere between the name and the warning posted near the church portico.

"The passion for setting people right is in itself an afflictive disease" ("Snakes, Mongooses . . ."). Marianne Moore tells us this, but the diagnosis is simply one of the symptoms. The cure (and only a partial one at that) is in silence, in restraint, or in "distaste which takes no credit to itself" ("Snakes, Mongooses . . ."). This last is a difficult if not impossible attitude, yet concentration and humility often do achieve it for Marianne Moore. It is interesting to note how full her first volume of poems (1921) is of nasty caricature—"To Be Liked by You Would Be a Calamity," for example. Her early uncollected magazine publications also contain a number of agitated caricatures. She kept in the canon only "To a Steam Roller," "Those Various Scalpels," "Pedantic Literalist," and poems like "In These Days of Hard Trying" and "The Monkeys," and notably "Marriage," which although they contain bits of caricature and vehement distaste for certain qualities in people, do not take too much credit to themselves. The author in fact implicates her own methods in them, often as not, showing a personal understanding that has earned the right to judge.

Moore's harshest criticisms and strongest dislikes are often directed at picky criticism and unwillingness to praise. If we wanted to partake of nastiness ourselves, we would say this is because she was afraid her own product at times could not withstand criticism or earn wholehearted praise. She would try to ignore us; it is fair enough, as we are also invited to ignore her. Her shield is her humility. If we do not ignore her, it is because we feel the integrity behind the poems despite obscurity, willfulness, pain, platitude, and the rest.

Heroism demands an ironic vision that can absorb the paradox of not liking to dislike, that can find humor as well as seriousness in the "heroic" griffoned-in-the-dark statement: "Like does not like like that is obnoxious" ("The Pangolin"). The hero has a hard time making herself clear, her armor is always getting in the way, disguising her meaning, insisting too much on itself; yet if the hero has a single virtue it is knowing clearly what she likes and where she will go with her liking. The critic should know what *she* likes.

Sometimes one's distaste is mild and one is predisposed to tolerance, as Moore is in "People's Surroundings," where the poet, not enamoured of the fussiness of rich people's houses, says simply, "One has one's preferences in the matter of bad furniture/ and this is not one's choice." And a critic might say that one has one's preferences in the matter of obscure poems, and this is not one's choice. "Blessed Is the Man" begins emphatically with the statement that he is blessed "who does not sit in the seat of the scoffer—/ the man

who does not denigrate, depreciate, denunciate." But if the poem does not
mean to *denunciate* "brazen authors, downright soiled and downright spoiled
. . . the old quasi-modish counterfeit," it is hard to say exactly what the poem
does mean to say about them. "Blessed the unaccommodating man," and
Marianne Moore is blessed for this. And "blessed the geniuses who know that
egomania is not a duty"; she is blessed again.

The hero must perform "The Labours of Hercules" in a world that is
full of people who need to be improved: "to *popularize* the mule . . . to
persuade one of austere taste . . . to *persuade* those self-wrought Midases of
brains/ whose fourteen-carat ignorance aspires to rise in value . . . to *teach* the
bard . . . to *prove* to the high priests of caste . . . to *teach* the patron-saints-to-
atheists . . . to *convince* snake-charming controversialists." (italics mine). Not
a model of tolerance, often in fact banging you over the head with it, the
hero is a rhetorician.

In the animal poems, in poems about people's surroundings, works of
art and artists, in the long rhetorical essay called "Marriage," Marianne Moore
tries to set a world of manners and forms in order. The hero-rhetorician may
fail, as Daniel Webster did, to bring things into final harmony, yet despite
personal failing, he was a variety of hero who could see both sides of a problem. We may feel in the end that Marianne Moore herself has failed to bring
the poem "Marriage" together. Still, she has seen all sides of her argument,
and she never claimed it was a poem—just some "statements that took [her]
fancy which [she] tried to arrange plausibly." What can you say to that kind
of rhetoric? It is economical and heroic, to say the least, and most.

Marianne Moore's work is a lifelong exposition of paradox, and no
matter how much careful observation she lavishes on the objects that illustrate her various paradoxes, no matter how much precise illusion is given
shape through her disarming rhetoric, the paradoxes still remain and are always interesting. Perhaps paradox itself is the rock crystal thing that the hero
is seen to see. It is accuracy and mystery well married; it is naked in its objective transparence, but armored in the untouchable axial law that made it.

The desire for the purity of the rock crystal is an impulse toward criticism that is not self-congratulatory or other-abasing. "In the Days of Prismatic Color" presents a wish for such critical simplicity. It speaks of the days
"not . . . of Adam and Eve, but when Adam was alone," for solitude is a pre-
requisite of the most accurate perception. It was then that "there was no
smoke and color was fine . . . because of its originality . . . plain to see and
account for." The poem goes on to lament that "it is no longer that"; that
complexity is a "pestilence" bewildering us with the "fallacy that insistence/
is the measure of achievement and that all/ truth must be dark." The task of

the hero as critic is to make her way through the false complexities of the world and her fear of them to the rock crystal thing.

William Carlos Williams in his essay on Moore remarks:

> Local color . . . is merely a variant serving to locate an acme point of white penetration. The intensification of desire toward this purity is . . . a quality present in much or even all that Miss Moore does. . . . The unessential is put rapidly aside as the eye searches between for illumination.[4]

We may not always feel this very clearly in the poems of Marianne Moore, because in their complementary intensifications of desire for accuracy, they present us with complicated knots of imagery, of local color and self-qualifying language, "yet with x-ray-like inquisitive intensity upon it, the surfaces go back" ("People's Surroundings"). "In these noncommittal, personal-impersonal expressions of appearance, the eye knows what to skip" ("People's Surroundings"). Even if the eye has a hard time occasionally—getting through all the appearances, the verbal foliage—we know that the surface is at most "noncommittal"; the real commitment is to truth, and truth that is something deeper and more permanent than art. Kenneth Burke notes:

> Truth in art is not the discovery of facts, not an addition to human knowledge in the scientific sense of the word. It is, rather, the exercise of human propriety, the formulation of symbols which rigidify our sense of poise and rhythm.[5]

It is to this truth of style that Marianne Moore is committed, this external propriety and poise and grace, but there is a "spiritual poise" ever beneath the surfaces; "Melanchthon" asks where the center is to be found, acknowledging that external poise is centered in pride. Marianne Moore's answer, in all the poems, would be that spiritual poise is to be found in the truth that informs our judgments, and our symbols of value on the deepest level. Likes, dislikes, or divinations—it is something given.

> Truth is no Apollo
> Belvedere, no formal thing. The wave may go over it if
> it likes.
> Know that it will be there when it says,
> "I shall be there when the wave has gone by."
> ("In the Days of Prismatic Color")

The hero as critic, as sightseer or knight or artist, is ideally solitary and free. Her solitude, however, is not entirely her own, as it must be dedicated to the truth of relationships and affections in the world at large. Her freedom is in "relinquishing what one would keep" ("His Shield"), in coveting nothing that she has let go, "whose faith is different from possessiveness—of a kind not framed by 'things which do appear'—" ("Blessed Is the Man"). Like the sea in a chasm, she finds her continuing in her surrendering ("What Are Years?"), yet there are things she must not surrender, such as her essential solitude, her mystery, and her armor. "Rather dead than spotted."

Hannah Arendt sees alienation as taking two forms, flight from the earth into the universe and flight from the earth into the self.[6] Marianne Moore's hero knows both sorts of alienation, one escaping to the abstraction of motto and axiom—the universal truth that can withstand any temporary destructive wave, and the other escaping into the mysterious armor of the self, the integrity of a very personal vision. Both extremes, however, are importantly mediated by the earth between them, the things which *do* appear and in their own objectivity allow the hero to form judgments, to organize rhetorically both her metaphysical and personal-spiritual visions. She can always return to the earth for substantiation of her self.

Erich Neumann describes, with great relevance to our conclusions about Moore's hero, the relationship between the creative man's commitments to the community of the world and those to his own private vision:

> The creative man's bond with the root and foundation of the collectivity is perhaps most beautifully expressed in Hölderlin's words: "The thoughts of the communal spirit come to a quiet end in the poet's soul." But the creative man's product as part of his development, is always bound up with his "mere individuality," his childhood, his personal experience, his ego's tendencies toward love and hate, his heights and his shadow. For the alertness of his consciousness permits the creative man more than the average man to "know himself" and "suffer from himself." His lasting dependence on his self fortifies him against seduction by a collective ego ideal, but makes him all the more sensitive to the realization that he is inadequate to himself, to the "self." Through this suffering from his shadow, from the wounds that have been open since childhood—these are the gates through which flows the stream of the unconscious, yet the ego never ceases to suffer from them—the creative man arrives at the humility that prevents him from overestimating his ego, because he knows that he is too much at the mercy of his wholeness, of the unknown self within him.[7]

Hercules and Jonah, the minor prophets, Ireland, Daniel Webster, dancers and baseball players and scientists, Leonardo and Presbyter John: all these figures have a heroism in common: they have ways of making order—physical or spiritual—out of disorder. They are more closely related than is apparent when they are seen, as they are in Moore's poems, as figures who have been both brave and defensive, explorative in their self-expressions, yet circumscribed by certain necessary tasks. Heroes manage to stand out as individuals in a world that is crushing of individuality, yet their lives are dedicated to the community also, of art, politics, morals. They manage to endure and to teach how to endure despite confusions of sense and shortages of affection. They know how to fight, how to armor themselves with, and in, skill, how to disarm with honesty and precision of action. In short, they have *style*; and it is a style of being in the world, and not any one heroic act that defines them. For animals heroism consists in merely being. For women and men it consists also in seeing and in being seen, in hearing and in being heard, in knowing how to take defeats and where to seek victories consistent with one's image of oneself.

There is only one poem called by Marianne Moore "The Hero," but in effect all the poems she wrote might claim this as some sort of subtitle. It is telling that the hero of the poem "The Hero" is an anonymous character, for the hero can be anybody at any time who shares the hero's devotion to vision and to the "rock crystal thing." Heroes have pasts and futures. This is clear from the poem; all her past sensations gather in her, preparing her with responses to her fathering fate, her apprehensions, her convictions. We must acknowledge the value of childhood and of limitations in general, turn the wishes born of both into actions. These actions are heroic when they express both the personal desire of the hero, fulfilling some need in her, and connect also with the desires of a community of potential heroes. Thus the wish and the limitation become a dance, a poem, a Brooklyn bridge or icosasphere, Bach's Solfegietto, or a knight in quest of modest armor.

The hero is not uniformly successful (this would defeat the knowledge gained through defeat), but she is uniformly herself and brimming with a light constantly her own. Animals do this naturally; the hero learns from them, and the hero learns from the examples of other heroes by imaginative identification, by a personal understanding of the work of the hero, an ability to judge with objectivity and love. The hero says again and again to herself what Marianne Moore says at the end of "In the Days of Prismatic Color": "I shall be there when the wave has gone by." "Truth" will be there, with its own style of being there, and with its own responding nature. This is the truth, informal but strong, of the hero of all Moore's quests.

In Marianne Moore's world, as in most other people's worlds, there is no heroism without efforts, specifically efforts of affection, because the world is basically a disaffecting place, a disordered and disturbing place. One who can forge style, honor, and conscience out of such a given mess of materials, who can, moreover, move comfortably between the precisions and specificities of objects and the abstractions which pertain to one's self, is heroic. Marianne Moore does not always seem to move comfortably between the extremes of particulars and abstractions in her poems; she does not always succeed in pulling an order and a clarity out of a bag of disorder and obscurity, yet the efforts of affection for the world and for the other minds in it are always in evidence, and a great amount of heroism is to be found in those efforts themselves, just as a great amount of poetry is to be found in unconscious fastidiousness. This is true even when a poem as a whole is judged to be something less than whole.

Marianne Moore may be seen as a knight set upon finding the Grail in a waste land of letters. The meaning of her particular Grail is meaning itself, a vessel into which the self may be safely placed, from which the self can safely speak. It is the knight, the one of high ideals who *acts,* who goes out of her way to find and conquer the rumored dragon, that carries home the prize of meaning. She is willing to fight because she trusts her powers of defense. She is willing sometimes to retreat because she understands the death that resides in too much aggressiveness. She is willing simply to talk when the solitude of battle or retreat is too painful.

I have noted the recurrence of the image of a king or of kingship in Moore's poems, but it is to be noted also that the king is never the hero by virtue of kingship alone. The king is more often a person in absentia. "The king is dead" ("No Swan So Fine"), or he is at the bottom of Guatavita Lake ("The Plumet Basilisk"), or he is, as he is to any working knight, somewhere distant, at the place of the quest's origin and the place to which the knight hopes to return. The king is a father, an origin, or a Father, an end, that we know only through rumor or on faith. He does not play a real part in the acts of the hero, or in the poems of Marianne Moore, but we feel the presence of some high or far mind to which the poems must be submitted for approval, a sort of ur-editor.

The king may represent the spiritual poise within us whose center we cannot locate because it is essentially everywhere, but whose presence is felt as possibility. The circumference of "spiritual poise" is of course nowhere; there is always another circle of reference to be drawn upon in any figure of reality. It is between the extremes of an inner center and an infinity of complexions outside the self, that the style and the heroism of Moore's poems move. She is ever self-conscious and ever self-effacing. We can never hope to locate the exact center of this self of which she and we are conscious, nor can we begin to set limits on just what in the miraculous abundance of the world her self will see fit to take to itself. There is a mechanism of "picking and choosing" that activates any poem of hers (or anyone's), but the mechanism itself is dark. The world from which this particular self can pick and choose is infinite, or infinitely light, including everything that can be seen or imagined and any combination of these.

Unconscious fastidiousness is the critical apparatus of the hero, and it would be far less than realistic to demand consistency from it as well as honesty. In Marianne Moore's comment on Cummings in the Cummings issue of the *Harvard Wake* (Spring 1946, #5) she mentions the "heroic" aspect of his work. Here is her contribution to the issue in its entirety:

> E. E. Cummings is a concentrate of titanic significance, "a posi-
> tive character"; and only ingenuousness could attempt to suggest
> in a word, the "heroic" aspect of his paintings, his poems, and his
> resistances. He does not make aesthetic mistakes.

He may make other kinds of mistakes, but it is not her duty to mention those. "Positiveness" has a great deal to do with heroism. The following comment expands this idea with respect to Cummings in Moore's review of *One Times One*:

> for poetry is a flowering and its truth is "a cry of a whole soul,"
> not dogma; it is a positiveness that is joy, that we have in bird-
> songs and should have in ourselves; it is a "cry of alive with a trill
> like until" and is a poet's secret, "for his joy is more than joy."
> Defined by this book in what it says of life in general "such is a
> poet and shall be and is."[8]

Such "heroism," such will to survive, "is exhausting, yet/ it contradicts a greed" ("He 'Digesteth Harde Yron'"); as if praise could, if strong and truthful enough, assuage the guilt of acquisition, of possession. Life itself is acquisition, and as Stevens notes in his *Adagia,* "Happiness is an acquisition." To the extent that something is acquired it also can be lost; one needs to praise and to see continually and with accuracy in order not to lose the gift and the vision.

The poem "Saint Nicholas," although not perhaps one of Moore's best

and most memorable poems, does show particularly well her desire to have
and to praise, a method of having and a method of praising that are her own.
Her method of having is to be given; this poem is in the form of a letter to
Santa Claus full of elaborate praise for each thing imaginatively requested.
She asks first for a chameleon:

> might I, if you can find it, be given
> a chameleon with tail
> that curls like a watch spring; and vertical
> on the body—including the face—pale
> tiger-stripes, about seven;
> (the melanin in the skin
> having been shaded from the sun by thin
> bars; the spinal dome
> beaded along the ridge
> as if it were platinum)?

All she asks really is that Saint Nicholas be able to *imagine* giving her such a
thing. If he were God, certainly he would be able to make such a chameleon
from her instructions. She realizes that no chameleon might be forthcoming
(a modest precaution) and delineates her second choice with as much precision as the first. It is something to wear, a modest armor to which she has
given a great amount of careful thought. Might she have a suit of *qiviut*, she
inquires, and with it "a taslon shirt, the drip-dry fruit/ of research second to
none;/ sewn, I hope, by Excello." Her demands are exacting, the motivation
admittedly childlike, the gifts somehow prepaid by the intensity of her wish
and her interest in their construction. The gift of creation itself would seem
to be best repaid by a kind of re-creation. Moore's re-creations are modest
and unconsciously fastidious; they represent a proper mode of action for an
uninsistent and contemplative hero.

The requests that the hero makes of the saint may be more fantastic,
though; finally she realizes she might as well ask for a miracle surpassing nature and technology:

> The moon should come here. Let him
> make the trip down, spread on my dark floor some dim
> marvel, and if a success
> that I stoop to pick up and wear,
> I could ask nothing more.

"Saint Nicholas," a late poem, asks for armor that is less materially tough than the elephant-skin of "Melanchthon" or the "mirror-of-steel uninsistence" of "Armor's Undermining Modesty," but more spiritually, magically impenetrable. The taslon shirt also has magic, and her last request, for a post-card reproduction of St. Hubert "in velvet and tense with restraint" is for an armor of miracle and spirit. This St. Hubert was "startled into a saint" by his vision of "a stag with figure entwined." The saint and hero are one and they are startled into themselves by a vision, of rock crystal, of scientific accuracy of construction, of divinity suddenly emerging from the forest of the common world.

The hero is entitled to ask a lot from the world; her asking is exhausting, and her vision is; but it contradicts greed as it fulfills a real desire for experience including experience of the self and the deepest wishes of the self —to be given gifts of modern science, of nature, and of spirituality. Poetry's or heroism's "truth is 'a cry of a whole soul,' not dogma." "External poise" and "spiritual poise" may finally be seen as having the same center and same exterior, both humbly and well armored in a moonlight cloak or saint's velvet lifted from a post card. These things come strangely from the world and go back into it strangely, as poems. The hero is medium.

As medium, the hero is critic, ushering her subjects from the world into art and from art back into the world. Her life is a continual allegory. The criticism itself that she may provide, her particular values, her subjects and objects, are not the message of her work as much as she herself is. She pays for the gift of creation, as has been seen, by herself creating, or by creating her self. Marianne Moore, in a review of T. S. Eliot's *Sacred Wood,* speaks of the close connection between creation and criticism:

> in what it *[The Sacred Wood]* reveals as a definition of criticism it is especially rich. The connection between criticism and creation is very close; criticism naturally deals with creation but it is equally true that criticism inspires creation. A genuine achievement in criticism is an achievement in creation; as Mr. Eliot says, "it is to be expected that the critic and the creative artist would frequently be the same person." Much light is thrown on the problems of art in Mr. Eliot's citing of Aristotle as an example of the perfect critic—perfect by reason of his having the scientific mind. Too much cannot be said for the necessity in the artist, of exact science.[9]

We shall always come back to "science" in the work of Marianne Moore, because science was to her a method of knowledge indispensable to her comprehensively evaluative mode of poetry. Moral sense may be uppermost, but it must be informed with the greatest possible exactitude about the state of things in the physical world. In order to make spiritual acknowledgment of creation, it must make technical acknowledgments—how it was done, how it is to be done. This technique links the past and the future as well as the matter and the spirit of all worldly phenomena. If "science" is accurate observation of the world's developing, temporary balance, and eventual dissolution, and "prophecy" the accurate observation of those processes on a spiritual level, then poetry, if it is to contain the truest of all observations, must put them together. The confusion is accurate and necessary. Confusion, submitted to poetry by unconfusion, confusion affectionately admitted, leads to the development and expression of the whole soul. It must acknowledge the desolation and loss described in such poems as "The Fish" as well as the "plan/ deep set within the heart of man" ecstasy of "Sun." It must see how the pangolin walks strangely on the edges of his feet and how the icosasphere is welded together. It must see:

> Sun and moon and day and night and man and beast
>   each with a splendor
>   which man in all his vileness cannot
>   set aside; each with an excellence!

("The Pangolin")

The hero, at the mercy of both her "efforts of affection" and her efforts of integration, is at the mercy of her own peculiar fate, to be drawn out of herself to observe and judge, and alternately withdrawn into herself again, also to observe and judge. Her fate is to keep these outward and inward expressions of herself balanced and integral. This is where verse becomes fate, where "foiled explosiveness becomes a kind of prophet" ("Then the Ermine"). Fate, like all the paradoxes contained in Marianne Moore's poetry, is irresolvable or unexplodable, because it contains both origin and end. We cannot see both at once. Howard Nemerov has remarked:

> Sometimes it appears to candid reflexion that great works of art give no meaning, but give instead, like the world of nature and history itself, materials whose arrangement suggests a tropism toward meaning, order and form; give, often in a tantalizing way the prospect of meaning somewhere beyond, beyond.[10]

Marianne Moore's best poems—"The Plumet Basilisk," "Marriage," "The Pangolin," among others—seem to do this, as does her work when thought of as a whole, the expression of a whole life of searching for particular illuminations, for the Grail of American letters and American conscience.

In the poem "By Disposition of Angels" she speaks of "these unparticularities praise cannot violate . . . how by darkness a star is perfected." And we feel that, as often as not, it is the darkness, the silences, the freely admitted mysteries surrounding the observable world or the necessarily elliptical poem that most nearly perfect them. "Foiled explosiveness" is "a perfecter and so a concealer" of our fate, of ourselves *from* ourselves.

> Mysteries expound mysteries.
> ("By Disposition of Angels")

and

> the Gordian knot need not be cut.
> ("Charity Overcoming Envy")

Wallace Stevens describes a hero that is not unrelated to Marianne Moore's hero, and in fact quite like herself:

> The highest man with nothing higher
> Than himself, his self, the self that embraces
> The self of the hero, the solar single,
> Man-sun, man-moon, man-earth, man-ocean,
> Makes poems on the syllable *fa* or
> Jumps from the clouds or, from his window,
> Sees the petty gildings on February . . .
> The man-sun being hero rejects that
> False empire . . . These are the works and pastimes
> Of the highest self: he studies the paper
> On the wall, the lemons on the table.
> This is his day. With nothing lost, he
> Arrives at the man-man as he wanted.
> This is his night and meditation.
> ("Examination of the Hero in a Time of War")

The hero's night and meditation may not be exactly our night and meditation, nor were they meant to be. His day, his lemons, his wallpaper, are his. Perhaps in reading the poems of Marianne Moore or Wallace Stevens, the *Cantos* of Ezra Pound, William Carlos Williams' *Paterson,* or James Joyce's *Finnegans Wake,* we are reading something literally less than literature in that the privacies of their authors and heroes preclude the absolute incandescence and coherence of, say Dante or Shakespeare. Yet they do give us heroes; they are our modern heroes, casting as much light as they can into dark places, making of diligent confusion a light unity. They give us the pleasures of watching single minds in their single-mindedness penetrating what each considers to be its own "rock crystal thing." The explosiveness of most modern literary efforts is not completely foiled, and the prophecy inherent in each may be sadly entropic as each dissolves into inexpressible complexity and obscurity dragging the single self along with it.

An acknowledged multiplicity may be disturbing to some, yet it gives us the choice of our lives where literature is concerned. Taken to be given, and given to be taken, "literature is a phase of life," and "where there is personal liking we go." Picking and choosing among the figures our age has given us, we may be refreshed to encounter Marianne Moore, whose still, small, and relatively unexploded voice somehow comes through all the shared confusions of intelligence to give us not only choice but also conviction with humor where

> bedizened or stark
> naked, man, the self, the being we call human, writing-
> master to this world, griffons a dark
> "Like does not like like that is obnoxious"; . . .

> Not afraid of anything is he,
>   and then goes cowering forth, tread paced to meet an obstacle
> at every step. Consistent with the
>   formula—warm blood, no gills, two pairs of hands and a few
>   hairs—that
> is a mammal; there he sits in his own habitat,
>   serge-clad, strong-shod. The prey of fear, he, always
>   curtailed, extinguished, thwarted by the dusk, work
>   partly done,

says to the alternating blaze,
  "Again the sun!
    anew each day; and new and new and new,
    that comes into and steadies my soul."

                         ("The Pangolin")

The animal-poet-hero's soul is thus steadied that its necessary forays into the darkness may be courageously made, that integration with its fate may be sought and satisfying, that rock crystal may be seen through to see it through, and that the apprehending of all may take place among the confusions of the world at large. Weaving in and out of our essential solitudes, such tasks take no less than heroic efforts: those toward survival, toward communication, toward discoveries of all sorts, and toward realizing ourselves in the graceful style or painful paradox of another's striking grasp. Beyond all this fiddle and filling the place of the genuine, the soul is steadied for its efforts of affection.

NOTES

1 —   INTRODUCTIONS

1. Marianne Moore, *A Marianne Moore Reader* (New York: Viking, 1961), p. 255.

2. *Ibid.*, p. 258.

3. William Carlos Williams, *The Autobiography of William Carlos Williams* (New York: Random House, 1951), p. 148.

4. Alfred Kreymborg, *Troubadour* (New York: Liveright, 1925), p. 252.

5. Wallace Stevens, "About One of Marianne Moore's Poems," *The Quarterly Review* 4 (2) (1948):147.

6. T. S. Eliot, introduction to Marianne Moore's *Selected Poems* (New York: Macmillan, 1935).

7. *Tipyn O'Bob* 6 (7) (May 1909).

8. Trumbull Stickney, quoted by I. A. Richards, "Poetic Process and Literary Analysis," in *Style in Language,* edited by Thomas Sebeok (Cambridge, Mass.: MIT Press, 1960), p. 15.

9. Donald Hall, "Interview with Marianne Moore," in *Marianne Moore,* edited by Charles Tomlinson (Englewood Cliffs, N.J.: Prentice-Hall, 1969), p. 23.

10. Ezra Pound, *The Literary Essays of Ezra Pound* (New York: New Directions, 1954), pp. 48 and 56.

11. Elizabeth Sewell, *The Human Metaphor* (Notre Dame, Ind.: University of Notre Dame Press, 1964), p. 68.

12. Elizabeth Sewell, quoting from *Die Lehringe zu Sais,* in *The Orphic Voice* (New Haven: Yale University Press, 1960), p. 204.

13. Moore, *Reader*, p. 214.

14. A distinction suggested by Stephen Spender in *The Making of a Poem* (London: H. Hamilton, 1955), p. 43.

2 —   STYLING STYLE

1. Paul Zweig, discussing Kierkegaard in *The Heresy of Self Love* (New York: Basic Books, 1968), p. 187, develops a similar idea: "By holding up the mirror to himself he [Kierkegaard] hoped to reinforce the 'interior action' which he already thought of as the 'divine side of man,' thereby cultivating his 'unknown god,' his individuality. This meant also to cultivate a means for grasping the peculiar rhythms of 'inwardness.' Kierkegaard's first reflection on literary style shows clearly that he knew how much of his struggle was to be lived in words, 'for isn't the primary virtue of a writer always to

have a style of his own, that is to say, a means of expression and exposition modeled on his very individuality?'"

2. Leo Spitzer, *Linguistics and Literary History* (Princeton, N.J.: Princeton University Press, 1974), pp. 19-20.

3. Roland Barthes, "Style and Its Image" in *Symposium on Literary Style,* edited by Seymour Chatman (New York: Oxford University Press, 1971), pp. 9-10.

4. John Keats, letter to George and Thomas Keats, 21, 27 (?) December, 1817, in *Selected Poems And Letters,* edited by Douglas Bush (Cambridge, Mass.: Houghton Mifflin, 1959), p. 261.

5. Marianne Moore, *Predilections* (New York: Viking, 1955), p. 3.

6. M. Merleau-Ponty, *The Phenomenology of Perception,* translated by Colin Smith (London: Routledge and Kegan Paul, 1974), p. 193.

7. Spitzer, *Linguistics,* p. 28.

8. Roland Barthes, *S/Z,* translated by Richard Miller (New York: Hill and Wang, 1974), pp. 11 and 4.

9. Louis T. Milic, "Rhetorical Choice and Stylistic Option," in *Symposium on Literary Style,* edited by Seymour Chatman (New York: Oxford University Press, 1971), pp. 77-80.

10. M. J. Tambimuttu, ed., *Festschrift for Marianne Moore's Seventy-Seventh Birthday* (New York: Tambimuttu & Mass, 1964), p. 117.

11. I owe this observation to Kenneth Burke, who notices this elephant's trunk as "not merely a *thing,* but as an *act,*" in his essay on Marianne Moore in *A Grammar of Motives and a Grammar of Rhetoric* (Cleveland: Meridian Books, 1962), p. 498.

12. Josephine Miles, "Style as Style," in *Symposium on Literary Style,* edited by Seymour Chatman (New York: Oxford University Press, 1971), p. 27.

13. Ivan Fónagy, "The Functions of Vocal Style," in *ibid.,* pp. 159-71.

14. Moore, *Predilections,* p. 135.

15. Northrop Frye, *The Well-Tempered Critic* (Bloomington: Indiana University Press, 1963).

16. Moore, *Predilections,* p. 69.

17. Barthes, "Style and Its Image," in *Symposium on Literary Style,* edited by Chatman.

18. Stillman Drake, "The Role of Music in Galileo's Experiments," *Scientific American* 232 (6) (June 1975):98-104.

19. Fónagy, "The Functions of Vocal Style," in *Symposium on Literary Style,* edited by Chatman.

20. Marianne Moore, *A Marianne Moore Reader* (New York: Viking, 1961), pp. 263 and 273.

21. Ernest Becker, *The Denial of Death* (New York: Free Press, 1973), p. 237.

22. M. A. K. Halliday, "Linguistic Function and Literary Style," in *Symposium on Literary Style,* edited by Chatman, pp. 332-34.

23. Moore, *Predilections,* pp. 26-30.

24. *Ibid.,* p. 57.

25. Frye, *Well-Tempered Critic,* pp. 30 and 68.

26. Moore, *Predilections,* p. 112.

27. Moore, *Reader,* pp. 171 and 174.

28. *Ibid.,* p. 57.

29. Moore, *Predilections,* p. 39.

30. Hugh Kenner, *A Homemade World* (New York: Knopf, 1975), pp. 102 and 104.

31. Moore, *Reader*, p. 196.

32. Paul Ricoeur, *Freud and Philosophy: An Essay in Interpretation*, translated by Denis Savage (New Haven: Yale University Press, 1970), p. 93.

33. Moore, *Predilections*, p. 39.

34. Owen Barfield, *On Poetic Diction* (London: Faber and Faber, 1952), p. 171.

35. Moore, *Predilections*, p. 15.

36. *Ibid.*, p. 47.

37. *Ibid.*, p. 13.

38. Moore, *Reader*, p. 271.

39. Moore, *Predilections*, pp. 7, 13, and 143.

40. Moore, *Reader*, p. 172.

41. Moore, *Predilections*, pp. 87-88.

42. *Ibid.*, p. 148.

43. Moore, *Reader*, p. 200.

44. Elizabeth Sewell, *The Orphic Voice* (New Haven: Yale University Press, 1960), p. 20.

45. Moore, *Predilections*, p. 68.

46. Moore, *Reader*, p. 273.

47. Kenneth Burke, *A Grammar of Motives and a Grammar of Rhetoric* (Cleveland: Meridian Books, 1962), p. 498.

48. Moore, *Reader*, p. 198.

49. Merleau-Ponty, *The Phenomenology of Perception*, p. 179.

50. Moore, *Reader*, p. 181.

51. Moore, *Predilections*, p. 145.

52. Moore, *Reader*, p. 175.

53. Kenneth Burke, *The Philosophy of Literary Form* (New York: Vintage, 1957), p. 39.

54. Moore, *Reader*, p. 273.

55. Burke, *Philosophy of Literary Form*, p. 53.

56. Norman Holland, *The Dynamics of Literary Response* (New York: Oxford University Press, 1968), pp. 135-36.

57. Moore, *Predilections*, p. 118.

58. Randall Jarrell, "Her Shield," in *Marianne Moore*, edited by Charles Tomlinson (Englewood Cliffs, N.J.: Prentice-Hall, 1969), p. 120.

59. Moore, *Predilections*, p. 83.

60. *Ibid.*, p. 13.

61. Aniela Jaffé, *The Myth of Meaning* (London: Hodder and Stoughton, 1970), p. 66.

62. Moore, *Predilections*, p. 23.

63. Mary Esther Harding, *Psychic Energy* (New York: Pantheon Books, 1948), p. 93.

64. T. S. Eliot, "Tradition and the Individual Talent," in *On Poetry and Poets* (New York: Farrar Straus and Cudahy, 1957).

65. Jaffé, *The Myth of Meaning*, p. 94.

66. Moore, *Predilections*, pp. 132-33.

3 — TAMING ANIMALS

1. Anna Freud, *The Ego and the Mechanisms of Defense,* translated by Cecil Bains (New York: International Universities Press, 1946).

2. Elizabeth Sewell, *The Human Metaphor* (Notre Dame, Ind.: University of Notre Dame Press, 1964), p. 114.

3. T. S. Eliot, *On Poetry and Poets* (New York: Farrar Straus and Cudahy, 1957), p. 30.

4. Marianne Moore, "A Virtuoso of Make-Believe," in *T. S. Eliot: A Symposium,* edited by Richard March and M. J. Tambimuttu (Chicago: Regnery, 1949), pp. 179-80.

5. See Edmund Wilson's "The Poetry of Drouth" in *The Dial* (December 1925) and T. S. Eliot's introduction to Marianne Moore's *Selected Poems* (1935).

6. Marianne Moore, "The World Imagined . . . Because We Are Poor," *Poetry New York* 4 (1951):7.

7. Elaine Sanceau, *Portugal in Search of Prester John* (London: Hutchinson, 1943), pp. 7-8.

8. Marianne Moore, *Tell Me, Tell Me* (New York: Viking, 1966), p. 48.

9. Marianne Moore, "Some Answers to Questions Posed by Howard Nemerov," in *Poets on Poetry,* edited by Howard Nemerov (New York: Basic Books, 1966).

10. Moore, "The World Imagined, . . ." p. 8.

4 — FIGHTING AFFECTIONS

1. Allen Tate, *The Man of Letters in the Modern World* (New York: Meridian Books, 1953), pp. 287-88.

2. Kenneth Burke, *The Philosophy of Literary Form* (New York: Vintage, 1957), p. 77.

3. Elizabeth Sewell, *The Orphic Voice* (New Haven: Yale University Press, 1960), p. 4.

4. Marianne Moore, *Predilections* (New York: Viking, 1955), p. 8.

5. Henry James, preface to *The American.*

6. William Hazlitt, "On Burke's Style," in *William Hazlitt, Essayist and Critic: Selections from His Writings* (London: F. Warne, 1889), pp. 294-95.

7. Burke, *The Philosophy of Literary Form,* p. 238.

8. Vivienne Koch has suggested that the "nomad" disposed to settle on the hand for life is a reference to Ezra Pound's proposal to H.D.'s father when Pound and H.D. were students at the University of Pennsylvania. H.D.'s father allegedly referred to Ezra as a "nomad." Ms. Koch's article, "The Peaceable Kingdom of Marianne Moore," appears in *The Quarterly Review of Literature* 4 (2) (1948):167n. 11.

9. Donald Hall, *Marianne Moore: The Cage and the Animal* (New York: Pegasus, 1970), p. 129.

10. Marianne Moore, *The Dial* 70 (1922), p. 621.

11. In *The Complete Poems* these lines read "Mars is excessive/ is being preventive," but the *is* should probably be read *in* as it appears in the first version of the poem, in *The Nation* in 1950.

12. Allison Heisch, "Queen Elizabeth I: Parliamentary Rhetoric and the Exercise of Power" in *Signs* 1 (1) (Autumn 1975):32.

13. Kurt Seligmann, *The History of Magic* (New York: Pantheon Books, 1948), pp. 332 and 472.

5 —   APPREHENDING HEROES

1. Marguerite Young, "An Afternoon with Marianne Moore," in *Festschrift for Marianne Moore's Seventy-Seventh Birthday,* edited by M. J. Tambimuttu (New York: Tambimuttu & Mass, 1964), p. 64.

2. T. S. Eliot, *The Use of Poetry and the Use of Criticism* (London: Faber and Faber, 1948), p. 155.

3. Howard Nemerov, ed., *Poets On Poetry* (New York: Basic Books, 1966).

4. Charles Tomlinson, ed., *Marianne Moore* (Englewood Cliffs, N.J.: Prentice-Hall, 1969), p. 53.

5. Kenneth Burke, *Counterstatement* (Chicago: University of Chicago Press, 1957), p. 42.

6. Referred to by Elizabeth Sewell in *The Human Metaphor* (Notre Dame, Ind.: University of Notre Dame Press, 1964), p. 53.

7. Erich Neumann, *Art and the Creative Unconscious* (New York: Pantheon Books, 1959), p. 194.

8. Marianne Moore, *Predilections* (New York: Viking, 1955), p. 143.

9. Marianne Moore, *The Dial,* (March 1921), p. 336.

10. Howard Nemerov, *Reflexions on Poetry and Poetics* (New Brunswick: Rutgers University Press, 1972), p. 30.

BIBLIOGRAPHY

BOOKS BY MARIANNE MOORE

Poems. London: The Egoist Press, 1921.
Marriage. London: Manikin, 1923.
Observations. New York: The Dial Press, 1924.
Selected Poems. New York: Macmillan, 1935; introduction by T. S. Eliot.
What Are Years. New York: Macmillan, 1941.
Nevertheless. New York: Macmillan, 1944.
Collected Poems. New York: Macmillan, 1951.
The Fables of La Fontaine. New York: Viking, 1954.
Predilections. New York: Viking, 1955.
Like a Bulwark. New York: Viking, 1956.
O to Be a Dragon. New York: Viking, 1959.
A Marianne Moore Reader. New York: Viking, 1961.
The Absentee. New York: House of Books, 1962.
Puss in Boots, The Sleeping Beauty, and Cinderella. New York: Macmillan, 1963; a translation and adaptation of the tales of Charles Perrault.
Tell Me, Tell Me: Granite, Steel, and Other Topics. New York: Viking, 1966.
The Complete Poems of Marianne Moore. New York: Macmillan and Viking, 1967.

UNCOLLECTED POEMS BY MARIANNE MOORE

"Appellate Jurisdiction." *Poetry* 6:71, May 1915.
"Apropos of Mice." *Bruno's Weekly* 3:1137, October 7, 1916.
"The Beast of Burden." *Lantern* (Bryn Mawr College) 22:57, Spring, 1913.
"Blake." *Others* 1, no. 6:105, December 1915.
"Counsel to a Bachelor." *Poetry* 6:71, May 1915.
"Diogenes." *Contemporary Verse* 1:6, January 1916.
"Ennui." *Tipyn O'Bob* (Bryn Mawr College) 6, no. 5:7, March 1909.
"Holes Bored in a Workbag by the Scissors." *Bruno's Weekly* 3:1137, October 7, 1916.
"In 'designing a cloak to cloak his designs,' you wrested from oblivion a coat of immortality for your own use." *Bruno's Weekly* 3:1233, December 30, 1916.
"The Just Man And." *Bruno's Weekly* 3:1233, December 30, 1916.

"Masks." *Contemporary Verse* 1:6, January, 1916.

"My Lantern." *Lantern* (Bryn Mawr College) 18:28, Spring 1910.

"My Senses Do Not Deceive Me." *Lantern* (Bryn Mawr College) 18:103, Spring 1910.

"Pigeons." *Poetry* 47:61-65, November 1935.

"Pretiolae." *Wake* no. 9:4, 1950.

"Progress." *Tipyn O'Bob* (Bryn Mawr College) 6, no. 8:10, June 1909.

"Qui s'excuse, s'accuse." *Lantern* (Bryn Mawr College) 18:103, Spring 1910.

"Quoting an Also Private Thought." *University of Kansas City Review* 16, no. 3:163, Spring 1950.

"A Red Flower." *Tipyn O'Bob* (Bryn Mawr College) 6, no. 7:14, May 1909.

"The Sentimentalist." *Tipyn O'Bob* (Bryn Mawr College) 5, no. 6:26, April 1908.

"That Harp You Play So Well." *Poetry* 6:70, May 1915.

"To a Friend in the Making." *Others* 1:105, December 1915.

"To a Man Working His Way Through the Crowd." *Egoist* 2:62, April 1, 1915.

"To Come after a Sonnet." *Tipyn O'Bob* (Bryn Mawr College) 4, no. 4:15, February 1907.

"To My Cup-Bearer." *Tipyn O'Bob* (Bryn Mawr College) 5, no. 6:21, April 1908.

"Tunica Pllio Proprior." *Lantern* (Bryn Mawr College) 18:102, Spring 1910.

"Under a Patched Sail." *Tipyn O'Bob* (Bryn Mawr College) 4, no. 4:12, February 1907.

"We Call Them the Brave." *The Nation* 172:423, May 5, 1951.

"You Say You Said." *Little Review* 5, no. 8:21, December 1918.

SELECTED MISCELLANEOUS ESSAYS AND REVIEWS BY MARIANNE MOORE

"The Accented Syllable." *Egoist* 3:151-52, October 1916.

"The Bright Immortal Olive." *Dial* 79:170-72, August 1925; review of H.D.

"Development." *Dial* 70:588-90, May 1921; review of Bryher.

"A Draft of XXX Cantos." *Criterion* 13: 482-85, April 1934; review of Ezra Pound's *A Draft of XXX Cantos.*

"Emily Dickinson." *Poetry* 41:219-26, January 1933.

"The Hawk and the Butterfly." *Westminster Magazine* 23:63-66, Spring 1934; concerns William Butler Yeats.

"Henry James as a Characteristic American." *Hound and Horn* 7:363-72, April-June 1934.

"Is the Real the Actual?" *Dial* 73:620-22, December 1922; concerns the sculptures of Alfeo Faggi.

"People Stare Carefully." *Dial* 80:49-52, January 1926; review of E. E. Cummings' *Poems.*

"A Portrait of George Moore." *Dial* 73:664-68, December 1922.

"The Sacred Wood." *Dial* 70:336-39, March 1921; review of T. S. Eliot's *The Sacred Wood.*

"The Spare American Emotion." *Dial* 80:153-56, February 1926; review of Gertrude Stein's *The Making of Americans.*

"A Virtuoso of Make Believe." *T. S. Eliot: A Symposium,* compiled by Richard March and M. J. Tambimuttu. Chicago: Regnery, 1949, pp. 179-80.

"Well Moused, Lion." *Dial* 76:84-91, January 1924; review of Wallace Stevens' *Harmo-nium.*

"'The World Imagined . . . Since We Are Poor.' The Auroras of Autumn: a note of this metaphor." *Poetry New York* no. 4:7-9, 1951; concerns Wallace Stevens' *The Auroras of Autumn.*

INDEX

MARIANNE MOORE

Poet of Affection

was composed in 10-point IBM Selectric Journal Roman Medium and
leaded two points by Metricomp Studios;
printed on 55-pound P & S Litho, B-32 shade,
by Vicks Lithograph and Printing Corp.;
Smyth-sewn and bound over boards in Permalin Permacote Cambric
by Vail-Ballou Press, Inc.;
and published by

SYRACUSE UNIVERSITY PRESS
Syracuse, New York 13210